The Open Mind

Interactive Readings and Focused Writings

Third Edition

By Laura Knight, Carol Friend and Beatrice Machunze
Mercer County Community College

Windsor Press
Windsor, NJ

Cover Photography and Design by Joseph Eschenberg

Printed in the United State of America.

10 9 8 7 6 5 4 3 2

Windsor Press and Publishing
PO Box 332
Windsor, NJ 08561-0332

~ Acknowledgements ~

~ The English Dept. faculty at Mercer County Community College for their encouragement and suggestions, especially Robin Schore for his extensive suggestions, editing, and proofreading

~ Michael Shea for providing the basis of this book through his text *Composing the Curriculum*

~ Dr. Sidney Weinstein for sharing his story with us

~ Joseph Eschenberg for photographing the book cover and Hayley Eschenberg for posing for the cover

~ Our families for their patience while we completed the book

~ And to all those who helped with the book but aren't mentioned here—a hearty appreciation for all you did.

TABLE OF CONTENTS

HUMANITIES

NATURAL SCIENCE

PART THREE: GRAMMAR, PUNCTUATION AND OTHER CONVENTIONS OF WRITING

THE OPEN MIND

Preface

The Open Mind is a textbook designed with you—the college reading and writing student—in mind. We wrote it for you. It is intended to be used by students in both introductory college reading and writing courses.

We prepared the textbook with the expectation that the learning in these classes would compliment and reinforce each other. Whereas the reading professor may find her focus to be primarily on such issues as comprehension, retention, and critical thinking, and the writing professor on such points as thesis statement, support, organization, and clarity, it is clear that both professors are engaging you in thinking about words and their meaning and how to use them to understand the written text as well as author it.

The curriculum of most academic institutions is broken down into three areas: the natural sciences (the world of nature that man does not control); the social sciences (how groups of people interact); and the humanities (works that are manmade, such as art, music, dance and literature). To be a "citizen of the world," you must learn to read and write in all three areas and this text will help you to achieve this.

Laura D. Knight
Carol Friend
Beatrice Machunze

Introduction to Reading and Writing

We like words. We like to talk and we like to read. We don't necessarily use "big words," but we do like the way some words look and sound: *ubiquitous*, *obsolete*, and *conundrum*.

Sometimes we love the way writers make us feel through their words. We love hearing the voices or the characters or the narrator of the story. We even like imagining who these writers are--even though we can't see them.

Writers are special people, but so are readers. We readers have an important job to perform and that is to enjoy and understand the writer's words, ideas and stories. Language is the main tool of this trade--the trade of writing and reading. We trade our ideas. We write, you read or conversely, you write and we read. That's a special exchange between people.

Read the following poem "Catch" by Robert Francis:

Two boys, uncoached are tossing a poem together,
Overhand, underhand, backhand, sleight of hand, every hand,
Teasing with attitudes, latitudes, interludes, altitudes,
High, make him fly off the ground for it, low, make him stoop,
Make him scoop it up, make him as-almost-as-possible miss it,
Fast, let him sting from it, not, now fool him slowly,
Anything, everything tricky, risky, nonchalant,
Anything under the sun to outwit the prosy,
Over the tree and the long sweet cadence down,
Over his head, make him scramble to pick up the meaning,
And now, like a posy, a pretty one plump in his hands.

A paraphrase of this poem might be that a game of catch is similar to a poet's relationship to his/her reader. The words, like a ball, are "thrown" in a variety of ways to keep up the interest and challenge the reader. If the "game" is to be appealing and interesting, monotony and staleness in word choice, sentence structure and ideas must be avoided. The same holds true for writers and readers of prose. As a writer, you should strive to make your writing interesting and engaging. As a reader, you should look for plays on words, meaningful repetitions and other methods the author uses to engage your intellect.

In this textbook, you will read short pieces from different parts of the world and written over many centuries. You may be familiar with some of the authors or topics, or they may all be new to you. In either case, view the readings in this text as a way to see and understand parts of the world without traveling around the world or back in time.

Interactive
Reading

Interactive Reading

~~ **"Mark Twain observed that there is no difference between those who choose not to read and those who can't read.** ~~

An "interactive" reader is one who actively engages with the text through critical thinking. Good readers see, hear, feel, touch and taste the language of the reading. They have developed interactive strategies to comprehend the text and ways in which to respond to the text, mostly through thinking, talking and writing their reactions to the text. Good readers are developed, not born. In order to be a critical reader, you use several reading strategies such as **activating your background knowledge (schema), establishing your purpose, developing questions, predicting what is to come, thinking about your thinking, discovering the author's point of view, examining language and vocabulary meanings, understanding connotation and denotation, identifying and appreciating inferences, marking text, writing notes for textbooks (Cornell Notes),** and **writing summaries or essays.**

Activate Your Schema

One of the most important tools readers rely on when they read new material is thinking about their own past experiences or background knowledge (**schema**). Readers use their background knowledge as a tool or guidepost for reading new material.

Here's an example: You've just been invited to a party of a friend's friend. You know your friend, but you don't know her friend. Now you have to decide whether to go to the party since you won't know anyone there except your one friend. You decide to go because you want to enlarge your experiences. In going you will use your past experiences (schema) of party-going to feel comfortable and relaxed.

This example illustrates the background knowledge. You do have similar past experiences–going to parties–although you have never been to this hostess's party. Reading can be like this. You rely on your background knowledge or schema to make the new material more accessible and understandable to you—the reader.

In reading circles, this process is called **activating schema**. When you activate your schema, you become hooked into the reading. The selections in this book will activate your schema by encouraging you to relate the knowledge you already have to the new knowledge and information you will attain.

Establish Your Purpose

In order to establish your purpose, you must first figure out the author's reasoning and writing method or style. To determine this purpose, ask yourself, "Am I being persuaded, informed, entertained, or possibly all three?" Once you have determined the writer's style or purpose, you are ready to determine your own purpose for the reading. Most textbooks have questions following the readings. Reading them can help you determine your purpose, but even without the questions, you can establish your purpose by matching it to the writer's style. Once you have established your purpose, you will have a road map of how to consciously read the piece. As you consciously read, keep the style and purpose in mind.

Develop Questions

Reading interactively requires formulating questions either in the margin of the book or in your mind of who, what, where, why, when and how ("the 5 W's") about the reading. You do this to interact with the text. For example, if the chapter heading is "Causes of the American Revolution," you can turn it into questions: **What** were the causes of the American Revolution?" **How** many causes were there? **Why** was there an American Revolution? **Who** were involved? **Where** did the main causes take place? If you are consciously searching for the answers to these questions, you will better understand the material and retain in your memory what you read. You also stay hooked into the reading, much the same way you are hooked into a conversation when you actively ask questions.

Predict What is to Come

Any thinking process (including thinking when reading) begins with what the subject is and what you think is going to happen to the subject. Based on the information in the text that you are given, you make an educated guess as to what will happen. If your prediction is close to what actually happens, then you know that you are actively thinking about the material and accurately comprehending the author's points. In addition, if your predictions about the topic or details contained in the reading are close to what happens in the reading, then you are more apt to retain the material. When you activate your schema, establish your purpose, and ask questions, then you should be able to predict what is to come. These processes are all interrelated.

Thinking about Thinking

Thinking about thinking, also known as **metacognition**, means that you are conscious of your mind's action of thinking. Rather than just letting the words flow over you without consciously thinking about their meaning and impact, you think about them and what they mean. You are aware of your reading process. For example, if you are driving, not only are you looking at the road ahead, you are looking in your rear and side mirrors to actively be aware of what is around you. The reading process is like this—it requires the same conscious mental processing, for without it you will not comprehend the words on the page. As your thinking about the reading evolves, your comprehension problems will lessen because your mind and eyes are working together to interact effectively with the text.

Point of View

Every writer has a view of the world and of the subject matter of which he/she writes. For example, a basketball game may be described from many different points of view. A player on each side may describe it, a spectator may describe it or the referee may describe it. Each gives us a picture of the game. Depending on who is describing the game, we will see a slightly different game. As readers, we need to think about the point of view of the author. This is also called author's perspective. Once you, the reader, know the author's viewpoint, you can follow his/her thesis or argument and determine if your perspective or point of view is the same or different from the author's. By determining your point of view (perspective) and the author's point of view (perspective), you are actively engaged in the text.

Vocabulary Words in Context

Some problems readers face is not knowing the text's vocabulary. Here are some ways to unravel the meaning of an unfamiliar word or words. "Vocabulary words in context" means you, the reader, can make an intelligent guess at the meaning of the word from the gist of the words around it. It's best not to interrupt your reading process to look up every unknown word right away in the dictionary. Mark unfamiliar words and then try these steps for making an "educated guess" at the meaning as you go. You'll acquire some real understanding of how words are used rather than just learning long vocabulary lists. Eventually you will confirm your guesses with a dictionary.

1. First, **SOUND** the word out. Use simple phonics to attempt saying it—try a couple of ways. You might recognize the word when you hear it.

2. Next, look at the **CONTEXT**. Guess at the word's meaning from the way it is used in the sentence. You may find that an informal definition is worked in near the word or maybe you will see the meaning reflected in the next idea, or you may just be able to determine its meaning by the way the passage continues.

3. If you can't understand what you're reading after using the above steps, pause and turn to the **DICTIONARY** or the textbook may have a glossary list. When you find your word, skim through the whole entry and find the most relevant meaning. Check the pronunciation, too.

4. Then reinforce your understanding by **WRITING** a usable, brief definition or synonym in the margin of your reading.

You should also use the dictionary as a final step even if you have been able to guess well enough to keep going in your reading. When you stop after a section of reading to make notes, check your understanding of any words that aren't yet absolutely clear.

Connotation and Denotation

From Latin *de* meaning "apart," *con* meaning "together" and *notatio/notationis* meaning "marking," denotation is the literal meaning of a word; think of it as the "dictionary meaning" and connotation is the attitude, the emotionalism we associate with a word. You should be aware of the connotation of words while you read; you'll get a sense of the writer's point of view toward that subject by the words he/she uses. For example, the word "home" literally means one's residence or where one lives. This is its denotation. The connotation of the word might bring to mind feelings of security and comfort and serenity.

Another way to view connotation and denotation is when you examine pairs of words that are essentially similar in meaning, but different in the favorable or unfavorable attitudes they evoke in most people. Listed below are pairs of works that evoke negative or positive feelings. For each pair place a plus sign after the word that conveys a favorable attitude and a minus sign after the word that carries a less favorable attitude:

Refreshing	_____	Chilly	_____
Politician	_____	Statesman	_____
Lazy	_____	Leisurely	_____
Serious	_____	Grim	_____
Mock	_____	Tease	_____

Another way to get a feel for the connotations of words and improve your word choice is by practicing shifting your viewpoint so that you can describe the same object both favorably and unfavorably. You can do this by first using words with a positive connotation and then switching to words with a negative connotation.

For the phrases below, write a short description that is favorable and then a short description that is unfavorable. For example, you might describe a ripe banana as sweet or mushy, depending on the desired connotation.

1. A hamburger made in a fast-food restaurant
2. A group of three or four teenagers walking down the street together
3. A PE teacher

Inference

Being able to tell the connotative meaning of words while you read enhances the interactive nature of the reading process. An inference is an implied meaning arising out of what is suggested in the text. Figurative language—such as metaphor, simile and analogy, as well as irony—is used to form inferences. Writers frequently use inference to add a layer of meaning to their thoughts. You may have heard of this process of reading inference as "reading between the lines." For example, sometimes a vivid description of an event tells more about how the characters in a story "feel" than the author could describe directly. Good writers use inference, and good readers can identify and understand the inference used.

Marking the Text

Before you settle into your favorite chair, you need to learn how to read at the college level. Of course you know how to decode the sounds on the page. You also may be able to interpret what you're reading as a way to interact with the writer, and sometimes you are actively engaged in the story or essay, reading critically, and consequently, your thinking becomes activated. At the college level, the way you are expected to read differs from the reading you have done in the past. The reading you do for your classes will require you to interact with the text. To do this you are expected to mark your textbooks.

Always grab a pen or pencil before you start to read. Write directly in the book, usually in the margin. Although this may go against everything you've been taught about books, marking the text while you read is not only all right, but it is one of the most important steps in your understanding of the material. Marking the text will help you to focus on the reading and your thinking process (metacognition). You will be actively engaging with the author's words, thoughts, and ideas. A connection will be established between you and the text. In marking text you are exercising the interactive reading process.

You will want to underline passages or words with a highlighter. However, you should use care with highlighting so that only the important ideas—not most of the text—is accented.

Here is a chart of some of the markings you may want to use in this and your other textbooks. You may come up with your own symbolic system for marking text:

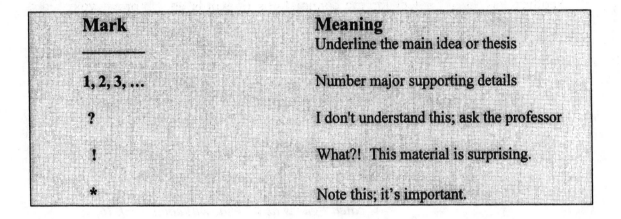

Mark	Meaning
————	Underline the main idea or thesis
1, 2, 3, ...	Number major supporting details
?	I don't understand this; ask the professor
!	What?! This material is surprising.
*	Note this; it's important.

Now, when you are in class, the important passages or the confusing passages or the surprising passages will stand out and you'll be able to **contribute to** and **understand** the discussion of the piece. Of course, when you are home sitting down to study for a test or writing an essay, again you will be able to quickly find the important passages you noted.

Note Taking

Taking notes while reading a textbook will keep you even more actively engaged in the dialogue you are having with the author. First you identify the main points and terms necessary to know during class and while you study. Then you include them in your notes. Lastly, you explain each term or main point in summary sentences. Note taking may take longer than simply marking the text, but it will directly reinforce what you are reading. By taking notes, you strengthen your comprehension and provide the most direct way to remember the material for examinations.

There are several note-taking systems, both for lectures and textbooks. One that is most useful is the **Cornell Note Taking Method**. For our purposes, we will focus on the strategies for taking Cornell Notes from textbooks. When you are in class taking notes, apply these same steps.

The Method

1. Draw a line or fold your paper 2-3 inches from the left column. This section is for key words and phrases. On the other 5-6 inches on the right of the vertical line, write the summary sentences, definitions or explanations that follow the terms you listed on the left.
2. Decide what to write on the right side of the line corresponding to these three ideas, ask yourself, "What have I read?" and "What are the most important ideas here?" Try to phrase the definition or explanation in your own words. However,

if you are trying to memorize terms and concepts, then it is better to quote the material right from the textbook. Add the page number after the sentence you wrote or quoted. This will make it easy for you to find the material when you are going to study for a test or to include it in an essay.

3. Review what you have written and underline key words or phrases on the right side of the line that you will need to recall for examinations.

Here's an example of Cornell Note Taking:

Activate schema	*Use my frame of reference or past experiences to make the new ideas easier to understand (5)*
Establish purpose	*Figure out the author's reasoning and writing style. Ask—"Am I being persuaded, informed, entertained, or all three?" (5)*
Predict what is to come	*Based on what I've read, make an informed "educated" guess as to what will come next. (6)*

SUMMARY WRITING

One of the most valuable ways to respond to a writer's story or article is through your own writing. Your purpose in writing a summary is to show your understanding of what you have read and to do this in approximately 1/10th of the words of the original. In a summary you demonstrate that you can identify and describe the **main ideas** or thesis or controlling ideas and the **major details** without adding in any opinions of your own.

Sometimes summary writing can be difficult because you must come up with your own words to express the full message of the reading. This is challenging at first because you will want to copy, but don't. You must use your own words to express your understanding of the text.

Remember, a summary should be short, including only the main and important points. For example, a summary of a 1,000-word article would be about 100-150 words. A shorter reading would have a shorter summary, and a longer reading would have a longer one.

Here are the steps to follow for good summary writing:

1. After reading the story or article, ask yourself who or what this is about. Once you have discovered that, write it down.

2. Next, ask yourself what major problem or idea is being discussed and write it down. At this point you have identified the main idea or thesis of the story or article.

3. This next step is crucial because it is here that you must decide what important details the writer discusses that support his/her article or short story. Read each paragraph as a unit of thought and underline the main idea for each paragraph. As you reread or review the article or short story, look for where you underlined in

the text and add these points to your notes. These "main ideas" are your major supporting points.

4. Once you have identified these major points, write them in your own words. Do not "cheat" at this point and "borrow" the author's words. This is plagiarism. Also, do not make judgments or conclusions about the work. Your opinions about the topic are not called for here.

5. You are almost done with the summary, but you still have two more important steps. Read all your notes and underlinings; then stop to think. (It isn't the product but the process. If you spend 5-10 minutes, maybe more, thinking about what you have read and looking at your writing from summary steps 1-3, you will be ready to write your summary.)

6. Based on your notes and beginning with the title and author of the original, write the first draft of your summary.

7. Revise your summary: check to see that you have excluded all detail, used your own words without adding your opinion and included all the main points.

Here is an example of a summary of the short story "Salvation," by Langston Hughes, which is in your book.

The short story "Salvation" by Langston Hughes describes the guilt and betrayal twelve-year old Langston Hughes feels after he lies about seeing Jesus while in church.

Langston's Aunt Reed brings him to her church to be "saved from sin." As he sits with the other children, he is waiting for a literal sign from Jesus. He wants to see him. He sits and waits while the other children go up to the platform, saying they have been saved. Finally he and his friend Wesley are the only two children left on the sinner's bench. Wesley gets up because he's "tired of sitting." Langston is the last child and everyone in the church is encouraging and pressuring him to get up to show he has been saved. The room is hot and it is getting late. Langston is still waiting for a literal sign. He realizes that Wesley obviously wasn't "saved" and God didn't strike him down for lying, so he goes to the platform with the other children. Everyone rejoices, while he feels shame and guilt.

At the end of the story, Langston cries while in his room that night. His aunt thinks this is because the Holy Ghost has come into his life. But Langston cries because he has lied about being saved and Jesus didn't come to him when he needed him.

Focused Writing

Focused Writing

~~ **"Exercise the writing muscle every day, even if it's only a letter, note, title list, character sketch, journal entry. Writers are like dancers, like athletes. Without that exercise, the muscles seize up." Jane Yolen** ~~

We humans are the only animals who write. We write to describe, to tell stories, to define, to explain, to persuade, to teach, to make sense of the world around us. We write to communicate with an audience that isn't in front of us, and therefore, what we write must be clear so the reader does not misunderstand our point.

You may like to write or perhaps the very thought of it scares you. Most writers aren't "born" that way; they become writers by learning and practicing. You too can become a good writer if you are willing to practice the skills needed.

Part of the two-way communication between a reader and a writer is activated when the reader becomes the writer. In this case, you, "the reader," are being asked to interact more completely with the text when you become engaged in the writing process. By responding to what you have read in writing, you more fully comprehend what the message is and how it makes you think and feel.

In our society, people in every profession need to write for one reason or another. In business, executives write memos, letters, and reports. Police officers write reports about the crimes they are investigating. Artists write proposals to gain funding. Nurses write notes about their patients. This is the age of written communication, and those who can write well tend to excel in their field because they can express themselves well. Because writing doesn't have the face-to-face contact of speaking, it is a more formalized way of conveying ideas, employing certain conventions that informed readers expect you to follow, such as capital letters to start sentences and the appropriate punctuation to end them.

Good writing is effective when it makes a point, follows standard conventions and uses clear language. The excerpt "My Teacher's Genius" by Helen Keller has many powerful words and sentences which when put together explain to us, the readers, the joy Helen Keller felt while beginning to learn about her world. She uses the senses (even though she does not have two of them) to describe her feelings about life and nature. If we were given a dry, dull description of her experiences, chances are we would be loathe to read on, but since she is able to tell us her story so vividly and creatively, we are willing to continue learning about her experiences. As a writer, try to "see" and "hear" the language of your essays and think consciously of your intentions towards your audience. If you think about what you want to say and then think of interesting ways to say it, you will be on your way to becoming a creatively conscious writer.

The Essay

Most of the writing you will do in college is in the form of an essay. Essays have certain characteristics:

- They are fairly brief, generally from two to thirty pages—long enough to develop a point, yet short enough to read in one sitting.
- They are non-fiction.

- They make a point.
- They are interesting to read.

INTRODUCTORY PARAGRAPH
   Catchy lead-in -- makes the reader want to continue
   Transitional sentence—brings the reader from the lead-in to the thesis
   Thesis statement -- explains what the essay is about

FIRST BODY PARAGRAPH
   Topic sentence -- contains the focus of the paragraph
   Supporting sentences -- give back-up points for topic sentence
   Detail sentences -- give specific examples
   Transitional sentences/words—bring the reader to the next idea

SECOND BODY PARAGRAPH
   Topic sentence
   Supporting sentences
   Detail sentences
   Transitional sentences/words—bring the reader to the next idea

THIRD BODY PARAGRAPH
   Topic sentence
   Supporting sentences
   Detail sentences
   Transitional sentences/words—bring the reader to the next idea

You add as many body paragraphs as you need.

CONCLUSION
   Gives closure to the essay. May summarize the main point and tie into the introduction. Does not add any new information.

Parts of the Essay

All essays have an organization. The most common and most useful is the "introduction-body-conclusion" format.

Introductions
"Grabber" Lead-Ins

An interesting introduction is one that "grabs" the reader's attention and makes the reader want to continue reading. You should make a point to write an engaging introduction by using one of these methods:

- Telling a brief, related story (narration)
- Using a related quotation

- Citing a relevant current event
- Relating a fact or statistic
- Posing a question

The Thesis Statement

The thesis statement is the sentence that explains what your essay will be about. It always contains two parts: the **subject** and your **opinion** or judgment about that subject. It tells the reader what point you are going to make. Do not write a sentence that is a fact because you won't have an opinion to prove and support in the body of the essay. Usually, but not always, it is placed at the end of the introductory paragraph. Every essay must have a thesis statement, even if it is only implied.

Your thesis statement should <u>never</u> announce your topic ("I am going to write about…." "This essay is about…." "In this paper I am going to tell you about…."). Also, don't rely on your title to be the subject of the first sentence of the introduction. For example, if your title is "The Importance of Recycling," your first sentence cannot be "It is important for the environment." "It" (a pronoun) doesn't have a noun to refer to because the title doesn't count as part of the body of the essay. You must restate the topic: "Recycling is important for the environment."

Following the list below can help you to write an effective thesis statement:

- Write the main idea of the essay assignment in your own words.
- In about 20 words, write the main point that you want to make in your essay, keeping your answer to #1 in mind.
- Write your thesis statement in one or two sentences, making sure you have one main point that includes an opinion or judgment.
- Check to see if your thesis statement
    a. answers the assignment ___ yes ___ no
    b. has one subject ___ yes ___ no
    c. gives an opinion, not a statement of fact ___ yes ___ no

Remember, you can rewrite and revise your thesis statement whenever you want during the writing process.

Practice 2: Look at the following sentences and decide if they would make good thesis statements. Mark **T** if you think yes and **X** if you think no. Revise the sentences you marked with an X so they will be good thesis statements.

___ 1. There are elements of risk in picking up a stranger along the highway. _____

_____

___ 2. In this essay, I am going to explain to you why *Moby Dick* is one of the greatest novels every written. ___ *Moby Dick, A great*

novel in time, _____

___ 3. George Washington was first Commander-in-Chief of the American colonies.

_____

4. Foreign-born American citizens often occupy less prominent positions in the country's social, economic, and political life. _____

_____

5. Let me explain about the role of women during World War I. _____

Women, Strong and Brave, their hard fought time during WWI.

In summary, the thesis statement

- has a subject and an opinion (or judgment) about the subject
- tells what the essay is about
- does not announce the topic

Body

Learning to write paragraphs is an important step to writing well because paragraphs are the basic building blocks of essays. The body of an essay contains paragraphs with the ideas that support your thesis statement. Each body paragraph is held together by its topic sentence, the statement that focuses the paragraph. If you were to skim an article to get its main points, most likely you would read the first sentence or two of each paragraph. Usually the main idea of the paragraph, the topic sentence, is located in the first sentence or two.

Like a thesis statement, the topic sentence contains a subject and an opinion. All of the sentences in the paragraph explain the point made in the topic sentence. All of the sentences are relevant to the topic of the paragraph. In other words, **no sentence is about anything else.**

To c onvince your r eader o f t he s oundness o f your p oint, you n eed t o a dd s entences that support the topic sentence. Although there is no set number of sentences for a paragraph, aim for six to eight supporting sentences per paragraph. Each sentence should be specific and give lots of detail. Some of them may be examples or quotations from your sources.

In a typical essay, you will have two to five body paragraphs to support your thesis statement (refer to the chart on essay structure). Of course, you may have more, depending on the topic of your essay.

Here are some tips about body paragraphs:

- A new paragraph is most often started when a new point is begun.
- A new paragraph is sometimes started to give readers' eyes a rest. A long paragraph might be broken up for this reason.
- A paragraph can be one sentence long if you a re trying to e mphasize a point.
- Each paragraph should have a topic sentence.

Here are some points at which you can start a paragraph:

- <u>Shifts in time.</u> Look for spots where you have written words such as *at that time, then*, or *afterward*, or have given other time signals.

- Shifts in place. Look for spots where you have written *another place* or *on the other side* or have used words that point to places.
- Shift in direction. Look for spots where you have written *on the other hand*, *nevertheless*, or *however*, or have indicated contrast.
- Shifts in emphasis or focus. Look for spots where you have shifted to a new point, perhaps used words such as *another*, *in addition*, or *not only*.

Signal words such as these are called **transitional words** or **transitional expressions.**

Practice 1: Develop the following points by showing (not telling) your reader what you mean.

Topic: I can't decide whether I should fix up my old car or replace it with a new one.

1.   My old car is inexpensive to own and operate.

    a.   My car is inexpensive to operate and very old.

    b. _____

    c. _____

2.   However, a new car would have many conveniences that my old car lacks.

    a.   A new car has many conveniences that

    b.   my old car dosent have,

    c. _____

Practice 2:

Topic: I need to decide whether to move into my own apartment or continue to live at home. Both seem to have advantages.

1.   Moving into my own apartment would mean that I would have more privacy.

    a.   My privacy is why I want to move

    b.   into my own apartment,

    c. _____

2.   On the other hand, living at home would assure me company and support.

    a.   Living at home would assure me

    b.   company and support,

    c. _____

Conclusion

Every essay needs some type of conclusion. Usually the conclusion echoes the idea in the thesis statement, but uses different words. It may take an idea from the introduction (sometimes from the "grabber" introduction) and go back to it, this time with the reader having the additional knowledge supplied in the body paragraphs.

Some "don'ts" for writing conclusions:
- Don't write "In conclusion…." Since it's the last paragraph, the reader already knows that this is the end of the essay.
- Don't add new information. If you've discovered a wonderful point, add it to the body of the essay.
- Don't repeat your introduction word for word or point by point. That's just plain boring.

The Writing Process

~~ "You can only learn to be a better writer by actually writing." Doris Lessing ~~

All writers think about their subject, prewrite in some form, outline, draft, edit, draft, revise and draft and edit again. And then they have to proofread! This is called the writing cycle or the writing process.

The writing process consists of **prewriting**, **organizing ideas**, **drafting**, **revising**, and **proofreading**. The process is not straightforward but cyclical: you may have to go back to draft again before moving on to the next step.

Prewriting

Freewriting, brainstorming, and asking questions are all ways to generate ideas about your topic.

Freewriting is an effective cure for writer's block. You write about your topic without stopping for ten minutes. Just keep writing for ten minutes. If you get stuck, you can write your name over and over or "I can't think of anything" until a thought pops into your head. *Ideas will come to you from deep inside.* Once the ten minutes are up, read what you've written and pull out the valid and interesting ideas.

From the reading "Sister Flowers," here's an example of a freewrite about someone who is "the measure of what a human being can be":

I don't know what to write about. I cant think of anyone. No one no one no one. Except my fifth grade teacher Mr. Morgan. May be I could write about him. He made leaning fun but he didn't put up with any nonsense either. He was his own person. He knew a lot about what we were leanring and he always actied like we were the best students he could have. I wanted to be like him. Smart. Funny. Distinquished. I guess I did do think he is what a human could be. In his class I reaslized I would be anything I wanted if I was willing to work for it.

Brainstorming is thinking about your topic and then writing a list of every word or phrase that comes to mind. Don't stop writing the list until you have at least 10 words or phrases. Don't worry if the words/phrases aren't related or aren't in the "right" order, and don't try to write sentences. You are generating ideas that will become a part of your essay here.

Here's an example of brainstorming about suffering an emotional injury:

1. *angry with Maneesh*
2. *betrayed me by telling a secret*
3. *didn't keep promise*
4. *other friends noticed I changed*
5. *made me angry w/everyone*
6. *not trusting*
7. *thought about who I wanted to be*
8. *he isn't worth it*
9. *moved on*
10. *felt free*
11. *made me smarter not bitter*

Asking questions is based on the six "W"s journalists use to gather information for a story: Who? What? Where? Why? When? and How? By answering these questions, you will generate ideas for your essay.

Here's an example of asking questions about a ceremony in which you participated:

Who?:   *Me*
What?:   *High school graduation/award ceremony*
Where?:   *Hightstown High School*
Why?:   *Won Artist Award/finished 4 yrs. of h.s. (yeah)*
When?:   *June 12, 2004*
How?:   *My painting voted the best by students and art teachers.*
            Finished all my courses – passed all of them.

Organizing Your Ideas

Once you have enough ideas from your prewriting activities, you need to put them in some type of order that will make sense. You can accomplish this through either an **informal outline** or a **map**.

An **informal outline** does not have to have the same structure as a formal outline, but it gives you a way to see how your essay will progress from idea to idea. Outlines are easier to change than drafts, and once they are finished, you don't have to worry about what comes next in your essay because it is right there in the informal outline. Here's an example of an informal outline for the topic "Similarities in Creation Stories":

Similarities and Differences in Creation Stories
INTRO: (Remember to add a "catchy" intro) Thesis: The creation stories of the Maori Indians and the Judeo-Christian religion have many similarities and some differences

BODY:
1. *Similarities*
   - A. *Both explain how the earth, sun, sky, water were created*
   - B. *Both have a god or gods doing the creating*
   - C. *Both tell how the god/gods' children are formed*
2. *Differences*
   - A. *Maori has many gods; Judeo-Christian has one*
   - B. *Maori uses more lyrical language, while Judeo-Christian uses more straightforward language.*

CONCLUSION: (Remember to tie into the "catchy" lead-in)—They have more similarities than differences.

A writing or essay map uses each word or phrase you've chosen to represent each idea in a visual scheme. Each idea is "mapped" in connecting bubbles. Your main idea will be in the middle, and the supporting ideas come out from it.

Here's a map about the advantages of using the school's Writing Center:

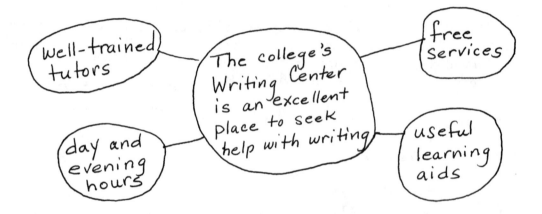

Drafting

Once you are satisfied with your prewriting and organizing efforts and you have sufficient support for each paragraph, you should write your first draft. **In one sitting,** using your outline or map as a guide, **write an entire draft of your essay.**

At this point don't be overly concerned with spelling, punctuation, or grammar (although if you see an obvious mistake, feel free to correct it). You'll get to that step soon. Here is where you want a complete draft, something that looks like an essay with paragraphs and complete sentences and capital letters. You want something you'll be able to edit, and unless you have a complete work, you won't be able to do that. If you find you don't have enough ideas, go back to the prewriting strategies to generate more ideas.

If you plan well, you should be able to leave the draft for a day or two before you approach it again. By leaving it for a day or two, you can gain an insight into its strengths and weaknesses.

Transitional Expressions

Transitional expressions add bridges to your ideas. They help your reader see the progression from one idea to the next.

Purpose	Transitional Words
to add	also, and, and then, as well, besides, beyond that, first (second, third, last, and so on), for one thing, furthermore, in addition, moreover, next
to compare	also, as well, both (neither), in the same way, likewise, similarly
to contrast	although, be that as it may, but, even though, however, in contrast, nevertheless, on the contrary, on the other hand, yet, whereas
to concede (a point)	certainly, granted that, of course, no doubt, to be sure
to emphasize	above all, especially, in fact, in particular, indeed, most important, surely
to illustrate	as a case in point, as an illustration, for example, for instance, in particular, one such, yet another

Revising

The word revising comes from the Latin *revisere* meaning, "to visit again, look at again." That is just what you are doing when you revise your essay. When you were drafting, you were concerned with the whole essay. When revising, you are looking at specific areas of the draft to see if they make sense, if they flow, and if they supply enough examples that are specific.

Follow these steps for revising your essay:
1. Read the introduction. Have you used a "grabber" opener? Do you have an identifiable thesis statement? Does the thesis have a subject and an opinion about that subject?
2. Read each body paragraph separately. Does the point you make in the topic sentence (you do have a topic sentence, right?) support the thesis statement? Do you have specific examples, facts, or necessary information to support your point? Have you used the clearest words for that point?
3. Read the body paragraphs as a unit. Do the paragraphs flow together? Have you put your paragraphs in the order that would be most effective?
4. Are your sentences awkward? Is the sentence structure varied? Is your word choice free from slang and clichés? Do the words mean what you think they do?

(If you are not sure, look them up in the dictionary.) You can read about these techniques in the Grammar Section of this book.

5. Read the conclusion. Does your conclusion give a sense of completeness? Have you reemphasized the ideas that are most important? Have you added any new information? (If you have, take it out of the conclusion and add it to the appropriate place in the body of the essay.)

Once you've answered these questions and revised your draft to reflect the changes, you are ready to proofread your essay.

Proofreading

Now that the larger issues—your organization, structure, flow and support—are in order, it is time to proofread your essay for errors that have slipped by you.

Here is a list of important areas you should check before handing your essay in to your professor:

- Are all your words spelled correctly?
- Have you used the correct punctuation?
- Do all your sentences have a subject, verb, and complete thought?
- Have you used standard American English (no slang)?
- Do your sentences all begin with a capital letter and end with one of the three final punctuation marks (. ! ?)?

If you know that you have a particular problem with punctuation or subject-verb agreement, for example, you should be especially diligent in checking your essay in these areas. Some students find it effective to proofread by starting at the **end** of the essay and sentence by sentence read up to the beginning. This way they don't get caught up in the content and miss mistakes. Once you've proofread thoroughly, you are ready to hand in your essay, knowing that you've given your ideas the time and attention that they deserve.

An Overview of the Writing Process

1. After you've read the assignment, grab a blank sheet or two of paper, find a comfortable chair, and prewrite about the assignment for 10 to 15 minutes. Don't worry about what you write—just let yourself go. Remember not to stop writing the entire time; don't cross out words as you go; don't correct your spelling; don't police yourself in anyway. Most of all, don't be afraid of what you're writing; no one else will ever see it. At the end of this time, stop. Read what you've written.

2. You are looking at the information that will be used in your essay (honestly!). Underline, circle or put checks in the margins next to those ideas you think you should keep and see if you can piece together an organization for your ideas. You may need to prewrite again if you don't have enough information. If so, get a new sheet

of paper, sit in the same comfy chair (or at the computer with the screen darkened if you choose) and repeat step one.

3. Based on the information you've gathered from the prewriting activities, organize your ideas in outline form.

4. Now you have to start writing. Following your outline, write your first draft in one sitting. If you follow through on this, you will feel superb—a sense of accomplishment—after you've completed the draft. If you feel comfortable, share your ideas with your classmates or a trusted friend. Maybe you're unsure of a line you've written. Ask your classmates or friends for their opinion.

5. Now comes the hard part: revision. Look over your draft critically. This means **honestly** evaluating its strengths and weakness.

6. When you're confident about the content of your essay, remember to revise it for word choice and specificity.

7. Next you need to proofread your essay for the details (did you accidentally write the same same word twice? Or did you transpose lettres?). Give it one final read, looking just for those little errors. If you are using a word processor, be sure you are reading the hard (paper) copy, and not the computer screen.

8. You're ready to hand it in.

Sample Essay

Below is a sample of a student's writing at the end of the semester. Note the catchy introduction, the developed body paragraphs, and a conclusion that ties the essay together and looks back to the introduction. Also note that the essay is carefully proofread, with few sentence, grammatical or mechanical errors.

Basket Weaving is My Major

How often has a student been asked in a humorous tone, "Are you majoring in basket weaving?" Strangely, can we not compare basket weaving to the studies of humanities, natural science, and social science? Each strand of a basket is insignificant; however, when woven together the sum of its smaller parts creates a foundation, gives strength, and produces a form—the end result. The individual strands of a basket are woven so tightly together that it is difficult to see where one strand begins and where another ends. We can say the same for the studies of humanities, social science and natural science; each relying heavily upon one another, intricately woven together, often difficult to see the dividing lines, but just as the strands of a basket are individual, so are these sciences.

During the semester, in order to further understand the concept of natural science, we were required to write an essay regarding the forces of nature. As I wrote "Love Prevails a Nor'easter," I found the studies of social science and humanities entwined. Just as

26

the storm's violence and uncontrollable forces refers to natural science, the wedding refers to social science. It is through our society, our family, and groups of people that we learn the norms of our culture. Our culture tells us how we should celebrate a wedding: a bride dressed in white and the ceremony in a church is expected in some cultures. Social science studies cultures, societies, and the environment in which we grow, and how each forms our beliefs, expectations and perceptions. Clearly, a wedding celebration is learned, passed down from generation to generation, and therefore falls into the realms of social science.

To further blur the dividing line, just as I have shown that a wedding could be related to social science, the wedding may fall into the realm of humanities. If we say humanities is the study of humanly made things, made purely for enjoyment, often referred to as works of art, we think of music, painting, literature, and theater. Can humanities not cross this line? If we expand our view of art and think of the word masterpiece, this wedding clearly was a masterpiece. Each flower chosen for its exquisite beauty, each centerpiece perfectly arranged, and details of each room exhuded the artful details of intense construction to create an overwhelming feeling of awe. Not just the norm or how one is expected to celebrate a wedding, but instead, this bride created an illusion that made us feel as though we walked into a watercolor canvas of a little piece of heaven. Such beauty, difficult to describe, was created for our complete enjoyment. Yes, the wedding was a social event, but the visionary talent, which the bride labored over for her guests' enjoyment, was a true masterpiece—a work of art. As seen here, this example of humanities is a fine line, and debatable, but a dividing line nonetheless. Thinking back, I wonder if it is even possible to write without including all three sciences.

Socrates used the three sciences to help us learn what we do not even know we know, and/or do not know. Plato's written work of Socrates' teachings clearly falls into the realms of humanities. Socrates develops vivid pictures in our mind. He uses the sun, moon, reflection, the cave, and pain, all of which fall into the area of natural science, to teach social science. He helps us see what we could not possibly have seen without guidance. Socrates, through the vivid description of the cave, leads us to understand our individual environment and how it can develop our own perceptions of the world. He shows us that our views are so limited that we only see what we are accustomed to see. Our perception created by our surroundings and our experiences in life is depicted clearly in that cave. How perfect is the analogy of using shadows to represent our perception? This clearly helps us understand what we see is only the surface of things. Shadows have no details, rarely do we look for details, or even if we search for the details; we will not fully understand the real pictures because we can only see through our eyes. I contemplate whether will we ever really see the complete picture, the way things really are, or will we always be blinded by the sun—our views.

Sadly, I realized we would never see the true picture; we will always wear our own shades. It was our final assignment, to draw what we saw in the "The Allegory of the Cave," that gave me a clearer understanding of this concept. However, with my newly acquired knowledge and great understanding, it only brought me so far, and in its place were new questions and new ideas. While drawing the reflections in the water, I realized if I were to look at my reflection in the water, although it has not changed, someone else would view my reflection differently. No two people will see the same reflection.

Humanities, social science, and natural science can be studied individually; however, it is together that the studies are more complete—the sum of their smaller parts creates the end results. As I attempt to untangle their intricate weave, I realize that with more knowledge, comes more questions; is this not what Socrates refers to when he implies that the greatest gift of all is to learn not only what we do not know, but also learn what we didn't even know we didn't know? I know this—the next time someone asks me if I major in basket weaving, my reply will be, "Yes, it is the intricate weave of humanities, social science, and natural science."

USES OF LANGUAGE

Using Specific Language

Mark Twain said, "The difference between the right word and the almost right word is the difference between lightning and the lightning bug." The more specific the words you choose (keeping in mind their connotation as well as their denotation) the clearer your writing will be.

Practice 1: Each of the sentences below is vague. Underline the subject and the verb in each sentence and substitute more specific terms. If possible, add a descriptive word or phrase.

1. The person walked. _The person walked very slow._
2. The animal made a noise. _the Tiger animal's noise was loud the most_
3. The store had many people in it. _The store was very crowded._
4. A guy went into a building. _A person walked into that building._
5. The thing moved. _The thing moved around the room._

Practice 2: Each of the sentences below is vague. Underline the subject and the verb in each sentence and substitute more specific terms. If possible, add a descriptive word or phrase:

1. The woman said stuff. _The woman said nice things._
2. The machine made a noise. _The machine was very loud._
3. The thing was old. _The thing was very old._
4. The animal went out. _The animal went out of the room._
5. The stuff didn't work. _The stuff didn't work as we thought they would._

Practice 3: Carefully read through the entire opening paragraphs of George Orwell's _1984_ several times. Then fill in each blank with a word that makes the most sense, but choose it carefully so that your reader will have a clear picture of your idea.

28

It was a ___bright___ cold ___Day___ in April, and the clocks were striking thirteen. Winston Smith, his chin ___nuzzled___ into his ___breast___ in an effort to escape the ___vile___ wind, slipped ___quickly___ ly through the ___glass___ doors of Victory Mansions, though not ___quickly___ ly enough to ___prevent___ a swirl of ___gritty___ dust from entering along with him.

The hallway smelt of ___boiled___ cabbage and ___old rags___ ___rag___ mats. At one end of it a ___colored___ poster, too large for indoor display had been ___tacked___ to the wall. It ___depicted___ ___simp___ ly a(n) ___enormous___ face, more than a ___meter___ wide: the face of a man about forty-five, with a ___heavy___ ___black___ mustache and ___ruggedly___ ly handsome features. Winston ___made___ for the stairs. It was ___no___ use trying the lift. Even at the ___best___ of ___times___ it was seldom working, and at present the electric current was ___cut off___ during ___daylight daytime___ hours. It was part of the _____ drive in _____ion for Hate Week. The _____ was _____ flights up, and Winston, who was _____-nine, and had a varicose ulcer _____ his _____ knee went _____ly, resting _____ times on the way. On each landing, _____ the lift shaft, the poster _____ the _____ face stared _____ the _____. It was one of those pictures which are so _____ that the eyes follow you about when you move. BIG BROTHER IS WATCHING YOU, the caption _____ it ran.

Here are the original opening paragraphs from *1984*:

It was a bright cold day in April, and the clocks were striking thirteen. Winston Smith, his chin nuzzled into his breast in an effort to escape the vile wind, slipped quickly through the glass doors of Victory Mansions, though not quickly enough to prevent a swirl of gritty dust from entering along with him.

The hallway smelt of boiled cabbage and old rag mats. At one end of it a colored poster, too large for indoor display, had been tacked to the wall. It depicted simply an enormous face, more than a meter wide: the face of a man of about forty-five, with a heavy black moustache and ruggedly handsome features. Winston made for the stairs. It was no use trying the lift. Even at the best of times it was seldom working, and at present the electric current was cut off during daylight hours. It was part of the economy drive in preparation for Hate Week. The flat was seven flights up, and Winston, who was thirty-nine and had a varicose ulcer above his right ankle, went slowly, resting several times on the way. On each landing, opposite the lift-shaft, the poster with the enormous face glazed from the wall. It was one of those pictures which are so contrived that the eyes follow you about when you move. BIG BROTHER IS WATCHING YOU, the caption beneath it ran.

Practice 4: For each underlined word or phrase in the following paragraph choose a more specific term.

My female relative, like some older people, thinks all her young relatives should know
My cousins sister, like some other people, cousins should know

how nice the good old days were before modern communication systems when she and
Beautiful ... Modern Communication Systems

my male relative were young. Every so often, my male sibling Frank watches her
Uncle ... time ... Uncle

coming up the thoroughfare. Then he frowns and says to me, "Here comes trouble,
Coming up the thoroughfare ... says

Denise!" She always walks into our eating area with a big salutation, but then she acts
Walks ... lunch ... Big salutation

like a member of the military. She likes to criticize. As soon as the evening meal is
Member of the military ... The evening meal

finished and the eating paraphernalia are done, my female relative tries to get our
Eating paraphernalia ... Done ... female relative

attention. If she doesn't, she touches the furniture, asks for silence, and begins to speak
Touches ... furniture

some words which go something like this: "These days a girl dresses in small pieces of
Some Words ... Small pieces

material and calls it wearing apparel! These days a boy shows his attentions to a girl he
Material ... Wearing Apparel

doesn't even know! When I was a girl, young people were a lot different." As soon as she leaves, Frank always <u>stands</u> up and <u>says</u>, "That woman <u>bothers my feelings</u>! The

_____

next <u>time</u> she <u>wants</u> to have a meal, tell her we <u>have to go out</u>."

_____

Practice 5: Use each of the following words in a focused, descriptive sentence. Include some details that would answer the questions who, what, were, when, how or why.

1. ...neighbors.

    My neighbors are very nice people.

2. My mother-in-law...

    My mother-in-law is very generous person.

3. The wolf...

    The wolf is very dangerous when he is mad.

4. ...exploded...

    The car exploded when it went of the cliff.

5. All the rivers...

    All the rivers are filled after the rain storm

6. ...tired sales clerk...

    _____

    _____

7. ...sleeps...

    The people sleep in the tent on their camping trip.

Cliché

A cliché is often a simile or metaphor characterized by its overuse. Because it so commonplace, it has lost its impact. Nothing will deaden your writing faster than using clichés. A cliché cannot communicate because people have heard the expression or idea so many times that they are no longer able to react to it. When you write, avoid trite, overused similes and metaphors.

Practice: Rewrite the following sentences, removing the cliché and replacing it with clear, vivid language.

1. Although the present was useless, Laura thought, "Never look a gift horse in the mouth."

   _____

   _____

2. When Carol heard the angry next-door-neighbor banging on her door, she told her daughter, "Here comes trouble; head for the hills!"

   _____

   _____

3. Bea was embarrassed as a blushing bride.

   Bea was embarrassed red

   _____

4. Kerrie said Marc was as cold as ice.

   Kerrie said Marc was heartless

   _____

5. After Rhea's boyfriend left her again, her best friend told her to wake up and smell the coffee.

   Get a grip

   _____

Slang

Slang is informal language consisting of words and expressions that are not considered appropriate for college writing. It is also considered non-standard speech because it differs from the accepted, easily-recognizable speech of the community.

Some examples of slang are phat, duh, awesome, win-win, skanky, icky, newbie, flame, spam, net-head and dude. Slang originates most often from television, computer-use, friends and groups, which use slang to show membership. Also, to define itself, each generation creates new words to describe the same things. There are "regionalisms" to slang; what has meaning in one part of the country or even the same city may be nonsensical in another. But beware: slang becomes "dead" every three to five years. If you want your writing to last, you should avoid slang. Groovy, man.

Practice: Change the slang (in italics) to standard American English.

1. The car was *a steal* for the money until owner *got wise* and *jacked up* the price.

    The car was priced good for the money

2. The basketball game was a *real wipeout*; we got our *butts kicked*.

    lose, we lost the game.

3. I *pushed the panic button* when the teacher called on me. I was *out to lunch*.

    Touched panic button, went

4. I work with so many *jerks that* it's a wonder I don't *flip out.*

    people

5. Marie *whipped right through* the multiple-choice questions, but the essay section *threw her a curve ball.*

    _____

    _____

Usage

Sometimes writers confuse words that sound similar or perhaps they have misunderstood their use. You should always be careful of the meanings of the words you use. Here is a short list of words that are often confused or misused:

Commonly Confused Words

a	use before nouns beginning with consonants
an	use before nouns beginning with vowels (a, e, i, o, u)
advice	a noun meaning opinion or counsel
advise	a verb meaning recommend or suggest
affect	a verb meaning to have an influence or to act on the emotions of
effect	a noun meaning something brought about by a cause; a result
all ready	completely prepared
already	previously; before

~~alright~~	should not be used; not a word
all right	written as two words; mean okay
being as	should not be used in college writing; informal; slang
since	means because
hear	perceive with the ear
here	in this place
~~irregardless~~	should not be used; not a word
regardless	in spite of everything; anyway
its	belonging to it
it's	the contraction of "it is" or "it has"
knew	past tense of know
new	not old
passed	went by; succeeded in; handed to
past	a time before the present
quiet	silent; hushed; still
quite	entirely; completely
than	shows comparison
then	next in time, space or order
their	belonging to them
there	at that place; a neutral word used with verbs such as *is, are, had*
they're	the contracted shortened form of "they are"
though	despite the fact that; although
thought	past tense of think
threw	past tense of throw
through	from one side to the other; finished
to	a verb part, as in "to smile"; toward
too	overly; also
two	the number 2
your	belonging to you
you're	the shortened form of "you are"
weather	atmospheric condition
whether	if it happens that; in case; if

where	in what place
were	past tense of the verb "to be"
wear	to have on
which	what particular one or ones
witch	a woman who practices sorcery
whose	belonging to whom
who's	the shortened form of "who is" and "who has"
would have	correct very formation
would of	mistakenly using "of" instead of "have"

Practice 1: Cross out the incorrectly used word and replace it with the correct one.

1. ~~Being as~~ _Since_ Anne is my sister, I let her borrow my car.

2. ~~Irregardless~~ _Regardless_ of whose fault it is, the broken window still needs to be replaced.

3. All people need to ~~except~~ _accept_ advice at some time in their life.

4. ~~Who's~~ _Whose_ books are on the desk?

5. If we were fives miles east, would the ~~whether~~ _weather_ be sunny?

Practice 2: Circle the correct word.

1. Kasey said she was feeling ((all right), alright).

2. Juan said he (though, (thought)) he could meet us after practice.

3. Leora (new, (knew)) if she studied, she would do well on the test.

4. Tomas chose to ((wear), were, where) a tuxedo to the New Year's Eve party.

5. First you add the sugar, and (than, (then)) you add the eggs.

Practice 3:
1. After we played football in the rain, we were (quiet, (quite)) a sight.

2. Mildred ((would have), would of) left at seven, but her alarm clock didn't ring.

3. I couldn't (here, (hear)) the directions, so I asked the steward to repeat them.

4. "Quick, put the package over (their, (there), (they're))!"

5. "You are (to, (two), too) big to be carried, "said the mother to her ((to), two, too)- year old.

Deconstructing and Constructing Readings

BEGINNING THOUGHTS ON THE NATURAL, SOCIAL SCIENCE, AND HUMANITIES

Michael Shea

1   Let us agree, for sake of thought, that the natural sciences are bodies of organized facts, definitions, formulas, and functions describing those things which human beings did not create and which constantly change according to their own force: cells and stars and seashores, for example; that, although these verbal and mathematical formulations are themselves a humanly-made part of Western culture, the natural forces they seek to describe, trace, or plot are not humanly made.

2   Though these statements may be more controversial, let us speculate, too, that the social sciences are also bodies of organized observations, facts, definitions, formulas describing the ways human beings tend to relate to one another in the many smaller societies (or social situations) that make up a Society; that the cultural artifacts that hold them together—tools, works of art, and customs and laws (including language conventions)—are humanly made.

3   And finally, in order to begin our humanities-inspired conversation, let us assume that humanities courses involve us in gathering around and carefully wording descriptions and observations of a humanly-made thing that exists purely to be enjoyed and admired as, together, we take collegial notice of what we see and hear—and think and imagine when engaging a verbal work of art. Such things are called works of art—"thought things": ideas and theories whose "stories" take the form of essays, as well as works of other literary, visual, and performing art. As Keats has written: they "tease us out of thought."

4   Is it also possible that we commit ourselves to considering and reconsidering these propositions carefully enough so that they might help us avoid incoherent, impressionistic, and purely self-referential statements relative to the topics whose meaning they underwrite and by which they are underwritten? In this way we will also discover that, though a topic like "story" is presented in *Composing the Curriculum* from the point of view of social sciences, it might also be "read" and "written out" from the point of view of the humanities—as Writing Prompt 4 may indicate: "Now that I think about it, I may have paid such close attention to her/his words…for a few reasons." This in contrast to the preceding prompt, Prompt 3, pointing to a social-science reading and writing: "Now that I think about it, she/he may have told this story to me in particular, in that particular place, at that particular time for a few reasons."

5   Similarly, the selection from Rachel Carson's influential work *Silent Spring*, "A Fable for Tomorrow," does indeed, address the concept of nature as proposed above—those things that humans did not create and that continue to metamorphose themselves according to their own force. At the same time, the discourse brought to life by its sentences does not seem to be science—bodies of organized facts, definitions, formulas, and functions.

38

6   The opening reference to a "town in America," and words like "families," "farmers," and "anglers," arise naturally out of the nature discussion, pointing to the kinds of humanly-made things studied as parts of the social sciences. However, these do not do their pointing in a scientific way. Rather, the discourse, with its version of a "once-upon-a-time" opening, moves in a more story-like, "fabulous" way, as the title itself, indicates so that we are invited to entertain the concept of nature by attending to, wondering at, and describing the movement of metaphor in the work. The excerpts from Diversity of Life, in contrast, do reveal themselves to be science—a portion of that recorded body of knowledge.

7   As students of the humanities, let us give witness in discerning ways to ideas and writings that have so enriched our lives—and those of the generations that have gone before us—even as they point us to more specialized study in the art and sciences.

LETTER TO PRESIDENT PIERCE, 1855

Chief Seattle

Vocabulary Words

sacred (par. 2)
reflection (par. 5)

henceforth (par. 6)
stench (par. 7)

1 How can you buy or sell the sky, the warmth of the land? The idea is strange to us. If we do not own the freshness of the air and the sparkle of the water, how can you buy them?

2 Every part of this earth is sacred to my people. Every shining pine needle, every sandy shore, every mist in the dark woods, every clearing and humming insect is holy in the memory and experience of my people. The sap which coursed through the trees carries the memories of the red man.

3 The white man's dead forget the country of their birth when they go to walk among the stars. Our dead never forget this beautiful earth, for it is the mother of the red man. We are part of the earth, and it is a part of us. The perfumed flowers are our sisters; the deer, the horse, the great eagle, these are our brothers. The rocky crests, the juices in the meadows, the body heat of the pony, and man—all belong to the same family.

4 So when the great white Chief in Washington sends word that he wishes to buy our land, he asks much of us. The great Chief sends word he will reserve us a place so that we can live comfortably to ourselves. He will be our father, and we will be his children. So we will consider your offer to buy our land. But it will not be easy. For this land is sacred to us.

5 This shining water that moves in the streams and the rivers is not just water but the blood of our ancestors. If we sell you land, you must remember that it is sacred, and you must teach your children that it is sacred and that each ghostly reflection in the clear water of the lakes tells of events and memories in the life of my people. The water's murmur is the voice of my father's father.

6 The rivers are our brothers; they quench our thirst. The rivers carry our canoes and feed our children. If we sell you our land, you must remember and teach your children, that the rivers are our brothers, and yours, and you must henceforth give the rivers the kindness you would give any brother. We know that the white man does not understand our ways. One portion of the land is the same to him as the next, for he is a stranger who comes in the night and takes from the land whatever he needs. The earth is not his brother, but his enemy, and when he has conquered it, he moves on. He leaves his fathers' graves, and his children's birthright is forgotten. The sight of your cities pains the eyes of the red man. But perhaps it is because the red man is a savage and does not understand.

7 There is no quiet place in the white man's cities. No place to hear the leaves of spring or the rustle of insect's wings. But perhaps because I am a savage and do not understand, the clatter only seems to insult the ears. The Indian prefers the soft sound of the wind darting over the face of the pond, the smell of the wind itself cleansed by a mid-day rain, or scented with the pinon pine. The air is precious to the red man. For all things share the same breath—the beasts, the trees, the man. Like a man dying for many days, he is numb to the stench.

[8] What is man without the beasts? If all the beasts were gone, men would die from great loneliness of spirit, for whatever happens to the beasts also happens to man. All things are connected. Whatever befalls the earth befalls the sons of the earth.

[9] It matters little where we pass the rest of our days; they are not many. A few more hours, a few more winters, and none of the children of the great tribes that once lived on this earth, or that roamed in small bands in the woods, will be left to mourn the graves of a people once as powerful and hopeful as yours.

[10] The whites, too, shall pass—perhaps sooner than other tribes. Continue to contaminate your bed, and you will one night suffocate in your own waste. When the buffalo are all slaughtered, the wild horses all tamed, the secret corners of the forest heavy with the scent of many men, and the view of the ripe hills blotted by talking wires, where is the thicket? Gone. Where is the eagle? Gone. And what is it to say goodbye to the swift and the hunt, the end of living and the beginning of survival? We might understand if we knew what it was that the white man dreams, what he describes to his children on the long winter nights, what visions he burns into their minds, so they will wish for tomorrow. But we are savages. The white man's dreams are hidden from us.

Thinking and Responding to the Reading

1. What is the Native American's relationship to nature? Explain.
2. What is the main idea of this letter?
3. Why does Chief Seattle refer to himself and his people as "savage"? Is this meant to be ironic? Explain why or why not.
4. What prediction does he make about the white man's life that is true today? Be specific.
5. Why does he believe that the white man's dreams are hidden?
6. Compare this story to Rachel Carson's "A Fable for Tomorrow." List the similarities.

Springboard for Composing

How would Chief Seattle describe his "home"? (Consider, among other features of this letter, his personification of natural elements). Where do you think Chief Seattle would call the white man's home? Are the Indian and the white man's needs met in these respective places?

DADDY TUCKED THE BLANKET

Randall Williams

Vocabulary Words

semirural (par. 2)	teetering (par. 9)	affluent (par. 21)
humiliating (par. 5)	deteriorating (par. 12)	grandeur (par. 23)
shiftless (par. 7)	futility (par. 13)	retrospect (par. 25)
articulate (par. 7)	psyche (par. 20)	

1   About the time I turned sixteen, my folks began to wonder why I didn't stay home any more. I always had an excuse for them, but what I didn't say was that I had found my freedom and I was getting out.

2   I went through four years of high school in semirural Alabama and became active in clubs and sports; I made a lot of friends and became a regular guy, if you know what I mean. But one thing was irregular about me. I managed those four years without ever having a friend visit at my house.

3   I was ashamed of where I lived. I had been ashamed for as long as I had been conscious of class.

4   We had a big family. There were several of us sleeping in one room, but that's not so bad if you get along, and we always did. As you get older, though, it gets worse.

5   Being poor is a humiliating experience for a young person trying hard to be accepted. Even now—several years removed—it is hard to talk about it. And I resent the weakness of these words to make you feel what it was really like.

6   We lived in a lot of old houses. We moved a lot because we were always looking for something just a little better than what we had. You have to understand that my folks worked harder than most people. My mother was always at home, but for her that was a full-time job—and no fun, either. But my father worked his head off from the time I can remember in construction and shops. It was hard, physical work.

7   I tell you this to show that we weren't shiftless. No matter how much money Daddy made, we never made much progress up the social ladder. I got out thanks to a college scholarship and because I was a little more articulate than the average.

8   I have seen my Daddy wrap copper wire through the soles of his boots to keep them together in the wintertime. He couldn't buy new boots because he had used the money for food and shoes for us. We lived like hell, but we went to school well-clothed and with a full stomach.

9   It really is hell to live in a house that was in bad shape ten years before you moved in. And a big family puts a lot of wear and tear on a new house, too, so you can imagine how one goes downhill if it is teetering when you move in. But we lived in houses that were sweltering in summer and freezing in winter. I woke up every morning for a year and a half with plaster on my face where it had fallen out of the ceiling during the night.

10   This wasn't during the Depression; this was in the late 60's and early 70's.

11   When we boys got old enough to learn trades in school, we would try to fix up the old house we lived in. But have you ever tried to paint a wall that crumbled when the

roller went across it? And bright paint emphasized the holes in the wall. You end up more frustrated than when you began, especially when you know that at best you might come up with only enough money to improve one of the six rooms in the house. And we might move out soon after, anyway.

12   The same goes for keeping a house like that clean. If you have a house full of kids and the house is deteriorating, you'll never keep it clean. Daddy used to yell at Mama about that, but she couldn't do anything. I think Daddy knew it inside, but he had to have an outlet for his rage somewhere, and at least yelling isn't as bad as hitting, which they never did to each other.

13   But if you have a kitchen which has no counter space and no hot water, you will have dirty dishes stacked up. That sounds like an excuse, but try it. You'll go mad from the sheer sense of futility. It's the same thing in a house with no closets. You can't keep clothes clean and rooms in order if they have to be stacked up with things.

14   Living in a bad house is generally worse on girls. For one thing, they traditionally help their mother with the housework. We boys could get outside and work in the fields or cut wood or even play ball and forget about living conditions. The sky was still pretty.

15   But the girls got the pressure, and as they got older it became worse. Would they accept dates knowing they had to "receive" the young man in a dirty hallway with broken windows, peeling wallpaper and a cracked ceiling? You have to live it to understand it, but it creates a shame which drives the soul of a young person inward.

16   I'm thankful none of us ever blamed our parents for this because it could have crippled our relationships. As it worked out, only the relationship between our parents was damaged. And I think the harshness which they expressed to each other was just an outlet to get rid of their anger at the trap their lives were in. It ruined their marriage because they had no one to yell at but each other. I knew other families where the kids got the abuse, but we were too much loved for that.

17   Once I was about sixteen and Mama and Daddy had had a particularly violent argument about the washing machine, which had broken down. Daddy was on the back porch—that's where the only water faucet was—trying to fix it and Mama had a washtub out there, washing school clothes for the next day and they were screaming at each other.

18   Later that night everyone was in bed and I heard Daddy get up from the couch where he was reading. I looked out from my bed across the hall and into their room. He was standing right over Mama and she was already asleep. He pulled the blanket up and tucked it around her shoulders and just stood there and tears were dropping off his cheeks and I thought I could faintly hear them splashing against the linoleum rug.

19   Now they're divorced.

20   I had courses in college where housing was discussed, but the sociologists never put enough emphasis on the impact living in substandard housing has on a person's psyche, especially children's.

21   Small children have a hard time understanding poverty. They want the same things children from more affluent families have. They want the same things they see advertised on television, and they don't understand why they can't have them.

22   Other children can be incredibly cruel. I was in elementary school in Georgia—and this is interesting because it is the only thing I remember about that particular school—when I was about eight or nine.

23   After Christmas vacation had ended, my teacher made each student describe all his or her Christmas presents. I became more and more uncomfortable as the privilege passed around the room toward me. Other children were reciting the names of the dolls they had been given, the kinds of bicycles and the grandeur of their games and toys. Some had lists which seemed to go on and on for hours.

24   It took me only a few seconds to tell the class that I had gotten for Christmas: a belt and a pair of gloves. And then I was laughed at—because I cried—by a roomful of children and a teacher. I never forgave them, and that night I made my mother cry when I told her about it.

25   In retrospect, I am grateful for that moment, but I remember wanting to die at the time.

Thinking and Responding to the Reading

1.   Why didn't Williams have friends visit him at his home?
2.   Why was it hard to keep the house clean? Fixed up?
3.   Why does the author say that children can be very cruel? Give specific examples.
4.   Why do you think Williams's parents separated even though it is obvious that they loved each other? What effect do you think it had on Williams?
5.   What is the meaning of the last paragraph? For which event, the classroom or his mother's tears, is he grateful? Why would he be grateful for either of these events?
6.   What is the main point of this essay? Do you think Williams's examples support this main point?

Springboard for Composing

In the first line of "Daddy Tucked the Blanket," Randall Williams writes: "...I didn't stay home any more." Do you think he considered the houses he had lived in "homes"? Were there some aspects of his living situation that you think define a home? What are your expectations of a home?

HOMELESS

Anna Quindlen

Vocabulary Words

rummaged (par. 1)	overactive (par. 3)	enfeebled (par. 5)
adrift (par. 2)	legacy (par. 3)	huddled (par. 7)
anonymous (par. 2)	ferocity (par. 4)	crux (par. 7)

1   Her name was Ann, and we met in the Port Authority Bus Terminal several Januarys ago. I was doing a story on homeless people. She said I was wasting my time talking to her; she was just passing through, although she'd been passing through for more than two weeks. To prove to me that this was true, she rummaged through a tote bag and a manila envelope and finally unfolded a sheet of typing paper and brought out her photographs.

2   They were not pictures of family, or friends, or even a dog or cat, its eyes brown-red in the flashbulb's light. They were of a house. It was like a thousand houses in a hundred towns, not a suburb, not a city, but somewhere in between with aluminum siding and a chain-link fence, a narrow driveway running up to a one-car garage and a patch of backyard. The house was yellow. I looked on the back for a date or a name, but neither was there. There was no need for discussion. I knew what she was trying to tell me, for it was something I had often felt. She was not adrift, alone, anonymous, although her bags and her raincoat with the grime shadowing its creases had made me believe that she was. She had a house, or at least once upon a time had had one. Inside were curtains, a couch, a stove, potholders. You are where you live. She was somebody.

3   I've never been very good at looking at the big picture, taking the global view, and I've always been a person with an overactive sense of place, the legacy of an Irish grandfather. So it is natural that the thing that seems most wrong with the world to me right now is that there are so many people with no homes. I'm not simply talking about shelter from the elements, or three square meals a day or a mailing address to which the welfare people can send the check—although I know that all these are important for survival. I'm talking about a home, about precisely those kinds of feelings that have wound up in cross-stitch and French knots on samplers over the years.

4   Home is where the heart is. There's no place like it. I love my home with a ferocity totally out of proportion to its appearance or location. I love dumb things about: the hot-water heater, the plastic rack you drain the dishes in, the roof over my head, which occasionally leaks. And yet it is precisely those dumb things that make it what it is—a place of certainty, stability, predictability, privacy, for me and for my family. It is where I live. What more can you say about a place than that? That is everything.

5   Yet it is something that we have been edging away from gradually during my lifetime and the lifetimes of my parents and grandparents. There was a time when where you lived was where you worked and where you grew the food you ate and even where you were buried. When that era passed, where you lived at least was where your parents had lived and where you would live with your children when you became enfeebled. Then, suddenly where you lived was where you lived for three years, until you could move on to something else and something else again.

6   And so we have come to something else again, to children who do not understand what it means to go to their rooms because they have never had a room, to men and women whose fantasy is a wall they can paint a color of their own choosing, to old people reduced to sitting on molded plastic chairs, their skin blue-white in the lights of a bus station, who pull pictures of houses out of their bags. Homes have stopped being homes. Now they are real estate.

7   People find it curious that those without homes would rather sleep sitting up on benches or huddled in doorways than go to shelters. Certainly some prefer to do so because they are emotionally ill, because they have been locked in before and they are damned if they will be locked in again. Others are afraid of the violence and trouble they may find there. But some seem to want something that is not available in shelters, and they will not compromise, not for a cot, or oatmeal, or a shower with special soap that kills the bugs. "One room," a woman with a baby who was sleeping on her sister's floor, once told me, "painted blue." That was the crux of it; not size or location, but pride of ownership. Painted blue.

8   This is a difficult problem, and some wise and compassionate people are working hard at it. But in the main I think we work around it, just as we walk around it when it is lying on the sidewalk or sitting in the bus terminal—the problem, that is. It has been customary to take people's pain and lessen our own participation in it by turning it into an issue, not a collection of human beings. We turn an adjective into a noun: the poor, not poor people; the homeless, not Ann or the man who lives in the box or the woman who sleeps on the subway grate.

9   Sometimes I think that we would be better off if we forgot about the broad strokes and concentrated on the details. Here is a woman without a bureau. There is a man with no mirror, no wall to hang it on. They are not the homeless. They are people who have no homes. No drawers that hold the spoons. No window to look out upon the world. My God. That is everything.

Thinking and Responding to the Reading

1.   What is the main idea of this article? Where did you find this information?
2.   What is Ann trying to tell Quindlen by handing her the picture? Why is this important?
3.   What is Quindlen's attitude toward home?
4.   In paragraphs 5 and 6, Quindlen shows the transition of what homes used to be to what they are now. She breaks this progression into four parts. What are they?
5.   Explain the main idea of paragraphs 8 and 9. Do you agree with Quindlen's conclusion? Why or why not?
6.   What does she mean by "global view" (paragraph 3) and "broad strokes" (paragraph 9)?
7.   What is your definition of a homeless person?

Springboard for Composing

The last lines of paragraph 4, Quindlen states, "And yet it is precisely those dumb things that make [a home] what it is." Do you agree or disagree? Can you add to her list?

REPLY TO AN EVICTION NOTICE

Robert Flanagan

Vocabulary Words

camped (line 1)	cramped (line 3)	shrewdly (line 5)	gauged (line 9)
promoter (line 2)	endurances (line 3)	ungiving (line 5)	vantage (line 11)

1 My mother and father camped in such
2 in their time, landlord, promoter
3 of cramped endurances,
4 your rightful inheritance. Your father
5 purchased shrewdly and practiced ungiving
6 well. Mine did not.
7 So my sweaty bursts of living
8 are managed in rooms
9 gauged like parking meters, narrow as coin slots,
10 while from the landscaped, architect-designed
11 vantage of your home,
12 the town looks before you like a Monopoly board.
13 Ownership is your reward
14 And punishment; movement mine.

Thinking and Responding to the Reading

1. Whose voice is heard in the first line? What words make this clear?

2. In the second line we learn who is being addressed. Who is it? By the time we read the third and fourth lines we get a sense of the speaker's tone. What is it? What language has led you to this conclusion?

3. Though it is not stated, what was purchased? What does Flanagan mean by "practiced ungiving well"?

4. Why do you think the speaker refers to his existence as "bursts of living" and why are they "sweaty"? What later line supports this idea of impermanent existence?

5. *Gauge* has multiple meanings. Which one fits in this poem? What is the relationship between parking meters and these rooms? How does "narrow as coin slots" fit the picture? What does this simile imply?

6. Based on language from the poem, describe the landlord's home. Why did the poet use the word home and not house? What is the connotative difference? How does the speaker's voice change at this moment in the poem?

7. What do the last two lines suggest? How does the speaker feel about his fate?

8. From the speaker's point of view, of what would a home consist? Does it match your idea of a home?

 **Springboard for Composing**

How would the landlord define a home? Do you think the speaker could define it? If so, what qualities would he ascribe to it? Make your own list of a home's characteristics. Thinking about the differences between a "home" and a "house," discuss which one you live in. Explain why or in what ways it fits the term you chose.

SALVATION

Langston Hughes

Vocabulary Words

dire (par. 3)	rounder (par. 6)	serenely (par. 7)
gnarled (par. 4)	deacons (par. 6)	knickerbockered (par. 11)

1   I was saved from sin when I was going on thirteen. But not really saved. It happened like this. There was a big revival at my Auntie Reed's church. Every night for weeks there had been much preaching, singing, praying, and shouting, and some very hardened sinners had been brought to Christ, and the membership of the church had grown by leaps and bounds. Then just before the revival ended, they held a special meeting for children, "to bring the young lambs to the fold." My aunt spoke of it for days ahead. That night I was escorted to the front row and placed on the mourners' bench with all the other young sinners, who had not yet been brought to Jesus.

2   My aunt told me that when you were saved you saw a light, and something happened to you inside! And Jesus came into your life! And God was with you from then on! She said you could see and hear and feel Jesus in your soul. I believed her. I had heard a great many old people say the same thing and it seemed to me they ought to know. So I sat there calmly in the hot, crowded church, waiting for Jesus to come to me.

3   The preacher preached a wonderful rhythmical sermon, all moans and shouts and lonely cries and dire pictures of hell, and then he sang a song about the ninety and nine safe in the fold, but one little lamb was left out in the cold. Then he said: "Won't you come? Won't you come to Jesus? You lambs, won't you come?" And he held out his arms to all us young sinners there on the mourners' bench. And the little girls cried. And some of them jumped up and went to Jesus right away. But most of us just sat there.

4   A great many old people came and knelt around us and prayed, old women with jet-black faces and braided hair, old men with work-gnarled hands. And the church sang a song about the lower lights are burning, some poor sinners to be saved. And the whole building rocked with prayer and song.

5   Still I kept waiting to *see* Jesus.

6   Finally all the young people had gone to the altar and were saved, but one boy and me. He was a rounder's son named Westley. Westley and I were surrounded by sisters and deacons praying. It was very hot in the church, and getting late now. Finally Westley said to me in a whisper: "God damn! I'm tired o'sitting here. Let's get up and be saved." So he got up and was saved.

7   Then I was left all alone on the mourners' bench. My aunt came and knelt at my knees and cried, while prayers and song swirled all around me in the little church. The whole congregation prayed for me alone, in a mighty wail of moans and voices. And I kept waiting serenely for Jesus, waiting, waiting – but he didn't come. I wanted to see him, but nothing happened to me. Nothing! I wanted something to happen to me, but nothing happened.

8   I heard the songs and the minister saying: "Why don't you come? My dear child, why don't you come to Jesus? Jesus is waiting for you. He wants you. Why don't you come? Sister Reed, what is this child's name?"

9   "Langston," my aunt sobbed.

10   "Langston, why don't you come? Why don't you come and be saved? Oh, Lamb of Gold! Why don't you come?"

11   Now it was really getting late. I began to be ashamed of myself, holding everything up so long. I began to wonder what God thought about Westley, who certainly hadn't seen Jesus either, but who was now sitting proudly on the platform, swinging his knickerbockered legs and grinning down at me, surrounded by deacons and old women on their knees praying. God had not struck Westley dead for taking his name in vain or for lying in the temple. So I decided that maybe to save further trouble, I'd better lie, too, and say that Jesus had come, and get up and be saved.

12   So I got up.

13   Suddenly the whole room broke into a sea of shouting, as they saw me rise. Waves of rejoicing swept the place. Women leaped in the air. My aunt threw her arms around me. The minister took me by the hand and led me to the platform.

14   When things quieted down, in a hushed silence, punctuated by a few ecstatic "Amens," all the new young lambs were blessed in the name of God. Then joyous singing filled the room.

15   That night, for the first time in my life but one for I was a big boy twelve years old—I cried. I cried, in bed alone, and couldn't stop. I buried by head under the quilts, but my aunt heard me. She woke up and told my uncle I was crying because the Holy Ghost had come into my life, and because I had seen Jesus. But I was really crying because I couldn't bear to tell her that I had lied, that I had deceived everybody in the church, that I hadn't seen Jesus, and that now I didn't believe there was a Jesus anymore, since he didn't come to help me.

 Thinking and Responding to the Reading

1.   When Hughes writes about "lambs in the fold" and lambs in general he is using a figure of speech, a comparison. What is being compared? Is it useful as a figure of speech?

2.   The words "sin" (par. 1), "mourner" (par. 1) and "salvation" (title) all have connotations. What are connotations and what connotations do these words have for you?

3.   Why does Westley "see" Jesus? Why does Hughes come to Jesus?

4.   How does Hughes feel after his salvation?

5.   Does he finally believe in Jesus after his experience at the church? How do you know this?

6.   When writing a story or essay, transitions—words that bridge from action to action—are helpful for the reader to easily shift event to event or idea to idea. What transitions does Hughes use in this essay?

50

Springboard for Composing

In Hughes's essay on the ritual of being saved from sin, he suggests that sometimes we are forced to do things we do not wish to because of social pressures. As such, they can be harmful to us. Yet, is it possible that some type of learning springs from such situations? Think of an example from your life, and write about what happened. What were you pressured to do? What type of learning sprung from this situation?

NATIVE ORIGIN
from *MOHAWK TRAIL*

Beth Brant

Vocabulary Words

taboo (par. 2)	staunched (par. 13)	reverence (par. 16)
rituals (par. 5)	pliant (par. 15)	fecund (par. 18)

1   The old women are gathered in the Longhouse. First, the ritual kissing on the cheeks, eyes, the lips, the top of the head; that spot where the air parts in the middle like a wild river through a canyon.

2   A Grandmother sets the pot over the fire that has never gone out. To let the flames die is a taboo, a break of trust. The acorn shells have been roasted the night before. Grandmother pours the boiling water over the shells. An aroma rises and combines with the smell of wood, smoke, sweat, and the sharp-sweet odor of blood.

3   The acorn coffee steeps and grows strong and dark. The old women sit patiently in a circle, not speaking. Each set of eyes stares sharply into the air or the fire. Occasionally, a sigh is let loose from an open mouth. A Grandmother has a twitch in the corner of her eye. She rubs her nose, then, smooths her hair.

4   The coffee is ready. Cups are brought from a wooden cupboard. Each woman is given the steaming brew. They blow on the swirling liquid, then slurp the drink into hungry mouths. It tastes good. Hot, dark, strong. A little bitter, but that is all to the good.

5   The women begin talking among themselves. They are together to perform a ceremony. Rituals of old women take time. There is no hurry.

6   The magic things are brought out from pockets and pouches.

7   A turtle rattle made from a she-turtle who was a companion of the woman's mother. It died the night she died, both of them ancient and tough. Now, the daughter shakes the rattle, and mother and she-turtle live again.

8   A bundle containing a feather from a hermit thrush. This is a holy feather. Of all the birds in the sky, hermit thrush is the one who flew to the Spirit World. It was there she learned her beautiful song. She is clever and hides from sight. To have her feather is great magic. The women pass the feather. They tickle each other's chins and ears. Giggles and laughter erupt in the dwelling.

9   Bundles of corn, kernels of red, yellow, black. These also are passed from wrinkled hand to dry palm. Each woman holds the corn in her hand for a while before giving it to her sister.

10   Leaves of Witch Hazel and Jewelweed. Dandelion roots for chewing. Pearly Everlasting for smoking. These things are given careful attention. Much talk is generated over the old ways of preparing these gifts.

52

11   A woman gives a smile and brings a cradleboard from behind her back. There is nodding of heads and laughter and long-drawn-out "ahhhhhs." The cradleboard has a beaded back that a mother made in her ninth month. An old woman starts a song; the others join her:

        Little baby
        Little baby
        Ride on Mother's back
        Laugh, laugh
        Life is good
        Mother shields you
        Mother shields you.

12   A Grandmother wipes her eyes, another holds her hands and kisses the lifelines.

13   Inside the cradleboard are bunches of moss taken from a menstrual house. This moss has staunched lakes of blood that generations of women have squeezed from the wombs.

14   The acorn drink is reheated and passed once more. A woman adds wood to the fire. She holds her arms out to the flames. Another woman comes behind her with a warm blanket. She wraps it around her friend and hugs her shoulders. They stand before the fire.

15   A pelt of fur is brought forth. It once belonged to a beaver. She was found one morning, frozen in the ice, her lodge unfinished. The beaver was thawed and skinned. The women worked the hide until it was soft and pliant. It was the right size to wrap a newborn in, or to comfort old women on cold nights.

16   A piece of flint. An eagle bone whistle. A hank of black hair, cut in mourning. These are examined with reverence.

17   The oldest Grandmother removes a pouch from around her neck. She opens it with rusty fingers. She spreads the contents in her lap. Fistful of dark earth.

18   It smells clean, fecund. The women inhale the odor. The metallic taste of iron is on their tongues, like a sting.

19   The oldest Grandmother scoops the earth back into her pouch. She tugs at the string. It closes. The pouch lies between her breasts, warming her skin. Her breasts are supple and soft for one so old. Not long ago, she nursed a sister back to health. A child drank from her and was healed of evil spirits that entered her as she lay innocent and dreaming.

20   The ceremony is over. The magic things are put in their places. The women kiss and touch each other's faces. They go out into the night. The moon and stars are parts of Sky Woman. She glows—never dimming, never retreating.

21   The Grandmothers gather inside the Longhouse. They tend the fire.

Thinking and Responding to the Reading

1.   Brant uses all of the five senses to describe the ritual. Find five words or phrases where she uses a sense to describe.

2.   Brant also uses many metaphors to explain the ritual. Find three and explain each.

3. What is the ritual in this essay? (Brant does not tell the reader outright.) How did you infer this?
4. What evidence in the essay can you find to support your answer to question 3.
5. What aspects of this ritual teach us a lesson about life or death? Explain.

Springboard for Composing

The old women's gathering for a ceremony has taken place many times before and will in all likelihood continue to do so in the years to come. What is the importance of such a ritual to those involved? Why do we repeat these same formalities over and over again? Brainstorm some rituals in your culture. Chose one and discuss how this ritual played an important part in connecting you to your community and culture.

from *THE WAY TO RAINY MOUNTAIN*

N. Scott Momaday

Vocabulary Words

writhe (par. 1)	unrelenting (par. 3)	reverence (par. 9)	indulge (par. 12)
sacred (par. 3)	humiliation (par. 3)	wariness (par. 9)	compensation (par. 12)
preeminently (par. 3)	affliction (par. 3)	inherently (par. 10)	servitude (par. 12)
disposition (par. 3)	brooding (par. 3)	sentinel (par. 11)	purled (par. 14)
grim (par. 3)	tenuous (par. 8)	enmities (par. 12)	

1   A single knoll rises out of the plain in Oklahoma, north and west of the Wichita range. For my people, the Kiowas, it is an old landmark, and they gave it the name Rainy Mountain. The hardest weather in the world is there. Winter brings blizzards, hot tornadic winds arise in the spring, and in summer the prairie is an anvil's edge. The grass turns brittle and brown, and it cracks beneath your feet. There are greenbelts along the rivers and creeks, linear groves of hickory and pecan, willow and witchhazel. At a distance in July or August the steaming foliage seems almost to writhe in fire. Great green and yellow grasshoppers are everywhere in the tall grass, popping up like corn to sting the flesh, and tortoises crawl about on the red earth, going nowhere in the plenty of time. Loneliness is an aspect of the land. All things in the plain are isolate; there is no confusion of objects in the eye, but one hill or one tree or one man. To look upon that landscape in the early morning, with the sun at your back, is to lose the sense of proportion. Your imagination comes to life, and this, you think, is where Creation was begun.

————

2   I returned to Rainy Mountain in July. My grandmother had died in the spring, and I wanted to be at her grave. She had lived to be very old and at last infirm. Her only living daughter was with her when she died, and I was told that in death her face was that of a child.

3   I like to think of her as a child. When she was born, the Kiowas were living the last great moment of their history. For more than a hundred years they had controlled the open range from the Smoky Hill River to the Red, from the headwaters of the Canadian to the fork of the Arkansas and Cimarron. In alliance with the Comanches, they had ruled the whole of the Southern Plains. War was their sacred business, and they were the finest horsemen the world has every known. But warfare for the Kiowas was preeminently a matter of disposition rather than of survival, and they never understood the grim, unrelenting advance of the U.S. Cavalry. When at last, divided and ill provisioned, they were driven onto the Staked Plains in the cold of autumn, they fell into panic. In Palo Duro Canyon they abandoned their crucial stores to pillage and had nothing then but their lives. In order to save themselves, they surrendered to the soldiers at Fort Sill and were imprisoned in the old stone corral that now stands as a military museum. My grandmother was spared the humiliation of those high gray walls by eight or ten years, but she must have known from birth the affliction of defeat, the dark brooding of old warriors.

[4] Her name was Aho, and she belonged to the last culture to evolve in North America. Her forebears came down from the high country in western Montana nearly three centuries ago. They were a mountain people, a mysterious tribe of hunters whose language has never been classified in any major group. In the late seventeenth century they began a long migration to the south and east. It was a journey toward the dawn, and it led to a golden age. Along the way the Kiowas were befriended by the Crows, who gave them the culture and religion of the Plains. They acquired horses; and their ancient nomadic spirit was suddenly free of the ground. They acquired Tai-me, the sacred sundance doll, from that moment the object and symbol of their worship, and so shared in the divinity of the sun. Not least, they acquired the sense of destiny, therefore courage and pride. When they entered upon the Southern Plains they had been transformed. No longer were they slaves to the simple necessity of survival; they were a lordly and dangerous society of fighters and thieves, hunters and priests of the sun. According to their origin myth, they entered the world through a hollow log. From one point of view, their migration was the fruit of an old prophecy, for indeed they emerged from a sunless world.

———

[5] Though my grandmother lived out her long life in the shadow of Rainy Mountain, the immense landscape of the continental interior lay like memory in her blood. She could tell of the Crows, whom she had never seen, and of the Black Hills, where she had never been. I wanted to see in reality what she had seen more perfectly in the mind's eye, and drove fifteen hundred miles to begin my pilgrimage.

[6] A dark mist lay over the Black Hills, and the land was like iron. At the top of a ridge I caught sight of Devil's Tower upthrust against the gray sky as if in the birth of time the core of the earth had broken through its crust and the motion of the world was begun. There are things in nature that engender an awful quiet in the heart of man; Devil's Tower is one of them. Two centuries ago, because of their need to explain it, the Kiowas made a legend at the base of the rock. My grandmother said:

[7] Eight children were there at play, seven sisters and their brother. Suddenly the boy was struck dumb; he trembled and began to run upon his hands and feet. His fingers became claws, and his body was covered with fur. There was a bear where the boy had been. The sisters were terrified; they ran, and the bear after them. They came to the stump of a great tree, and the tree spoke to them. It bade them climb upon it, and as they did so, it began to rise into the air. The bear came to kill them, but they were just beyond its reach. It reared against the tree and scored the bark all around with its claws. The seven sisters were borne into the sky, and they became the stars of the Big Dipper.

[8] From that moment, and so long as the legend lives, the Kiowas have kinsmen in the night sky. Whatever they were in the mountains, they could be no more. However tenuous their well-being, however much they had suffered and would suffer again, they had found a way out of the wilderness.

[9] My grandmother had a reverence for the sun, a holy regard that now is all but gone out of mankind. There was a wariness in her, and an ancient awe. She was a Christian in her later years, but she had come a long way about, and she never forgot her birthright. As a child she had been to the sun dances, she had taken part in that annual rite, and by it she had learned the restoration of her people in the presence of Tai-me. She was about seven when the last Kiowa sun dance was held in 1887 on the Washita River above Rainy

Mountain Creek. The buffalo were gone. In order to consummate the ancient sacrifice—to impale the head of a buffalo bull upon the Tai-me tree—a delegation of old men journeyed into Texas, there to beg and barter for an animal from the Goodnight herd. She was ten when the Kiowas came together for the last time as a living sun-dance culture. They could find no buffalo; they had to hang an old hide from the sacred tree. Before the dance could begin, a company of soldiers rode out from Fort Sill under orders to disperse the tribe. Forbidden without cause the essential act of their faith, having seen the wild herds slaughtered and left to rot upon the ground, the Kiowas backed away forever from the tree. That was July 20, 1890, at the great bend of the Washita. My grandmother was there. Without bitterness, and for as long as she lived, she bore a vision of deicide.

[10]   Now that I can have her only in memory, I see my grandmother in the several postures that were peculiar to her: standing at the wood stove on a winter morning and turning meat in a great iron skillet; sitting at the south window, bent above her beadwork and afterwards, when her vision failed, looking down for a long time into the fold of her hands; going out upon a cane, very slowly as she did when the weight of age came upon her; praying. I remember her most often at prayer. She made long, rambling prayers out of suffering and hope, having seen many things. I was never sure that I had the right to hear, so exclusive were they of all mere custom and company. The last time I saw her she prayed standing by the side of her bed at night, naked to the waist, the light of a kerosene lamp moving upon her dark skin. Her long black hair, always drawn and braided in the day, lay upon her shoulders and against her breasts like a shawl. I do not speak Kiowa, and I never understood her prayers, but there was something inherently sad in the sound, some merest hesitation upon the syllables of sorrow. She began in a high and descending pitch, exhausting her breath to silence; then again and again—and always the same intensity of effort, of something that is, and is not, like urgency in the human voice. Transported so in the dancing light among the shadows of her room, she seemed beyond the reach of time. But that was illusion; I think I knew then that I should not see her again.

[11]   Houses are like sentinels in the plain, old keepers of the weather watch. There, in a very little while, wood takes on the appearance of great age. All colors wear soon away in the wind and rain, and then the wood is burned gray and the grain appears and the nails turn red with rust. The window panes are black and opaque; you imagine there is nothing within, and indeed there are many ghosts, bones given up to the land. They stand here and there against the sky, and you approach them for a longer time than you expect. They belong in the distance; it is their domain.

[12]   Once there was a lot of sound in my grandmother's house, a lot of coming and going, feasting and talk. The summers there were full of excitement and reunion. The Kiowas are a summer people; they abide the cold and keep to themselves, but when the season turns and the land becomes warm and vital they cannot hold still; an old love of going returns upon them. The aged visitors who came to my grandmother's house when I was a child were made of lean and leather, and they bore themselves upright. They wore great black hats and bright ample shirts that shook in the wind. They rubbed fat upon their hair and wound their braids with strips of colored cloth. Some of them painted their faces and carried the scars of old and cherished enmities. They were an old council of warlords, come to remind and be reminded of who they were. Their wives and daughters served them well. The women might indulge themselves; gossip was at once the mark and compensation of their servitude. They made loud and elaborate talk among them-

selves, full of jest and gesture, fright and false alarm. They went abroad in fringed and flowered shawls, bright beadwork and German silver. They were at home in the kitchen, and they prepared meals that were banquets.

13   There was frequent prayer meetings, and nocturnal feasts. When I was a child I played with my cousins outside, where the lamplight fell upon the ground and the singing of the old people rose up around us and carried away into the darkness. There were a lot of good things to eat, a lot of laughter and surprise. And afterwards, when the quiet returned, I lay down with my grandmother and could hear the frogs away by the river and feel the motion of the air.

———

14   Now there is a funeral silence in the rooms, the endless wake of some final word. The walls have closed in upon my grandmother's house. When I returned to it in morning, I saw for the first time in my life how small it was. It was late at night, and there was a white moon, nearly full. I sat for a long time on the stone steps by the kitchen door. From there I could see out across the land; I could see the long row of trees by the creek, the low light upon the rolling plains and the stars of the Big Dipper. Once I looked at the moon and caught sight of a strange thing. A cricket had perched upon the handrail, only a few inches away. My line of vision was such that the creature filled the moon like a fossil. It had gone there. I thought, to live and die, for there, of all places was its small definition made whole and eternal. A warm wind rose up and purled like the longing within me.

15   The next morning, I awoke at dawn and went out on the dirt road to Rainy Mountain. It was already hot, and the grasshoppers began to fill the air. Still, it was early in the morning, and birds sang out of the shadows. The long yellow grass on the mountain shone in the bright light, and a scissortail hied above the land. There, where it ought to be, at the end of a long and legendary way, was my grandmother's grave. She had at last succeeded to that holy ground. Here and there on the dark stones were ancestral names. Looking back once, I saw the mountain and came away.

Thinking and Responding to the Reading

1.   The title of this story is ironic. Tell why.
2.   What descriptions does Momaday give of the land, the Kiowa people and his grandmother?
3.   Why is he not returning to Rainy Mountain? What does he take away with him?
4.   What is the tone of this essay?
5.   Momaday uses metaphors and similes throughout. Find three and explain them.

Springboard for Composing

What do you know about your family's history and traditions? Are they important to you? Chose one and explain its importance to you and your ties to your family.

AROUND THE BLOCK

Sir Sidney Weinstein

Vocabulary Words

venture (par. 1)	assure (par. 2)	topography (par. 4)	invariably (par. 4)
font (par. 2)	vistas (par. 3)	conveyance (par. 4)	inviolate (par. 5)

1   I vividly recall my fears at being lost should I venture away from home. This was the time of the well-publicized kidnapping-murder trial at which Clarence Darrow defended Leopold and Loeb, and we children were warned by our parents to stay close to home. I was interested in finding a method to get back home where I walk out of sight of our apartment building. Being only four years old, I was not permitted to cross the street unaccompanied by an adult. I knew this, and I also reasoned that if I remained on the sidewalk I would be safe from cars and horse-drawn wagons. But how could I insure my return home if I lost sight of our apartment building?

2   I posed this question to my older brother Bernie, the six-year-old font of much of my knowledge. Bernie was quick to assure me that if I remained on the sidewalk, never crossing the street, and continued to walk, turning at the corners, I would return home safely. I was fascinated.

3   This knowledge was one of the most important facts of my young life, for it opened to me vistas of travel I never before imagined. I could leave home, secure in the knowledge that I could walk completely around the block—alone—St. Marks Place in New York City—and return safely home unaided by an adult.

4   Flush with this newfound knowledge, I ventured further: "If I walked in a straight line, could I walk around the world and come back home again?" (I already knew that the world was round as a ball.) I was assured by my unfailing six-year-old mentor that this was indeed the case. He did warn that since there were oceans, I would need a boat. And other geographic topography might mean I could need other types of transportation. But, despite my need for various types of conveyance, if I kept on my straight course, I would invariably return home.

5   I believe this information first demonstrated to me that valuable, inviolate rules of knowledge did exist, which if one heeded, could serve to ensure errorless paths—both geographic and intellectual—for life. This information guided me through my various paths in life.

Thinking and Responding to the Reading

1.   What is Weinstein's main point in this essay?
2.   Although Weinstein doesn't give a date of this event, he implies it in the essay. When do you think this story took place? Tell why using specific references in the essay.

3.   Paraphrase the sentence, "But despite my need for various types of conveyance, if I kept straight on my course, I would invariably return home."

4.   Do you agree if one follows a path through life using knowledge that one will be "ensured errorless paths"? Explain.

5.   Can you think of a time when you sought the advice of someone close to you? How did you apply this information?

Springboard for Composing

What qualities does a mentor have to have? What is the difference between a mentor and a friend? Can a friend be a mentor? Is a mentor a friend? A teacher and a mentor? Who is someone who has mentored you?

THE DAY I LEARNED HUMILITY

Raye McDonald

Vocabulary Words

humility (title)	flawlessly (par. 8)
impact (par. 1)	intently (par. 9)
pitiful sight to behold (par. 3)	

1   "This teacher only accepts a limited number of students. She is very tough and expects two hours of practice every day. You are very lucky to get an audience with her." I listened to my friend talk and her words made little impact on me. After all, I knew that my audition piece by the great jazz composer George Gershwin was impressive and that I could play it well enough to dazzle most anyone. And after all, I had been playing the piano for over thirty years!

2   The audition time was set for ten o'clock and when I arrived at the teacher's home at exactly that time, it was pouring down rain. I reached into the back seat of my car and grabbed my umbrella. Just as I opened it, my left thumb got caught in the handle and it pulled out a rather sizeable chunk of flesh. I found a tissue, wrapped it around the bleeding finger, grabbed my music and made a dash for the front porch. I rang the bell and waited.

3   Finally, she came to the door, and I was probably a pitiful sight to behold, standing there with a sagging umbrella and a bloody finger. She motioned for me to come inside and before I had a chance to introduce myself, she said, "You are exactly two and one half minutes late and you should never park at the front of this house. Put your things there." She motioned to a small chair sitting by the front door. I deposited everything but my music book and tried to let my eyes get used to the huge music studio that I was in.

4   There were two grand pianos sitting side by side and a lighted floor lamp stood next to one of them. The entire back wall was glass and provided the room with natural light. "You can move your car when the rain subsides. Please take a seat at that piano." She motioned to the one where the floor lamp was. "Is your piece memorized?"

5   "Yes, it is."

6   I handed her my book and she took a seat across the room from the piano. My thumb was still bleeding, and I knew that I had to tell her about it. "I cut my thumb on my umbrella and it is still bleeding. Do you have a bandage?" She disappeared into another room and quickly came back with the dressing. I thanked her and hurriedly applied the bandage to my finger.

7   I looked back at her and saw her looking at my music. "Well, I see you are going to play a ragtime piece by Gershwin. You may begin when you are ready."

8   The moment that I played the first few notes of the music, I knew everything was going to be just fine. The keys were very loose and even with the sore thumb, I played the piece flawlessly. When I finished, I dropped my hands into my lap, confident that she would give me a huge compliment, or maybe even applaud.

9   She was looking intently at the music and for at least five minutes, said nothing. My heart began to pound and my legs felt weak. And then she slowly arose from her chair, walked across the room toward me, looked intently into my eyes and said, "Yes, I can help you."

10   This is a true story. This master teacher revolutionized my playing ability and has had the most influence upon my musical life.

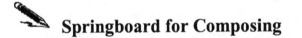

Thinking and Responding to the Reading

1. What does Raye McDonald expect to happen? What actually happens?
2. How does the teacher's first response to McDonald set the tone of their meeting?
3. Who is George Gershwin? What can we learn about the narrator from her choice of composers?
4. Do you think she was disappointed in the music teacher's response?
5. Have you had a teacher who taught you some humility? Describe this person and what you learned from him/her.

Springboard for Composing

Define the difference between the words humility and humiliation. Can a lesson in humility be a form of advice, instruction or guidance? Recall a criticism of yourself that served as a learning experience and expanded your perception of yourself and the world. Who was it? Where and when did this take place?

THE TEACHER WHO CHANGED MY LIFE

Nicholas Gage

Vocabulary Words

askance (par. 5)	war-ravaged (par. 7)	ecstatic (par. 11)
mentor (par. 5)	impoverished (par. 7)	balky (par. 16)
muse (par. 5)	thresh (par. 9)	bouzoukis (par. 19)
layabouts (par. 6)	mortified (par. 11)	catalyst (par. 21)

1   The person who set the course of my life in the new land I entered as a young war refugee—who, in fact, nearly dragged me onto the path that would bring all the blessings I've received in America—was a salty-tongued, no-nonsense school teacher named Marjorie Hurd. When I entered her classroom in 1953, I had been to six schools in five years, starting in the Greek village where I was born in 1939.

2   When I stepped off a ship in New York Harbor on a gray March day in 1949, I was an undersized 9-year-old in short pants who had lost his mother and was coming to live with the father he didn't know. My mother, Eleni Gatzoyiannis, had been imprisoned, tortured and shot by Communist guerrillas for sending me and three of my four sisters to freedom. She died so that her children could go to their father in the United States.

3   The portly, bald, well-dressed man who met me and my sisters seemed a foreign, authoritarian figure. I secretly resented him for not getting the whole family out of Greece early enough to save my mother. Ultimately, I would grow to love him and appreciate how he dealt with becoming a single parent at the age of 56, but at first our relationship was prickly, full of hostility.

4   As Father drove us to our new home—a tenement in Worcester, Mass.—and pointed out the huge brick building that would be our first school in America, I clutched my Greek notebooks from the refugee camp, hoping that my few years of schooling would impress my teachers in this cold, crowded country. They didn't. When my father led me and my 11-year-old sister to Greendale Elementary School, the grim-faced Yankee principal put the two of us in a class for the mentally retarded. There was no facility in those days for non-English-speaking children.

5   By the time I met Marjorie Hurd four years later, I had learned English, been placed in a normal, graded class and had even been chosen for the college preparatory track in the Worcester public school system. I was 13 years old when our father moved us yet again, and I entered Chandler Junior High shortly after the beginning of seventh grade. I found myself surrounded by richer, smarter and better-dressed classmates who looked askance at my strange clothes and heavy accent. Shortly after I arrived, we were told to select a hobby to pursue during "club hour" on Fridays. The idea of hobbies and clubs made no sense to my immigrant ears, but I decided to follow the prettiest girl in my class—the blue-eyed daughter of the local Lutheran minister. She led me through the door marked "Newspaper Club" and into the presence of Miss Hurd, the newspaper advisor and English teacher who would become my mentor and my muse.

6   A formidable, solidly built woman with salt-and-pepper hair, a steely eye and a flat Boston accent, Miss Hurd had no patience with layabouts. "What are all you goof-offs doing here?" she bellowed at the would-be journalists. "This is the Newspaper Club! We're going to put out a *newspaper.* So if there's anybody in this room who doesn't like work, I suggest you go across to the Glee Club now, because you're going to work your tails off here!"

7   I was soon under Miss Hurd's spell. She did indeed teach us to put out a newspaper, skills I honed during my next 25 years as a journalist. Soon I asked the principal to transfer me to her English class as well. There, she drilled us on grammar until I finally began to understand the logic and structure of the English language. She assigned stories for us to read and discuss; not tales of heroes, like the Greek myths I knew, but stories of underdogs—poor people, even immigrants, who seemed ordinary until a crisis drove them to do something extraordinary. She also introduced us to the literary wealth of Greece—giving me a new perspective on my war-ravaged, impoverished homeland. I began to be proud of my origins.

8   One day, after discussing how writers should write about what they know, she assigned us to compose an essay from our own experience. Fixing me with a stern look, she added, "Nick, I want you to write about what happened to your family in Greece." I had been trying to put those painful memories behind me and left the assignment until the last moment. Then, on a warm spring afternoon I sat in my room with a yellow pad and pencil and stared out the window at the buds on the trees. I wrote that the coming of spring always reminded me of the last time I said goodbye to my mother on a green and gold day in 1948.

9   I kept writing, one line after another, telling how the Communist guerrillas occupied our village, took our home and food, how my mother started planning our escape when she learned that the children were to be sent to re-education camps behind the Iron Curtain and how, at the last moment, she couldn't escape with us because the guerrillas sent her with a group of women to thresh wheat in a distant village. She promised she would try to get away on her own, she told me to be brave and hung a silver cross around my neck, and then she kissed me. I watched the line of women being led down into the ravine and up the other side, until they disappeared around the bend—my mother a tiny brown figure at the end who stopped for an instant to raise her hand in one last farewell.

10   I wrote about our nighttime escape down the mountain, across the minefields and into the lines of the Nationalist soldiers, who sent us to a refugee camp. It was there that we learned of our mother's execution. I felt very lucky to have come to America, I concluded, but every year, the coming of spring made me feel sad because it reminded me of the last time I saw my mother.

11   I handed in the essay, hoping never to see it again, but Miss Hurd had it published in the school paper. This mortified me at first, until I saw that my classmates reacted with sympathy and tact to my family's story. Without telling me, Miss Hurd also submitted the essay to a contest sponsored by the Freedoms Foundation at Valley Forge, Pa., and it won a medal. The Worcester paper wrote about the award and quoted my essay at length. My father, by then a "five-and-dime-store chef," as the paper described him, was ecstatic with pride, and the Worcester Greek community celebrated the honor to one of its own.

12   For the first time I began to understand the power of the written word. A secret ambition took root in me. One day, I vowed, I would go back to Greece, find out the details of my mother's death and write about her life, so her grandchildren would know of

her courage. Perhaps I would even track down the men who killed her and write of their crimes. Fulfilling that ambition would take me 30 years.

13   Meanwhile, I followed the literary path that Miss Hurd had so forcefully set me on. After junior high, I became the editor of my school paper at Classical High School and got a part-time job at the Worcester Telegram and Gazette. Although my father could only give me $50 and encouragement toward a college education, I managed to finance four years at Boston University with scholarships and part-time jobs in journalism. During my last year of college, an article I wrote about a friend who had died in the Philippines—the first person to lose his life working for the Peace Corps—led to my winning the Hearst Award for College Journalism. And the plaque was given to me in the White House by President John F. Kennedy.

14   For a refugee who had never seen a motorized vehicle or indoor plumbing until he was 9, this was an unimaginable honor. When the Worcester paper ran a picture of me standing next to President Kennedy, my father rushed out to buy a new suit in order to be properly dressed to receive the congratulations of the Worcester Greeks. He clipped out the photograph, had it laminated in plastic and carried it in his breast pocket for the rest of his life to show everyone he met. I found the much worn photo in his pocket on the day he died 20 years later.

15   In our isolated Greek village, my mother had bribed a cousin to teach her to read, for girls were not supposed to attend school beyond a certain age. She had always dreamed of her children receiving an education. She couldn't be there when I graduated from Boston University, but the person who came with my father and shared our joy was my former teacher, Marjorie Hurd. We celebrated not only my bachelor's degree but also the scholarship that paid my way to Columbia's Graduate School of Journalism. There, I met the woman who would eventually become my wife. At our wedding and at the baptisms of our three children, Marjorie Hurd was always there, dancing alongside the Greeks.

16   By then, she was Mrs. Rabidou, for she had married a widower when she was in her early 40s. That didn't distract her from her vocation of introducing young minds to English literature, however. She taught for a total of 41 years and continually would make a "project" of some balky student in whom she spied a spark of potential. Often these were students from the most troubled homes, yet she would alternately bully and charm each one with her own special brand of tough love until the spark caught fire. She retired in 1981 at the age of 62 but still avidly follows the lives and careers of former students while overseeing her adult stepchildren and driving her husband on camping trips to New Hampshire.

17   Miss Hurd was one of the first to call me on Dec. 10, 1987, when President Reagan, in his television address after the summit meeting with Gorbachev, told the nation that Eleni Gatzoyiannis' dying cry, "My children!" had helped inspire him to seek an arms agreement "for all the children of the world."

18   "I can't imagine a better monument for your mother," Miss Hurd said with an uncharacteristic catch in her voice.

19   Although a bad hip makes it impossible for her to join in the Greek dancing, Marjorie Hurd Rabidou is still an honored and enthusiastic guest at all family celebrations, including my 50th birthday picnic last summer, where the shishkebab was cooked on spits, clarinets and bouzoukis wailed, and costumed dancers led the guests in a serpentine line around our Colonial farmhouse, only 20 minutes from my first home in Worcester.

20   My sisters and I felt an aching void because my father was not there to lead the line, balancing a glass of wine on his head while he danced, the way he did at every celebration during his 92 years. But Miss Hurd was there, surveying the scene with quiet satisfaction. Although my parents are gone, her presence was a consolation, because I owe her so much.

21   This is truly the land of opportunity, and I would have enjoyed its bounty even if I hadn't walked into Miss Hurd's classroom in 1953. But she was the one who directed my grief and pain into writing, and if it weren't for her I wouldn't have become an investigative reporter and foreign correspondent, recorded the story of my mother's life and death in *Eleni* and now my father's story in *A Place for Us*, which is also a testament to the country that took us in. She was the catalyst that sent me into journalism and indirectly caused all the good things that came after. But Miss Hurd would probably deny this emphatically.

22   A few years ago, I answered the telephone and heard my former teacher's voice telling me, in that won't-take-no-for-an-answer tone of hers, that she had decided I was to write and deliver the eulogy at her funeral. I agreed (she didn't leave me any choice), but that's one assignment I never want to do. I hope, Miss Hurd, that you'll accept this remembrance instead.

Thinking and Responding to the Reading

1.   Explain the line, "For the first time I began to understand the power of the written word." What power is the speaker talking about? What can words do?

2.   List the honors Nick received over the years as a writer. Which one would you pick as the most important one? Which one would he pick? Do you both agree?

3.   What was Gage's purpose in writing about his mother and father's life especially since they were neither prominent nor famous people? What purposes does a biography serve?

4.   Towards the end of the story, Gage remarks, "This is truly the land of opportunity." Is this the only point of the story or are there others? Explain.

Springboard for Composing

Explain how, with Miss Hurd's mentoring, Nicholas becomes more comfortable in his new school as well as his adopted country. Now recall a time when you received someone's help to feel the same way other than your home. Consider these possibilities: your workplace, a relative's house, a rehab center, a dorm or a friend's house.

ADVICE TO YOUTH

Samuel L. Clemens

Vocabulary Words

didactic (par. 1)	painstaking (par. 5)	heedless (par. 6)
enduring (par. 1)	eminence (par. 5)	precepts (par. 8)
beseechingly (par. 1)	peerless (par. 5)	gratified (par. 8)
temperate (par. 5)	prevail (par. 5)	

1   Being told I would be expected to talk here, I inquired what sort of a talk I ought to make. They said it should be something suitable to youth—something didactic, instructive, or something in the nature of good advice. Very well. I have a few things in my mind which I have often longed to say for the instruction of the young: for it is one's tender early years that such things will best take root and be most enduring and most valuable. First, then, I will say to you, my young friends—and I say it beseechingly, urgingly—

2   Always obey you parents, when they are present. This is the best policy in the long run, because if you don't they will make you. Most parents think they know better than you do, and you can generally make more by humoring that superstition than you can by acting on your own better judgment.

3   Be respectful to your superiors, if you have any, also to strangers, and sometimes to others. If a person offends you, and you are in doubt as to whether it was intentional or not, do not resort to extreme measures; simply watch your chance and hit him with a brick. That will be sufficient. If you shall find that he had not intended any offense, come out frankly and confess yourself in the wrong when you struck him; acknowledge it like a man and say you didn't mean to. Yes, always avoid violence; in this age of charity and kindliness, the time has gone by for such things. Leave dynamite to the low and unrefined.

4   Go to bed early, get up early—this is wise. Some authorities say get up with the sun; some others say get up with one thing, some with another. But a lark is really the best thing to get up with. It gives you a splendid reputation with everybody to know that you get up with the lark; and if you get the right kind of a lark, and work at him right, you can easily train him to get up at half past nine, every time—it is no trick at all.

5   Now as to the matter of lying. You want to be very careful about lying; otherwise you are nearly sure to get caught. Once caught, you can never again be, in the eyes of the good and the pure, what you were before. Many a young person has injured himself permanently through a single clumsy and ill finished lie, the result of carelessness born of incomplete training. Some authorities hold that the young ought not to lie at all. That, of course, is putting it rather stronger than necessary; still, while I cannot go quite so far as that, I do maintain, and I believe I am right, that the young ought to be temperate in the use of this great art until practice and experience shall give them that confidence, elegance, and precision which alone can make the accomplishment graceful and profitable. Patience, diligence, painstaking attention to detail—these are the requirements; these, in

time, will make the student perfect; upon these, and upon these only, may he rely as the sure foundation for future eminence. Think what tedious years of study, thought, practice, experience, went to the equipment of that peerless old master who was able to impose upon the whole world the lofty and high sounding maxim that "truth is mighty and will prevail"—the most majestic compound fracture of fact which any of woman born has yet achieved. For the history of our race, and each individual's experience, are sown thick with evidence that a truth is not hard to kill and that a lie told well is immortal. There is in Boston a monument of the man who discovered anesthesia; many people are aware, in these latter days, that that man didn't discover it at all, but stole the discovery from another man. Is this truth mighty, and will it prevail? Ah no, my hearers, the monument is made of hardy material, but the lie it tells will outlast it a million years. An awkward, feeble, leaky lie is a thing which you ought to make it your unceasing study to avoid; such a lie as that has no more real permanence than an average truth. Why, you might as well tell the truth at once and be done with it. A feeble, stupid, preposterous lie will not live two years—except it be a slander upon somebody. It is indestructible, then, of course, but that is no merit of yours. A final word: begin your practice of this gracious and beautiful art early—begin now. If I had begun earlier, I could have learned how.

6   Never handle firearms carelessly. The sorrow and suffering that have been caused through the innocent but heedless handling of firearms by the young! Only four days ago, right in the next farmhouse to the one where I am spending the summer, a grandmother, old and gray and sweet, one of the loveliest spirits in the land, was sitting at her work, when her young grandson crept in and got down an old, battered, rusty gun which had not been touched for many years and was supposed not to be loaded, and pointed it at her, laughing and threatening to shoot. In her fright she ran screaming and pleading toward the door on the other side of the room; but as she passed him he placed the gun almost against her very breast and pulled the trigger! He had supposed it was not loaded. And he was right—it wasn't. So there wasn't any harm done. It is the only case of that kind I ever heard of. Therefore, just the same, don't you meddle with old unloaded firearms; they are the most deadly and unerring things that have ever been created by man. You don't have to take any pains at all with them; you don't have to have a rest, you don't have to have any sights on the gun, you don't have to take aim, even. No, you just pick out a relative and bang away, and you are sure to get him. A youth who can't hit a cathedral at thirty yards with a Gatling gun in three-quarters of an hour, can take up an old empty musket and bag his grandmother every time, at a hundred. Think what Waterloo would have been if one of the armies had been boys armed with old muskets supposed not to be loaded, and the other army had been composed of their female relations. The very thought of it makes one shudder.

7   There are many sorts of books; but good ones are the sort for the young to read. Remember that. They are a great, an inestimable, an unspeakable means of improvement. Therefore be careful in your selection, my young friends; be very careful; confine yourselves exclusively to Robertson's Sermons, Baxter's Saint's Rest, The Innocents Abroad, and works of that kind.

8   But I have said enough. I hope you will treasure up the instructions which I have given you, and make them a guide to your feet and a light to your understanding. Build your character thoughtfully and painstakingly upon these precepts, and by and by, when

68

you have got it built, you will be surprised and gratified to see how nicely and sharply it resembles everybody else's.

Thinking and Responding to the Reading

1. In the first paragraph, Clemens says he was requested to give a talk, "something suitable to youth—something didactic, instructive, or something in the nature of good advice." Is the advice he gives "didactic, instructive or something in the nature of good advice"? Or is it humorous? Explain.
2. Clemens is known for irony; this speech is a good example. Quote at least three instances of his uses of irony and explain each meaning.
3. In paragraph 5, why does Clemens say, "If I had begun earlier, I could have learned how…"? What does he mean by this?
4. Paraphrase paragraph 8, and then explain the inference in the paragraph.

Something that isn't exactly said but the term is hinted

Springboard for Composing

Think of a time when you mentored or imagined mentoring someone younger than yourself. What specific advice did or would you give this person so as to allow him or her to flourish? Try not to repeat what Clemens has written.

THE GETTYSBURG ADDRESS

Address delivered at the dedication of the cemetery at Gettysburg, Pennsylvania
November 19, 1863

Abraham Lincoln

Vocabulary Words

score (par. 1)
conceived (par. 1)
proposition (par. 1)
conceived (par. 2)

endure (par. 2)
consecrate (par. 3)
hallow (par. 3)
detract (par. 3)

devotion (par. 3)
in vain (par. 3)
perish (par. 3)

1   Four score and seven years ago our fathers brought forth on this continent a new nation, conceived in liberty and dedicated to the proposition that all men are created equal.

2   Now we are engaged in a great civil war, testing whether that nation or any nation so conceived and so dedicated can long endure. We are met on a great battlefield of that war. We have come to dedicate a portion of that field as a final resting-place for those who here gave their lives that that nation might live. It is altogether fitting and proper that we should do this.

3   But in a larger sense, we cannot dedicate, we cannot consecrate, we cannot hallow this ground. The brave men, living and dead who struggled here have consecrated it far above our poor power to add or detract. The world will little note nor long remember what we say here, but it can never forget what they did here. It is for us the living rather to be dedicated here to the unfinished work which they who fought here have thus far so nobly advanced. It is rather for us to be here dedicated to the great task remaining before us—that from these honored dead we take increased devotion to that cause for which they gave the last full measure of devotion—that we here highly resolve that these dead shall not have died in vain, that this nation under God shall have a new birth of freedom, and that government of the people, by the people, for the people shall not perish from the earth.

Thinking and Responding to the Reading

1.   Memorize The Gettysburg Address and be prepared to recite parts of it.
2.   Paraphrase the first sentence.
3.   Locate a sentence that has particular meaning for you. Explain its relationship to your social values and norms.
4.   What "great task" remains before Lincoln and the rest of the U.S.?
5.   What element of this "great task" have we achieved? What tasks remain?

70

Springboard for Composing

Surely you have heard or read from various sources that espouse the idea that all people are created equal. This is a difficult concept to truly comprehend. Are there any exceptions in your view? You have read, heard about and possibly even seen brave people giving up their lives in order to make a better world for the remaining living. What have you learned from these acts that more than likely a teacher could not teach you?

A HANGING

George Orwell

Vocabulary Words

sodden (par. 1)	solemn foolery (par. 10)	timorously (par. 15)	refractory (par. 22)
absurdly (par. 2)	servile (par. 11)	oscillated (par. 16)	anecdote (par. 24)
desolately (par. 3)	abominable (par. 13)	garrulously (par. 20)	amicably (par. 24)
pariah (par. 6)			

1   It was in Burma, sodden morning of the rains. A sickly light, like yellow tinfoil, was slanting over the high walls into the jail yard. We were waiting outside the condemned cells, a row of sheds fronted with double bars, like small animal cages. Each cell measured about ten feet by ten and was quite bare within except for a plank bed and a pot of drinking water. In some of them brown silent men were squatting at the inner bars, with their blankets draped round them. These were the condemned men, due to be hanged within the next week or two.

2   One prisoner had been brought out of his cell. He was a Hindu, a puny wisp of a man, with a shaven head and vague liquid eyes. He had a thick, sprouting moustache, absurdly too big for his body, rather like the moustache of a comic man on the films. Six tall Indian warders were guarding him and getting him ready for the gallows. Two of them stood by with rifles and fixed bayonets, while the others handcuffed him, passed a chain through his handcuffs and fixed it to their belts, and lashed his arms tight to his sides. They crowded very close about him, with their hands always on him in a careful, caressing grip, as though all the while feeling him to make sure he was there. It was like men handling a fish which is still alive and may jump back into the water. But he stood quite unresisting, yielding his arms limply to the ropes, as though he hardly noticed what was happening.

3   Eight o'clock struck and a bugle call, desolately thin in the wet air, floated from the distant barracks. The superintendent of the jail, who was standing apart from the rest of us, moodily prodding the gravel with his stick, raised his head at the sound. He was an army doctor, with a grey toothbrush moustache and a gruff voice. "For God's sake hurry up, Francis," he said irritably. "The man ought to have been dead by this time. Aren't you ready yet?"

4   Francis, the head jailer, a fat Dravidian in a white drill suit and gold spectacles, waved his black hand. "Yes, sir, yes sir," he bubbled. "All iss satisfactorily prepared. The hangman iss waiting. We shall proceed."

5   "Well, quick march, then. The prisoners can't get their breakfast till this job's over."

6   We set out for the gallows. Two warders marched on either side of the prisoner, with their rifles at the slope; two others marched close against him, gripping him by arm and shoulder, as though at once pushing and supporting him. The rest of us, magistrates and the like, followed behind. Suddenly, when we had gone ten yards, the procession stopped short without any order or warning. A dreadful thing had happened—a dog

came from goodness knows whence, had appeared in the yard. It came bounding among us with a loud volley of barks, and leapt round us wagging its whole body, wild with glee at finding so many human beings together. It was a large woolly dog, half Airedale, half pariah. For a moment it pranced round us, and then, before anyone could stop it, it had made a dash for the prisoner, and jumping up tried to lick his face. Everyone stood aghast, too taken aback even to grab at the dog.

7   "Who let that bloody brute in here?" said the superintendent angrily. "Catch it, someone!"

8   A warder, detached from the escort, charged clumsily after the dog, but it danced and gamboled just out of his reach, taking everything as part of the game. A young Eurasian jailer picked up a handful of gravel and tried to stone the dog away, but it dodged the stones and came after us again. Its yaps echoed from the jail walls. The prisoner, in the grasp of the two warders, looked on incuriously as though this was another formality of the hanging. It was several minutes before someone managed to catch the dog. Then we put my handkerchief through its collar and moved off once more, with the dog still straining and whimpering.

9   It was about forty yards to the gallows. I watched the bare brown back of the prisoner marching in front of me. He walked clumsily with his bound arms, but quite steadily, with that bobbing gait of the Indian who never straightens his knees. At each step his muscles slid neatly into place, the lock of hair on his scalp danced up and down, his feet printed themselves on the wet gravel. And once, in spite of the men who gripped him by each shoulder, he stepped slightly aside to avoid a puddle on the path.

10   It is curious, but till that moment I had never realized what it means to destroy a healthy, conscious man. When I saw the prisoner step aside to avoid the puddle, I saw the mystery, the unspeakable wrongness, of cutting a life short when it is in full tide. This man was not dying; he was alive just as we were alive. All the organs of his body were working–bowels digesting food, skin renewing itself, nails growing, tissues forming–all toiling away in solemn foolery. His nails would still be growing when he stood on the drop, when he was falling through the air with a tenth of a second to live. His eyes saw the yellow gravel and the grey walls, and his brain still remembered, foresaw, reasoned--reasoned even about puddles. He and we were a party of men walking together, seeing, hearing, feeling, understanding the same world; and in two minutes, with a sudden snap, one of us would be gone–one mind less, one world less.

11   The gallows stood in a small yard, separate from the main grounds of the prison, and overgrown with tall prickly weeds. It was a brick erection like three sides of a shed, with planking on top, and above that two beams and a crossbar with the rope dangling. The hangman, a grey-haired convict in the white uniform of the prison, was waiting beside his machine. He greeted us with a servile crouch as we entered. At a word from Francis the two warders, gripping the prisoner more closely than ever, half led, half pushed him to the gallows and helped him clumsily up the ladder. Then the hangman climbed up and fixed the rope round the prisoner's neck.

12   We stood waiting, five yards away. The warders had formed in a rough circle round the gallows. And then, when the noose was fixed, the prisoner began crying out on his god. It was a high, reiterated cry of "Ram! Ram! Ram! Ram!", not urgent and fearful like a prayer or a cry for help, but steady, rhythmical, almost like the tolling of a bell. The dog answered the sound with a whine. The hangman, still standing on the gallows,

produced a small cotton bag like a flour bag and drew it down over the prisoner's face. But the sound, muffled by the cloth, still persisted, over and over again: "Ram! Ram! Ram! Ram! Ram!"

13   The hangman climbed down and stood ready, holding the lever. Minutes seemed to pass. The steady, muffled crying from the prisoner went on and on, "Ram! Ram! Ram!" never faltering for an instant. The superintendent, his head on his chest, was slowly poking the ground with his stick; perhaps he was counting the cries, allowing the prisoner a fixed number–fifty, perhaps, or a hundred. Everyone had changed colour. The Indians had gone grey like bad coffee, and one or two of the bayonets were wavering. We looked at the lashed, hooded man on the drop, and listened to his cries--each cry another sound of life; the same thought was in all our minds: oh, kill him quickly, get it over, stop that abominable noise!

14   Suddenly the superintendent made up his mind. Throwing up his head he made a swift motion with his stick. "Chalo!" he shouted almost fiercely.

15   There was a clanking noise, and then dead silence. The prisoner had vanished, and the rope was twisting on itself. I let go of the dog, and it galloped immediately to the back of the gallows; but when it got there it stopped short, barked, and then retreated into a corner of the yard, where it stood among the weeds, looking timorously out at us. We went round the gallows to inspect the prisoner's body. He was dangling with his toes pointed straight downwards, very slowly revolving, as dead as a stone.

16   The superintendent reached out with his stick and poked the bare body; it oscillated, slightly. "He's all right," said the superintendent. He backed out from under the gallows, and blew out a deep breath. The moody look had gone out of his face quite suddenly. He glanced at his wrist-watch. "Eight minutes past eight. Well, that's all for this morning, thank God."

17   The warders unfixed bayonets and marched away. The dog, sobered and conscious of having misbehaved itself, slipped after them. We walked out of the gallows yard, past the condemned cells with their waiting prisoners, into the big central yard of the prison. The convicts, under the command of warders armed with lathis, were already receiving their breakfast. They squatted in long rows, each man holding a tin pannikin, while two warders with buckets marched round ladling out rice; it seemed quite a homely, jolly scene, after the hanging. An enormous relief had come upon us now that the job was done. One felt an impulse to sing, to break into a run, to snigger. All at once everyone began chattering gaily.

18   The Eurasian boy walking beside me nodded towards the way we had come, with a knowing smile: "Do you know, sir, our friend (he meant the dead man), when he heard his appeal had been dismissed, he pissed on the floor of his cell. From fright. – Kindly take one of my cigarettes, sir. Do you not admire my new silver case, sir? From the boxwallah, two rupees eight annas. Classy European style."

19   Several people laughed--at what, nobody seemed certain.

20   Francis was walking by the superintendent, talking garrulously. "Well, sir, all hass passed off with the utmost satisfactoriness. It wass all finished--flick! Like that. It is not always so–oah, no! I have known cases where the doctor wass obliged to go beneath the gallows and pull the prisoner's legs to ensure decease. Most disagreeable!"

21   "Wriggling about, eh? That's bad," said the superintendent.

22   "Ach, sir, it iss worse when they become refractory! One man, I recall, clung to the bars of hiss cage when we went to take him out. You will scarcely credit, sir, that it took six warders to dislodge him, three pulling at each leg. We reasoned with him. 'My dear fellow,' we said, 'think of all the pain and trouble you are causing to us!' But no, he would not listen! Ach, he was very troublesome!"

23   I found that I was laughing quite loudly. Everyone was laughing. Even the superintendent grinned in a tolerant way. "You'd better all come out and have a drink," he said quite genially. "I've got a bottle of whisky in the car. We could do with it."

24   We went through the big double gates of the prison, into the road. "Pulling at his legs!" exclaimed a Burmese magistrate suddenly, and burst into a loud chuckling. We all began laughing again. At that moment Francis's anecdote seemed extraordinarily funny. We all had a drink together, native and European alike, quite amicably. The dead man was a hundred yards away.

Thinking and Responding to the Reading

1.   What are the setting (place), and time period and conditions of "The Hanging?" Does knowing this help you to understand the story better?
2.   From the description of the hanging, state whether George Orwell is for or against capital punishment. Explain your answer.
3.   Who are the major characters? Would you include the dog? Why or why not?
4.   What is the significance of the prisoner stepping around the puddle?
5.   Orwell uses much figurative language, especially similes, in this essay. Find three similes in this essay and explain to what each simile refers.
6.   At the end of essay (par. 17-24), Orwell describes the behavior of the warders, superintendent and himself. What do you think he is feeling (ambivalent, disconsolate, elated, betrayed, alienated)? Then explain the last two sentences: "We all had a drink together, native and European alike, quite amicably. The dead man was a hundred yards away."

Springboard for Composing

Recall a time when you learned to work together, possibly despite differences of opinion, with members of a group (such as a youth group, a scout troop, a sports team, a choir or classmates) in order to execute a specific project. What happened? What did you do to make working together a smooth process? How did you resolve any differences?

CAPITAL PUNISHMENT

Carl Wellman

Vocabulary Words

inalienable (par. 1)
abolished (par. 2)
imposition (par. 2)
ambiguous (par. 3)
justifiability (par. 3)

virtuous (par. 4)
conscientiously (par 4)
heinous (par. 5)
plausible (par. 6)

depraved (par. 7)
inhibited (par. 8)
inclinations (par. 8)
salutary (par. 8)

inherent (par. 8)
deterrence (par. 9)
retribution (par. 9)
aggregate (par. 10)

1   Many people believe that, as the Declaration of Independence affirms, all human beings are born with an inalienable right to life. Presumably, the reason, or at least one of the reasons, that murder is wrong is that it is a violation of the victim's right to life. But what of the criminal's right to life? In most societies throughout history, the punishment for murder has been execution. If the murderer is a human being, and surely he is, and if his right to life is inalienable, as human rights are usually taken to be, then the murderer has a right to live that he has not forfeited by his criminal act. It would appear that capital punishment is as much a violation of the fundamental human right to life as murder itself. It seems to follow that the execution of a condemned criminal is always wrong. This raises the question of whether there are any circumstances that morally justify capital punishment.

2   This question is an issue of lively debate these days. Great Britain abolished the death penalty in 1969 for all crimes except wartime offenses such as treason or spying, but with the increase in crimes of violence, there has been a rising demand for the restoration of capital punishment for crimes such as the murder of a policeman or a child. In Furman v. Georgia (1972), the United States Supreme Court declared unconstitutional any statute imposing capital punishment at the discretion of the judge or jury, but it left undecided the constitutionality of the death penalty itself. As a result, many states have since then enacted new statutes making the imposition of the death penalty mandatory in the case of certain crimes such as first-degree murder or kidnapping. The morality and effectiveness of such statutes continues to be debated in Congress and in the state legislatures.

Defining the Problem

3   Let us try to define this specific moral problem more precisely. The expression "capital punishment" is ambiguous. It often refers to a certain kind of social institution. The institution of capital punishment is one pattern of punishment that forms part of the legal system in many, but not all, societies. It involves certain roles like those of the executioner and the criminal and certain rules such as the rule that only a person condemned to death by the courts is to be executed. One may well question the moral justifiability of this social institution, but this is not the question raised here. Instead, let us interpret the

us interpret the expression "capital punishment" as referring to a species of acts, acts of executing someone for conduct judged to be criminal.

[4] The question is whether such acts are right or wrong; this is not to ask whether such acts are virtuous or wicked. Presumably the act of executing an innocent person is wrong, ought not to be done, even when there may be nothing wicked in the act of an executioner who conscientiously performs his painful duty in complete ignorance of any judicial error. Again, even if it is granted that a given act of executing an incurably vicious criminal is right, it would not follow that there is any moral goodness in the act if the executioner performs it in order to enjoy the suffering of the victim rather than from a sense of duty to society. To ask whether an act ought or ought not to be done is not to ask whether it is morally praiseworthy or blameworthy. It is the former, the question of rightness or wrongness, that is at issue here.

[5] Finally, the question is whether capital punishment is ever right, whether there are any exceptional circumstances in which the act of executing a condemned criminal may be morally justifiable. No one could seriously maintain that capital punishment is always right, that condemned criminals should always be executed. An act of lynching performed by an enraged mob is a heinous wrong even when the mob has condemned its victim with a mock trial. In a less spectacular way, it is morally wrong to take a criminal's life for any trivial crime like shoplifting or speeding on the highway. The only serious alternatives are that it is always wrong to execute a condemned criminal, no matter how great his crime, and that, in a few cases, it is right to take a criminal's life for conduct judged to be very, very wrong. Hence, the question worth discussing is "Is capital punishment ever right?"

Arguments for Capital Punishment

[6] The classical and contemporary literature on the subject of capital punishment provides several very plausible arguments designed to prove that the act of executing a person for conduct judged to be criminal is sometimes right.

Prevention

[7] Capital punishment is sometimes morally justified as a means of preventing the criminal from committing additional crimes. By his past action the criminal has shown himself to be wicked and dangerous. Anyone depraved enough to murder or rape once is very likely to act in socially harmful ways again. The only sure way to prevent such a person from going on to murder or rape in the future is to execute him. Imprisonment is a far less effective means of protecting society from such dangerous criminals. Most prisoners are freed after a time—often having become more dangerous than when they entered prison—by parole, pardon or the expiration of their sentences. In any case, escape is always possible. And even within the confines of prison, a condemned criminal may murder or rape a guard, a fellow inmate or a visitor. Executing a condemned criminal is the only sure way to prevent him from committing additional acts of crime. Since it is only right to protect the innocent members of society from the most serious crimes, capital punishment is sometimes right.

Deterrence

[8]   Not only does capital punishment prevent the criminal himself from doing further harm to society, it also deters others from doing similar acts. Most people are tempted from time to time to do illegal and immoral acts; but the normal person is usually inhibited by conscience, or by fear of public condemnation, from serious wrongdoing. Some people, alas, require a stronger motive to overcome their criminal inclinations; and only the strongest threats of punishment can hold in check the strong emotions that cause the greatest crimes. Since almost everyone is terrified of death, capital punishment provides this salutary motive. The execution of one condemned criminal serves as an example to others of what may well befall them if they yield to their criminal impulses. Although very few potential criminals have personally witnessed executions, and fewer still have suffered them, the publicity given to the hanging or electrocution of condemned murderers and kidnappers has made almost everyone aware that the threat of the death penalty is no empty gesture. This knowledge, stimulating the deep and powerful fear of death inherent in human nature, deters potential criminals from the socially harmful acts they would otherwise commit. Since capital punishment sometimes deters potential criminals from doing socially harmful acts, and since it is right to protect society from seriously harmful acts, capital punishment is sometimes right.

Retribution

[9]   While the arguments from prevention and deterrence look to the future and attempt to justify capital punishment by an appeal to the future harm it will avoid, the argument from retribution looks to the past and tries to justify capital punishment as the right response to the wrong that has been done. Granted that society would be unjustified in taking a person's life in punishment for any trivial crime, capital punishment is just retribution for the greatest crimes. If one person has killed another, it is only fair that he give his own life in return. Kidnapping and rape are also so very wrong that the person who commits these acts deserves the greatest penalty, death. Justice demands that each individual be treated by others and by society as he deserves. The person who does good acts ought to be rewarded with good, and the person who does evil ought to suffer evil— each in proportion to the good or evil done. The conception of justice implicit in this argument has traditionally been illustrated by the figure of a blindfolded woman holding a set of balance scales. The woman is blindfolded so that she cannot recognize her friends and enemies and award the former more good and the latter more evil than they deserve. The balance scales symbolizes the element of retribution, the notion that good or evil are to be awarded in return for good or evil done. The total conception is that justice demands that each person receive what is due to him, that he receive an amount of good or evil that is equal to the good or evil he has done. Applied to punishment, this means that the punishment should fit the crime, that the evil inflicted upon the condemned criminal should be in proportion to the degree of harm he has done. Since the only penalty bad enough to equal the greatest crimes is death, and since justice requires that the criminal receive just retribution for his past misdeeds, and since it is right to do what justice requires, capital punishment is sometimes right.

Self-Defense

10   Capital punishment is sometimes right because it is sometimes an exercise of society's right to self-defense. Although it is generally wrong for one human being to take the life of another, there are exceptional cases where this is morally justified. A person has a right to kill his attacker if this is necessary to preserve his life or limb. Society, like the individual, has the right to preserve itself when its very existence is threatened. Now a murderer attacks, not only his individual victim, but society itself.   Since a society is constituted by an aggregate of individuals, to kill one or more individuals is already to begin to exterminate the society. Moreover, certain laws, such as the law prohibiting murder, are necessary if any collection of individuals are to live together in organized society. Hence, to break those laws that alone make the existence of society possible is to threaten that society with death. Capital punishment is sometimes right because it is right for society to exercise its right to self-defense, and in extreme cases capital punishment does defend the society from the attacks of a criminal that threatens its very existence.

Fulfilling a Duty

11   Executing a condemned criminal is sometimes right because it fulfills the duty of the executioner. Each of us plays many roles in society. I, for example, am a husband, a father, a citizen and a professor. Each social role brings with it certain duties. As a husband, my duties are at least to support my wife financially, to share certain household responsibilities, and to care for my wife in sickness and in health. To accept the position of professor in a university is to accept the duties of preparing lectures, grading tests and papers, holding regular office hours when students come for help in their studies, and doing original research as well. Similarly, the social role of public executioner brings with it certain duties, the chief of which is executing those condemned to death by the courts. No doubt it would be morally wrong for you or me to take the life of the criminal, no matter how guilty he might be. But it is right for the executioner to perform the act of capital punishment because he is acting in fulfillment of his duty as public executioner, and it is right to fulfill the duties of one's social role.

12   These are five arguments for capital punishment. It prevents the criminal from doing additional evil acts. It deters others from committing serious crimes. It is just retribution for the great wrong the criminal has done. It is society's act of killing in self-defense. And it fulfills the chief duty of the executioner. It is worth remembering that none of these arguments pretends to prove that all acts of capital punishment are right; each is intended to show only that it is sometimes right to execute a condemned criminal.

Thinking and Responding to the Reading

1.   Restate the problem Wellman asserts about capital punishment. What do you consider the problem or claim (argument) of the essay?
2.   List the premises which support the claim with facts, observations, and interpretations.

2. List the premises which support the claim with facts, observations, and interpretations.
3. Using the techniques to check for validity, analyze the validity of Wellman's argument.
4. Wellman uses both descriptive and prescriptive assumptions. List each and explain. Use Cornell Note Method if you like.
5. Do you agree with his argument? Explain your answer.
6. Compare Wellman's evidence concerning retribution to the evidence presented by Caryl Chessman in "A Letter to the Governor."

Springboard for Composing

What is your position on capital punishment? If you were serving on a jury case in which capital punishment could be the sentence imposed, how do you imagine yourself working together with your fellow jurors to achieve the required unanimous verdict?

A LETTER TO THE GOVERNOR

Caryl Chessman

Vocabulary Words

clemency (par. 2)	vengeance (par. 16)	pride (par. 25)
commutation (par. 2)	paradoxical evidence (par. 18)	vituperation (par. 25)
inevitable (par. 3)	barbarous (par. 18)	sardonically (par. 25)
oblivion (par. 3)	anachronism (par. 18)	sneered (par. 25)
confounding solution (par. 3)	cunning (par. 18)	remorseless (par. 25)
compelled (par. 5)	fiendish (par. 18)	reviled (par. 25)
grimly (par. 9)	hyperbole (par. 19)	internecine (par. 27)
reprieve (par. 12)	rationalize (par. 19)	vilified (par. 30)
reverberated (par. 13)	earnestly (par. 20)	redemption (par. 30)
sadistic (par. 13)	disavow (par. 20)	penologists (par. 33)
abolition (par. 15)	sever (par. 21)	futile (par. 34)
intercession (par. 15)	psychopath (par. 23)	degraded (par. 34)
defiance (par. 16)	endeavored (par. 23)	
wrath (par. 16)	ruthlessly (par. 24)	

Name: Caryl Chessman
Box 66565, San Quentin, Calif.

Date: February 26, 1960

The Hon. Edmund G. Brown
Governor of the State of California
State Capitol
Sacramento, California

Dear Governor Brown:

[1]   As you know, at approximately 4:45 p.m. on Thursday, February 19, 1960, I was removed from the Death Row Unit located on the fifth floor of the North Block here at San Quentin and locked in the small holding cell, just a few feet from the State's lethal gas chamber, where California's condemned spend their last night on earth. The death watch began. So far as I knew, I would be put to death at ten o'clock in the morning.

[2]   I was permitted to see an early edition of a Friday newspaper. Its headlines were large and black: CHESSMAN MUST DIE, BROWN SAYS. Again, only an hour earlier the members of the California Supreme Court had voted 4 to 3 against a recommendation to you for clemency. Thus, by a simple vote, you were foreclosed from exercising your commutation powers. The court had made its order "final forthwith." I had been notified of that action a few hours before being taken downstairs to the holding cell. In anticipation of it, I had put my affairs in order and executed a new will....

3 And death appeared inevitable. I held out no foolish, desperate hope for a life-sparing miracle. On the contrary, what sustained me, what made it possible for me to await the morning and oblivion with a detached, almost clinical calm was hope of an entirely different sort: the burning hope that my execution would lead to an objective reappraisal of the social validity or invalidity of capital punishment, and that such a reexamination would lead, in turn, to an awareness on the part of all Californians that Death Rows, and death chambers and executioners were unworthy of our society, that the former, in fact, were gross obscenities, solving nothing but rather confounding solution.

4 The minutes passed, the hours. The prison's Catholic Chaplain, Father Edward Dingberg, visited me. Associate Wardens Walter D. Archuff and Louis S. Nelson saw me for a few minutes. Dr. David G. Schmidt, San Quentin's chief psychiatrist, came in. Attorney George Davis conferred with me hurriedly, intending to return later. Warden Fred R. Dickson dropped by for a talk.

5 Contrary to published accounts that I consumed the condemned man's traditional hearty meal of "fried chicken, French fried potatoes, vegetable salad, coffee and two kinds of pie—apple and chocolate cream," I am compelled to confess these reports, seemingly attesting to my capacity as a trencherman, are somewhat exaggerated. Actually, my wants were more modest. I had a hamburger and a Coke about 7:30, and during the course of the evening I drank three cups of coffee. I also puffed on a cigar, although I normally do not smoke.

6 I waited. Midnight came. All my visitors had left but Warden Dickson. Then the telephone rang mutedly, and one of the death watch officers said, "It's for you, Warden." I watched Mr. Dickson disappear around a bend in the hallway. I paced the floor, my steps reduced to almost soundlessness by the cloth slippers. The radio outside the cell played quietly. Over it I had listened to a succession of newscasts. The news was all negative. One commentator reported Miss Asher had been unable to see you but, in vain, had talked with two members of your staff. A second commentator solemnly quoted you as having said, "Only an act of God can save Caryl Chessman now."

7 My eyes fell on the newspaper I had been allowed whose stark headline I quoted above. One of its front-page lead paragraphs read: "The world was disturbed last night as the hour for Caryl Chessman's execution drew near. Protests echoed from continent to continent." This San Francisco daily also reported: "There was little question that the Governor…was undergoing great emotional stress as Chessman's last hours ticked away," and "The mail—most of it running about three to one for clemency—continued to pour in. So did the telegrams and the zero hour telephone calls…."

8 On page two were pictures of the gas chamber and this account of how I could die in less than ten hours:

…He'll get a physical examination from the prison's chief physician, Dr. Herman H. Gross, at 9 A.M. and undoubtedly will once again be found to be in perfect condition.

At 9:45 A.M. come the last, formal visits from Warden Dickson and his aide to hear any last requests. Once again the chaplains will wait silently.

Over a carpeted floor, his stockinged feet should take the last walk at 10 A.M. on the dot.

There have been 164 people in the gas chamber before him, and experience gives the prison staff an almost split-second foretelling of the rest.

At 10:01 A.M. he should be in one of the two death chairs—B. in his case.

Two straps for each arm and leg, one across the chest and another for the waist. That, and the final slamming of the great iron door—less than three minutes.

At 10:03 ½ by schedule, Warden Dickson will nod at a guard and a lever will send the cyanide pellets into the sulfuric acid basins.

9   I smiled, grimly, I'm sure. I knew how it felt to be a dead man. Only the ritualized formalities of physically extinguishing my life with hydrochloric acid gas remained.

10   "Has the Warden gone?" I asked one of the death watch. "No," I was told, "he's still on the phone."

11   I gave no thought to the significance of the call. Then, audibly, I heard Warden Dickson say, "All right, Governor." A few seconds later the Warden reappeared. I'd glanced up from the paper I was reading. As he approached the cell, the Warden's face was a thoughtful mask.

12   "I have some news for you, Caryl." Mr. Dickson paused. "Oh?" I responded. He nodded, smiled. "The Governor has just granted you a 60-day reprieve."

13   The words had been spoken softly, but they crashed and reverberated in my mind like thunder in an echo chamber. Except possibly in a sadistic nightmare, they were words I truly never had expected to hear up to the instant of their utterance. I had been prepared to die; now I must be ready to go on living, I realized, for at least another 60 days.

14   I drew a deep breath as my thoughts raced. My words have been reported in the press: "Thank you. This is a great surprise. I really didn't expect it. Tell the Governor I thank him. I am surprised and grateful."

15   The Warden said he would see me again later in the morning. We said good-bye. Swiftly I was taken back upstairs in the elevator to Death Row. Swiftly, in the office, I changed into my regular clothing. Accompanied by the officers, I was passed through the "Bird Cage" with its double doors and multiplicity of bolts and bars and locks—into the Row proper. From most of the occupied cells, yellow light spilled out into the corridor. The condemned were awake, listening to their earphones, silent, waiting—for what? Somehow, even better than I, they had sensed their fate was tied to mine, and mine to a pressing social issue of far greater significance than what might, individually or collectively, happen to any or all of us. They had heard me say repeatedly that obviously the greatest hope for abolition of the death penalty lay with my death. They—even the tortured and troubled ones—knew this to be true. Their obvious course was to accept this fact and hope it might lead them out from the cold shadow of the gas chamber. But, as I later learned, they had sent you a telegram, urging your intercession in my behalf. They had refused to believe that death—even another's—was a solution. I don't know whether that telegram ever came to your attention in the flood of messages you were receiving. I do know it had a profound effect on me....

16   I continued along the corridor, stopping for a moment or two to speak to the occupant of each cell. The reaction was the same. Here was a genuine and spontaneous expression of brotherhood, commingled for them with a miracle. And make no mistake, Governor, I was for my doomed fellows no arrogant, swaggering hero returned after breathing defiance into the teeth of the cosmos. On the contrary, since they had come to know the man rather than the counterfeit black criminal legend, I was a flesh and blood human being whose appointment with man-imposed death had come to symbolize the critical and yet unresolved basic struggle of social man to rise above wrath and vengeance, to trust not the executioner, but their—mankind's—own reason and humanity in

building a saner world for their children and their children's children. These men had
been accused and convicted of homicidal violence, and so, better than any, they knew the
futility of such violence. Now, after a bitter contest, life in my case had claimed at least a
temporary victory....

[17]   We got the word [that] you had granted the reprieve because, since the people of
California were sharply divided on the issue, you wanted "to give the people...an opportunity, through the Legislature, to express themselves once more on capital punishment"....

[18]   And then, as well as in the hectic days to come, before there were calmer reflections
and clearer analysis, the paradoxical evidence mounted: While the Chessman case had
made evident the urgent need for a calm, careful and objective reexamination of the question whether capital punishment should not be discarded as a barbarous anachronism,
productive finally of nothing but division and uneasy doubt among us, my continued existence, if only for another few weeks, and the fearful Chessman legend, which portrayed
me as a cunning, fiendish, Cataline-like mocker of justice, threatened to throttle such a
reexamination and reevaluation at the outset.

[19]   I remain haunted by that paradox. Beyond the descriptive power of words, these
have been troubled and difficult days for me. I do not resort to hyperbole when I say they
have been hell, even more than the past 11 ½ years have been hell. I cannot escape the
fact I owe you my life for whatever days remain to me. I cannot forget that literally millions of people from nations around the world spoke out for me. In terms of the larger
social good that is your goal, my obligation is a heavy one, and I refuse to try to rational-
ize it away. Over and over I have asked myself the questions. What possibly can I do, if
anything, to divorce the ugly, emotional image of Caryl Chessman from the grave social
issue of capital punishment?" What can I say—and mean, and demonstrate?

[20]   ...I decided I can and I do, without theatrics, offer them my life. If the hysteria and
the mob wrath that surrounds the problem only can be prohibited by my death and if otherwise they agree that the death penalty be abolished, then I earnestly urge the members
of our legislature to frame their bill in such a way as to exclude me. This can be done
readily—for example, by a declaration in the law that anyone convicted of a capital offense during or subsequent to the year 1950, whose sentence of death remains in force
and unexecuted, shall be treated as though serving a sentence of life imprisonment. I
give my solemn word before the world that I will never challenge such a law in the courts
and I will disavow any attempt by any attorney purporting to act in my behalf.

[21]   ...If the legislators do not necessarily demand my death but do believe the final
question of my fate, under the California Constitution, should be resolved by yourself and
the majority opinion of the State Supreme Court, then I urge them so to indicate. This
way, by the passage of the type of bill mentioned above, they can sever the two problems....

[22]   Except for the days I was out to court, I have occupied a death cell continuously
since Saturday morning, July 3, 1948. I have had eight dates for execution in California's
lethal gas chamber fixed and then canceled, some in the very last hours. A ninth date
soon will be set. Ninety-odd men have taken that last, grim walk by my cell to their
deaths since I came to Death Row. If it gives them any satisfaction, Californians may be
assured my prolonged half-life in the shadow of the gas chamber has been an indescriba-
bly punishing ordeal. The shock of it, I think, has brought me to maturity; it has forced
upon me keen social awareness of the problem that, in exaggerated form, I am said to
typify.

23   I am now 38 years of age. I was 26 when arrested. Behind me is a long record of arrests. I am a graduate of California reform schools and prisons. I have been called a "criminal psychopath." Certainly, as a young man, I was a violent, rebellious, monumental damn fool. I was at odds with society; I resisted authority. I am ashamed of that past but I cannot change it. However, with my writings, I have tried to salvage something of social significance from it. Without shifting responsibility for my conduct, I endeavored in my first book to tell the story of my life and hence to explain how young men like myself got that way. I realized that Death Rows made sense only because people like Caryl Chessman didn't.

24   After being brought to the death house, the change in me and my outlook came slowly and painfully. Defiantly, I stood and fought in the courts for survival, asking no quarter and expecting none. But, ironically, to have any chance for survival, I had to turn to the law; I had to invoke the protections of the Constitution; I had to study, often as much as 18 to 20 hours a day; I had to learn to impose upon myself a harsh self-discipline; I had to think and to be ruthlessly honest with myself; in time, I forced myself to admit, "Chessman, you have been, and to some degree still are, an irrational, possible fool. What are you going to do about it?"

25   At that juncture, the traditional thing, the conventional response almost certainly would have been for me to confess my past folly and to beg for mercy. But I hesitated, not out of pride or false pride. I couldn't escape the fact that such a response on my part would, in practical effect, amount to affirmation that gas chambers and a system of justice ultimately based upon retribution possessed a genuine—rather than a mistakenly conceived and defended—social validity. I knew they did not possess such a validity. Without mock heroics, I became aware then that the great contribution I could make was to cause people, all people, to become angrily aware of places like Death Row and the administration of criminal justice in general. This, in my own way, I did: by continued total resistance. I was told I could not write another line for publication and I wrote anyway. When concerted efforts were made to suppress my manuscripts, I found a way to smuggle them from the prison. I intensified my court fight, winning some battles, losing others. Vituperation was heaped upon me. I became known as a mocker of justice. Editorial writers and public officials roundly denounced me. The public clamored for "this cunning fiend's" execution. Often I was half-mad with doubt; often I was ready to collapse with a brutal fatigue; often I sardonically sneered at myself and my goal. But I kept on somehow. A remorseless voice within told me, "This is your penance, fool—to be reviled and hated. This, if you call yourself a man, is the price you must pay."

26   I had certain advantages, and almost impossible handicaps. Among others, I had been convicted of unsavory sex offenses, sordid acts that, when recounted, inflamed the mind of the listener. They had inflamed the judge, the prosecutor, the jury. A Red Light Bandit—so-called because the bandit had operated, according to trial testimony, with a car equipped with a red spotlight such as those on police cars. He had accosted couples in lonely lovers' lanes. Armed with a gun, he would sometimes rob the couples, if they had any money. On two occasions testified to at my trial, he took the woman to his car. In one of these instances under threat of death, he compelled her, the victims to commit an unnatural sex act before letting her out and driving off. On a second occasion, he drove off with a 17-year-old girl to another secluded wooded area, compelled her, too, to commit a perverted sexual act and attempted to rape her. Then he let her out near her home. (This tragic young woman, who had a history of serious mental disturbance, was committed to a mental hospital some 19 months after her traumatic experience. "Today," the

wire services have quoted her mother as saying, "She just sits and stares"—lost in the withdrawn unreal world of the schizophrenic.)

27   It is no wonder, then, that the Red Light Bandit crimes so aroused judge, jury and prosecutor and antagonized them against the man accused of their commission. They angered and outraged me to an equal or greater degree, to an extent where in a red haze of emotion, I was unable to defend myself as effectively as otherwise I might. Stupidly and stubbornly, as well, I had withheld certain vital facts about my involvement in a violent internecine struggle for control of an illegal but police-protected bookmaking syndicate. The convict's code said I shouldn't talk, or name names. I didn't. Then, not by myself, other critical evidence got suppressed. Witnesses disappeared. And a damning net was drawn around me. The jury returned verdicts of guilty, doomed me. I was brought to Death Row, twice sentenced to death and to 15 consecutive prison terms. The question of guilt or innocence was closed unless I could somehow convince an appellate court I had been convicted illegally. Otherwise, branded a loathsome sex predator, I would die. I would have no chance to establish California had convicted the wrong man. It would make no difference that the description furnished the police of the bandit didn't remotely fit me; that the 17-year-old girl said her attacker had been "shorter than the usual man" and had weighed nearly 50 pounds less than the evidence showed I did, while I was six feet tall; or that she said the bandit had spoken with a slight accent, had appeared to be Italian and had a linear cut scar extending back from his right ear; or that this bandit usually gave his victims a look at his face before pulling up a handkerchief mask, while I just had been released from prison on parole and knew that, my photographs almost certainly would be the first shown robbery victims; or that I had absolutely no history as a sex offender; or that I had been refused the right to produce witnesses at the trial who would testify to my reputation for sexual normality as well as to produce expert psychiatric evidence that I did not possess the psychological disposition to commit sexual crimes, particularly those involving force or violence, and that I was not a psychopath.

28   All this made no difference. In the eyes of the law, I was guilty and would remain guilty unless I could win a new trial and acquittal. This galled me but it also drove and sustained me....

29   I wait to die. I remain locked in a death cell. More than 12 years have passed since my arrest. The State has spent nearly a million dollars in trying to kill me.

30   Now, in a few days, the California Legislature will be called into special session to consider abolition of capital punishment. Disturbed that a vote against the death penalty will be a vote for me, the man they believe has embarrassed their State and made a mockery of their laws, many legislators have vowed publicly to see that capital punishment is retained. I do not presume to tell them what to do; I do pray they will reconsider and reevaluate. I am more than willing that they separate me decisively from the greater issue. I am quite willing to die if that will bring about this desperately needed social reform. I do suggest that if our positions were reversed and they had found themselves occupying a death cell under the conditions I have they too, and honorably, would have done as I have done, even though it meant bringing the wrath of the State down upon them. Happily, they will never know what it means to be doomed, to be within hours and minutes of execution, to feel the full, terrible impact of mob wrath, to have a claim of innocence brushed impatiently aside, to be called a "monster" and vilified, to seek redemption, not through hypocritical groveling, but by a harder, perhaps impossible road, to win friends and want desperately to justify their friendship and their faith, to want to live and to be-

lieve, humbly, that within them is a gift for words that can enrich our literature and, their own case aside, contribute significantly to the pressing social problems of our day.

[31] I do not overstate when I say I gladly would die ten thousand gas chamber deaths if that would bring these truths into the hearts and minds of those who make our laws: A vote for either abolition or a moratorium is not an indication of approval of murder or other capital crimes, for the death penalty does not deter; it does not protect society. On the contrary, it leaves it defenseless, since as long as we have an executioner and a gas chamber, we will be content to believe that we can bury the problem with the offender. We will think that revenge is enough. It isn't. We must find why men kill and we must learn to prevent killing. We must become as intensely concerned with tomorrow's prospective victims as yesterday's actual ones. We must learn how to save lives and to salvage lives.

[32] As long as the death penalty is on our statute books, there will be too much emotionality and circus atmosphere tainting our administration of justice. And for those who doubt this, there is a ready and rational test at hand: Let a moratorium be ordered on the supreme penalty for a period of, say, five years. I am certain during that period there will be no rise in the per capita crimes. Rather, I am convinced the crime rate will drop appreciably, and that justice will function in a far more even-handed and fair way. The sensationalism inevitably attending capital cases will vanish. The citizen will be reassured. He will know that the man who has killed has been isolated. The accused is more likely, if he is guilty, to plead guilty. Our courts thus will be able to perform their duties more efficiently. And if an innocent man is later found to have been mistakenly convicted, it will not be too late to correct the error.

[33] Unfortunately, as investigation will confirm, too often it is the friendless and the fundless upon whom the death penalty is imposed. The man with means or who knows the angles does not come to Death Row. As well under our outmoded tests for legal sanity or insanity, too often the man who is executed is one who, while not legally insane, suffers from some serious mental disability. It needlessly demeans our society to engage in killing the mentally ill. Still further, among this group, as psychiatrists and penologists will attest, is the type of personality who is inflamed by the thought and threat of the gas chamber. His response to it, his overt expression of defiance, is to strike out homicidally. In effect, he gets his revenge in advance, and we in turn get ours after the tragedy.

[34] That is why so many thoughtful citizens advocate abolition or a moratorium. They feel, as I do, a sense of guilty responsibility at a lethal act that is both more than futile and less than futile when the State takes a life. They want their laws to express humanity's ideal of nobility, compassion, understanding and social awareness. They know that our laws can do so without endangering the citizens of California. The basis for their opposition to man's government killing man is thus, in the highest sense, ethical, social, practical and religious. They do not want to see their society needlessly degraded, their system of justice compromised.

[35] I must close, and in closing I again earnestly urge you to ask the Legislature to consider the question of capital punishment apart from Caryl Chessman and the Chessman case. I urge you to request that they consider framing their bill as suggested above, to exclude me. You can do this honorably by taking my life back into your hands alone. You can let *me* die. Indeed, as the matter now stands, you are powerless to do otherwise because of the present 4-3 vote against me in the California Supreme Court. But, at the same time, you can give your proposal to the Legislature for a chance.

36   It deserves that chance. It deserves your forceful leadership. You are right in the position you have taken. It is time to speak out, for too seldom does enlightened humanity in this age of fear and awesome nuclear devices have a spokesman with the courage to advocate that death and hate are not and never can be an answer to the problems that beset our civilization. Mankind and future generations ever will remain in your debt and ever will honor your name.

Yours respectfully,

/s/Caryl Chessman

Thinking and Responding to the Reading

1.   Paragraph 2 states, ..."California Supreme Court has voted 4 to 3 against a recommendation to you for clemency." Define clemency, and then explain this statement.
2.   In paragraph 3, Caryl Chessman states his thesis. Paraphrase it.
3.   In paragraph 9, he says, "I knew how it felt to be a dead man." What made him feel that?
4.   Chessman describes the Warden's face as a "thoughtful mask." What is the connotation of this description? What does he want the reader to see?
5.   In paragraph 18, Chessman discusses the paradox that a society faces in deciding the punishments for its criminals. Do you agree with him that "careful and objective reexamination of the question of capital punishment should not be discarded as a barbarous anachronism, productive finally of nothing but division and uneasy doubts among us..."? Explain.
6.   Chessman mentions the role of the media. How does he see its influence on the public's perceptions of the death penalty? What role do the media play in today's criminal cases?
7.   Based on his narration in paragraph 24, Chessman switches his narrative form from first person to third person. Given this information, is there possibly some doubt in your mind as to his guilt or innocence? Does he achieve some skepticism in your mind by writing in such a way?
8.   In paragraph 27, find the section where he casts doubts on his being the "Red Light Bandit." Paraphrase it. Of what does he state he is truly guilty?
9.   Chessman tells us that the State has spent nearly a million dollars trying to kill him. What is he implying by telling us this?
10.   In paragraphs 31-36, he concludes most of his argument against capital punishment. Cornell Note his conclusion or use the problem-solution diagram.
11.   State Chessman's overall claim (argument) and then list the major premises that support the claim.

Springboard for Composing

While in prison, Chessman learns to work with others to educate himself and ultimately the general public about his views of capital punishment. Chessman wrote, "I learned too late and only after coming to Death Row that each of us ever must be aware of the brotherhood of man . . . ." What methods do you think he may have used to work with others to achieve this goal? What methods have you used when working with others to achieve a goal? Be specific in stating what toward what goal you were working and what methods you used.

ONLY DAUGHTER

Sandra Cisneros

Vocabulary Words

anthology (par. 1)	retrospect (par. 5)	bouts (par. 9)
circumstance (par. 3)	putter (par. 5)	vials (par. 18)
destiny (par. 4)	philandering (par. 7)	

1   Once, several years ago, when I was just starting out my writing career, I was asked to write my own contributor's note for an anthology. I wrote: "I am the only daughter in a family of six sons. That explains everything."

2   Well, I've thought that ever since, and yes, it explains a lot to me, but for the reader's sake I should have written: "I am the only daughter in a Mexican family of six sons." Or even: "I am the only daughter of a Mexican father and a Mexican-American mother." Or: "I am the only daughter of a working-class family of nine." All of these had everything to do with who I am today.

3   I was/am the only daughter and only a daughter. Being an only daughter in a family of six sons forced me by circumstance to spend a lot of time by myself because my brothers felt it beneath them to play with a girl in public. But that aloneness, that loneliness, was good for a would-be-writer—it allowed me time to think and think, to imagine, to read and prepare myself.

4   Being only a daughter for my father meant my destiny would lead me to become someone's wife. That's what he believed. But when I was in the fifth grade and shared my plans for college with him, I was sure he understood. I remember by father saying. "*Que bueno, mi'ja*, that's good." That meant a lot to me, especially since my brothers thought the idea hilarious. What I didn't realize was that my father thought college was good for girls—good for finding a husband. After four years in college and two more in graduate school, and still no husband, my father shakes his head even now and says I wasted all that education.

5   In retrospect, I'm lucky my father believed daughters were meant for husbands. It meant it didn't matter if I majored in something silly like English. After all, I'd find a nice professional eventually, right? This allowed me the liberty to putter about embroidering my little poems and stories without my father interrupting with so much as a "What's that you're writing?"

6   But the truth is, I wanted him to interrupt. I wanted my father to understand what it was I was scribbling, to introduce me as "My only daughter, the writer." Not as "This is my only daughter. She teaches." *Es maestro*—teacher. Not even *profesora*.

7   In a sense, everything I have ever written has been for him, to win his approval even though I know my father can't read English words, even though my father's only reading includes the brown-ink *Esto* sports magazines from Mexico City and the bloody *¡Alama!* magazines that feature yet another sighting of *La Virgen de Gaudalupe* on a tortilla or a wife's revenge on her philandering husband by bashing his skull in with a molcajete (a kitchen mortar made of volcanic rock). Or the *fotonovelas*, the little picture paperbacks with tragedy and trauma erupting from the characters' mouths in bubbles.

90

8 A father represents, then, the public majority. A public who is disinterested in reading, and yet one whom I am writing about and for, and privately trying to woo.

9 When we were growing up in Chicago, we moved a lot because of my father. He suffered bouts of nostalgia. Then we'd have to let go of our flat, store the furniture with mother's relatives, load the station wagon with baggage and bologna sandwiches and head south. To Mexico City.

10 We came back, of course. To yet another Chicago flat, another Chicago neighborhood, another Catholic school. Each time, my father would seek out the parish priest in order to get a tuition break, and complain or boast: "I have seven sons."

11 He meant *siete hijos*, seven children, but he translated it as "sons." "I have seven sons." To anyone who would listen. The Sears Roebuck employee who sold us the washing machine. The short-order cook where my father ate his ham-and-eggs breakfasts. "I have seven sons." As if he deserved a medal from the state.

12 My papa. He didn't mean anything by the mistranslation. I'm sure. But somehow I could feel myself being erased. I'd tug my father's sleeve and whisper: "Not seven sons. Six! and one *daughter*."

13 When my oldest brother graduated from medical school, he fulfilled my father's dream that we study hard and use this—our heads, instead of this—our hands. Even now my father's hands are thick and yellow, stubbed by a history of hammer and nails and twine and coils and springs. "Use this," my father said, tapping his head, "and not this," showing us those hands. He always looked tired when he said it.

14 Wasn't college an investment? And hadn't I spent all those years in college? And if I didn't marry, what was it all for? Why would anyone go to college and then choose to be poor? Especially someone who had always been poor.

15 Last year, after ten years of writing professionally, the financial rewards started to trickle in. My second National Endowment for the Arts Fellowship. A guest professorship at the University of California, Berkeley. My book, which sold to a major New York publishing house.

16 At Christmas, I flew home to Chicago. The house was throbbing, same as always; hot tamales and sweet tamales hissing in my mother's pressure cooker, and everybody—my mother, six brothers, wives, babies, aunts, cousins—talking too loud and at the same time, like in a Fellini film, because that's just how we are.

17 I went upstairs to my father's room. One of my stories had just been translated into Spanish and published in an anthology of Chicano writing, and I wanted to show it to him. Ever since he recovered from a stroke two years ago, my father likes to spend his leisure hours horizontally. And that's how I found him, watching a Pedro Infante movie on Galavision and eating rice pudding.

18 There was a glass filled with milk on the bedside table. There were several vials of pills and balled Kleenex. And on the floor, one black sock and a plastic urinal that I didn't want to look at but looked at anyway. Pedro Infante was about to burst into song, and my father was laughing.

19 I'm not sure if it was because my story was translated into Spanish, or because it was published in Mexico, or perhaps because the story dealt with Tepeyac, the *colonia* my father was raised in and the house he grew up in, but at any rate, my father punched the mute button on his remote control and read my story.

²⁰ I sat on the bed next to my father and waited. He read it very slowly. As if he were reading each line over and over. He laughed at all the right places and read lines he liked out loud. He pointed and asked questions: "Is this So-and-so?" "Yes," I said. He kept reading.

²¹ When he was finally finished, after what seemed like hours, my father looked up and asked: "Where can we get more copies of this for the relatives?"

²² Of all the wonderful things that happened to me last year, that was the most wonderful.

Thinking and Responding to the Reading

1. Why does Cisneros's father say he has "seven sons"? How does Cisneros respond?
2. In paragraph 3 Cisneros says, "I was/am the only daughter and only a daughter." Explain the cultural implication of this statement.
3. What cultural and socio-economic values account for her father's treatment of her?
4. Why does her father want to distribute copies of Cisneros's story to the family?
5. Why does Cisneros write in paragraph 22, "Of all the wonderful things that happened to me last year, that was the most wonderful."

Springboard for Composing

Often the way parents raise their children is determined by their own heritage. As children begin their school years, one of the things they must learn is to live with, accept, and understand each other's different backgrounds. List the names of two or three classmates you have known who came from different backgrounds (religious, national or racial). Next to each one, record some characteristics of these students that you thought made them different from yourself. How old were you when you discovered these differences? What happened?

92

from *THE SCHOOL DAYS OF AN INDIAN GIRL*

Gertrude Simmons Bonnin (Zitkala Ša)

Vocabulary Words

throng (par. 2)	reproving (par. 4)	indignities (par. 16)
scrutinized (par. 3)	bedlam (par. 8)	imperative (par. 17)

I.   The Land of Red Apples

1   There were eight in our party of bronzed children who were going East with the missionaries. Among us were three young braves, two tall girls, and we three little ones, Judewin, Thowin, and I.

2   We had been very impatient to start on our journey to the Red Apple Country, which, we were told, lay a little beyond the great circular horizon of the Western prairie. Under a sky of rosy apples we dreamt of roaming as freely and happily as we had chased the cloud shadows on the Dakota plains. We had anticipated much pleasure from a ride on the iron horse, but the throng of staring palefaces disturbed and troubled us.

3   On the train, fair women, with tottering babies on each arm, stopped their haste and scrutinized the children of absent mothers. Large men, with heavy bundles in their hands, halted near by, and riveted their glassy blue eyes upon us.

4   I sank deep into the corner of my seat, for I resented being watched. Directly in front of me, children who were no larger than I hung themselves upon the backs of their seats, with their bold white faces toward me. Sometimes they took their forefingers out of their mouths and pointed at my moccasined feet. Their mothers, instead of reproving such rude curiosity, looked closely at me, and attracted their children's further notice to my blanket. This embarrassed me, and kept me constantly on the verge of tears.

5   I sat perfectly still, with my eyes downcast, daring only now and then to shoot long glances around me. Chancing to turn to the window at my side, I was quite breathless upon seeing one familiar object. It was the telegraph pole which strode by at short paces. Very near my mother's dwelling, along the edge of a road thickly bordered with wild sunflowers, some poles like these had been planted by white men. Often I had stopped, on my way down the road, to hold my ear against the pole, and hearing its low moaning, I used to wonder what the paleface had done to hurt it. Now I sat watching for each pole that glided by to be the last one.

----

6   We rode for several days, and it was night when we reached the school grounds. The lights from the windows of the large buildings fell upon some of the icicled trees that stood beneath them. We were led toward an open door, where the brightness of the lights within folded out over the heads of the excited palefaces who blocked the way. My body trembled more from fear than from the snow I trod upon.

----

7   I had arrived in the wonderful land of rosy skies, but I was not happy, as I had thought I should be. My long travel and the bewildering sights had exhausted me. I fell

asleep, heaving deep, tired sobs. My tears were left to dry themselves in streaks because neither my aunt nor my mother was near to wipe them away.

II.   *The Cutting of My Long Hair*

8   The first day in the land of apples was a bitter-cold one, for the snow still covered the ground, and the trees were bare. A large bell rang for breakfast, its loud metallic voice crashing through the belfry overhead and into our sensitive ears. The annoying clatter of shoes on bare floors gave us no peace. The constant clash of harsh noises, with an undercurrent of many voices murmuring an unknown tongue, made a bedlam within which I was securely tied. And though my spirit tore itself in struggling for its lost freedom, all was useless.

9   A paleface woman, with white hair, came up after us. We were placed in a line of girls who were marching into the dining room. There were Indian girls, in stiff shoes and closely clinging dresses. The small girls wore sleeved aprons and shingled [bobbed, cut short] hair. As I walked noiselessly in my soft moccasins, I felt like sinking to the floor, for my blanket had been stripped from my shoulders. I looked hard at the Indian girls, who seemed not to care that they were even more immodestly dressed than I, in their tightly fitting clothes. While we marched in, the boys entered at an opposite door. I watched for the three young braves who came in our party. I spied them in the rear ranks, looking as uncomfortable as I felt.

10   A small bell was tapped, and each of the pupils drew a chair from under the table. Supposing this act meant they were to be seated, I pulled out mine and at once slipped into it from one side. But when I turned my head I saw that I was the only one seated, and all the rest at our table remained standing. Just as I began to rise, looking shyly around to see how chairs were to be used, a second bell was sounded. All were seated at last, and I had to crawl back into my chair again. I heard a man's voice at one end of the hall, and I looked around to see him. But all the others hung their heads over their plates. As I glanced at the long chain of tables, I caught the eyes of a paleface woman upon me. Immediately I dropped my eyes, wondering why I was so keenly watched by the strange woman. The man ceased his mutterings, and then a third bell was tapped. Every one picked up his knife and fork and began eating. I began crying instead, for by this time I was afraid to venture anything more.

11   But this eating by formula was not the hardest trial in that first day. Late in the morning, my friend Judewin gave me a terrible warning. Judewin knew a few words of English; and she had overheard the paleface woman talk about cutting our long, heavy hair. Our mothers had taught us that only unskilled warriors who were captured had their hair shingled by the enemy. Among our people, short hair was worn by mourners, and shingled hair by cowards!

12   We discussed our fate some moments, and when Judewin said, "We have to submit because they are strong," I rebelled.

13   "No, I will not submit! I will struggle first!" I answered.

14   I watched my chance, and when no one noticed I disappeared. I crept up the stairs as quietly as I could in my squeaking shoes,--my moccasins had been exchanged for shoes. Along the hall I passed, without knowing whither I was going. Turning aside to an open door, I found a large room with three white beds in it. The windows were cov-

ered with dark green curtains, which made the room very dim. Thankful that no one was there, I directed my steps toward the corner farthest from the door. On my hands and knees I crawled under the bed, and cuddled myself in the dark corner.

15   From my hiding place I peered out, shuddering with fear whenever I heard footsteps near by. Though in the hall loud voices were calling my name, and I knew that even Judewin was searching for me, I did not open my mouth to answer. Then the steps were quickened and the voices became excited. The sounds came nearer and nearer. Women and girls entered the room. I held my breath, and watched them open closet doors and peep behind large trunks. Someone threw up the curtains, and the room was filled with sudden light. What caused them to stoop and look under the bed I do not know. I remember being dragged out, though I resisted by kicking and scratching wildly. In spite of myself, I was carried downstairs and tied fast in a chair.

16   I cried aloud, shaking my head all the while until I felt the cold blades of the scissors against my neck, and heard them gnaw off one of my thick braids. Then I lost my spirit. Since the day I was taken from my mother I had suffered extreme indignities. People had stared at me. I had been tossed about in the air like a wooden puppet. And now my long hair was shingled like a coward's! In my anguish I moaned for my mother, but no one came to comfort me. Not a soul reasoned quietly with me, as my own mother used to so; for now I was only one of many little animals driven by a herder.

III.   *The Snow Episode*

17   A short time after our arrival we three Dakotas were playing in the snow-drifts. We were all still deaf to the English language, excepting Judewin, who always heard such puzzling things. One morning we learned through her ears that we were forbidden to fall lengthwise in the snow, as we had been doing to see our own impressions. However, before many hours we had forgotten the order, and were having great sport in the snow, when a shrill voice called us. Looking up, we saw an imperative hand beckoning us into the house. We shook the snow off ourselves and started toward the woman as slowly as we dared.

18   Judewin said: "Now the paleface is angry with us. She is going to punish us for falling into the snow. If she looks straight into your eyes and talks loudly, you must wait until she stops. Then, after a tiny pause, say, 'No.'" The rest of the way we practiced upon the little word "no."

19   As it happened, Thowin was summoned to judgment first. The door shut behind her with a click.

20   Judewin and I stood silently listening at the keyhole. The paleface woman talked in very severe tones. Her words fell from her lips like crackling embers, and her inflection ran up like the small end of a switch. I understood her voice better than the things she was saying. I was certain we had made her very impatient with us. Judewin heard enough of the words to realize all too late that she had taught us the wrong reply.

21   "Oh, poor Thowin!" she gasped, as she put both hands over her ears.

22   Just then I heard Thowin's tremulous answer, "No."

23   With an angry exclamation, the woman gave her a hard spanking. Then she stopped to say something. Judewin said it was this: "Are you going to obey my word the next time?"

24   Thowin answered again with the only word at her command, "No."

25   This time the woman meant her blows to smart, for the poor frightened girl shrieked at the top of her voice. In the midst of the whipping the blows ceased abruptly, and the woman asked another question: "Are you going to fall in the snow again?"

26   Thowin gave her bad password another trial. We heard her say feebly, "No! No!"

27   With this the woman hid away her half-worn slipper, and let the child out, stroking her black shorn head. Perhaps it occurred to her that brute force is not the solution for such a problem. She did nothing to Judewin nor to me. She only returned to us our unhappy comrade and left us alone in the room.

28   During the first two or three seasons misunderstanding as ridiculous as this one of the snow episode frequently took place, bringing unjustifiable frights and punishments into our little lives.

Thinking and Responding to the Reading

1.   The narrator is an eight-year-old Dakota girl who travels east to attend a missionary school in the late 1800's. On her way to the missionary, the narrator encounters stares and pointing fingers. Why do the other travelers react this way (conflict values?, prejudice?, ignorance?, fear?)? Explain your answer.

2.   Name at least two other cultural differences she encounters and explain the differences to what she grew up with.

3.   The author uses many descriptive phrases, such as "great circular horizon of the Western prairie." Find two others that you think are particularly effective and explain their meanings.

4.   In "The Cutting of My Long Hair," why is the narrator so intent upon not having her hair shorn? Why do you think the missionaries cut her hair? What can you reasonably conclude about her cultural values as compared to the missionaries in terms of this section?

5.   In "The Snow Episode," explain the irony of Thowin's repeated answer of "No."

6.   Do the women realize the maltreatment they inflict on these three Dakota girls? Do you think they feel remorse for their actions? Why or why not?

7.   Look up the word *ethnocentricity*. Does its meaning apply to this story? Explain. What can you reasonably conclude from this definition?

 Springboard for Composing

At first, when we encounter a culture or a way of doing things differently than what we are used to, we may put up a resistance. List some of the ways we may resist and name several reasons why you think this happens.

SISTER FLOWERS

Maya Angelou

Vocabulary Words

sopped (par. 1)	incessantly (par. 11)	boggled (par. 27)
inedible (par. 1)	heath (par. 11)	leered (par. 32)
voile (par. 2)	morocco-bound (par. 11)	couched (par. 35)
benign (par. 4)	chifforobe (par. 17)	collective (par. 35)
unceremonious (par. 8)	sacrilegious (par. 17)	cascading (par. 37)
moors (par. 11)	infuse (par. 24)	aura (par. 42)

1   For nearly a year, I sopped around the house, the Store, the school and the church, like an old biscuit, dirty and inedible. Then I met, or rather got to know, the lady who threw me my first life line.

2   Mrs. Bertha Flowers was the aristocrat of Black Stamps. She had the grace of control to appear warm in the coldest weather, and on the Arkansas summer days it seemed she had a private breeze which swirled around, cooling her. She was thin without the taut look of wiry people, and her printed voile dresses and flowered hats were as right for her as denim overalls for a farmer. She was our side's answer to the richest white woman in town.

3   Her skin was a rich black that would have peeled like a plum if snagged, but then no one would have thought of getting close enough to Mrs. Flowers to ruffle her dress, let alone snag her skin. She didn't encourage familiarity. She wore gloves too.

4   I don't think I ever saw Mrs. Flowers laugh, but she smiled often. A slow widening of her thin black lips to show even, small white teeth, then the slow effortless closing. When she chose to smile on me, I always wanted to thank her. The action was so graceful and inclusively benign.

5   She was one of the few gentlewomen I have ever known, and has remained throughout my life the measure of what a human being can be.

6   Momma had a strange relationship with her. Most often when she passed on the road in front of the Store, she spoke to Momma in that soft yet carrying voice, "Good day, Mrs. Henderson." Momma responded with "How you, Sister Flowers?"

7   Mrs. Flowers didn't belong to our church, nor was she Momma's familiar. Why on earth did she insist on calling her Sister Flowers? Shame made me want to hide my face. Mrs. Flowers deserved better than to be called Sister. Then, Momma left out the verb. Why not ask, "How are you, Mrs. Flowers?" With the unbalanced passion of the young, I hated her for showing her ignorance to Mrs. Flowers. It didn't occur to me for many years that they were as alike as sisters, separated only by formal education.

8   Although I was upset, neither of the women was in the least shaken by what I thought an unceremonious greeting. Mrs. Flowers would continue her easy gait up the hill to her little bungalow, and Momma kept on shelling peas or doing whatever had brought her to the front porch.

9   Occasionally, though, Mrs. Flowers would drift off the road and down to the Store and Momma would say to me, "Sister, you go on and play." As I left I would hear the beginning of an intimate conversation, Momma persistently using the wrong verb, or none at all.

10   "Brother and Sister Wilcox is sho'ly the meanest—" "Is," Momma? "Is"? Oh, please, not "is," Momma, for two or more. But they talked, and from the side of the building where I waited for the ground to open up and swallow me, I heard the soft-voiced Mrs. Flowers and the textured voice of my grandmother merging and melting. They were interrupted from time to time by giggles that must have come from Mrs. Flowers (Momma never giggled in her life). Then she was gone.

11   She appealed to me because she was like people I had never met personally. Like women in English novels who walked the moors (whatever they were) with their loyal dogs racing at a respectful distance. Like the women who sat in front of roaring fire-places, drinking tea incessantly from silver trays full of scones and crumpets. Women who walked over the "heath" and read morocco-bound books and had two last names divided by a hyphen. It would be safe to say that she made me proud to be Negro, just by being herself.

12   She acted just as refined as whitefolks in the movies and books and she was more beautiful, for none of them could have come near that warm color without looking gray by comparison.

13   I was fortunate that I never saw her in the company of powhitefolks. For since they tend to think of their whiteness as an evenizer, I'm certain that I would have had to hear her spoken to commonly as Bertha, and my image of her would have been shattered like the unmendable Humpty-Dumpty.

14   One summer afternoon, sweet-milk fresh in my memory, she stopped at the Store to buy provisions. Another Negro woman of her health and age would have been expected to carry the paper sacks home in one hand, but Momma said, "Sister Flowers, I'll send Bailey up to your house with these things."

15   She smiled that slow dragging smile, "Thank you, Mrs. Henderson. I'd prefer Marguerite, though." My name was beautiful when she said it. "I've been meaning to talk to her, anyway." They gave each other age-group looks.

16   Momma said, "Well, that's all right then. Sister, go and change your dress. You going to Sister Flowers's."

17   The chifforobe was a maze. What on earth did one put on to go to Mrs. Flowers's house? I knew I shouldn't put on a Sunday dress. It might be sacrilegious. Certainly not a house dress, since I was already wearing a fresh one. I chose a school dress, naturally. It was formal without suggesting that going to Mrs. Flowers's house was equivalent to attending church.

18   I trusted myself back into the Store.

19   "Now, don't you look nice." I had chosen the right thing, for once....

20   There was a little path beside the rocky road, and Mrs. Flowers walked in front swinging her arms and picking her way over the stones.

21   She said, without turning her head, to me, "I hear you're doing very good school work, Marguerite, but that it's all written. The teachers report that they have trouble getting you to talk in class." We passed the triangular farm on our left and the path widened

98

to allow us to walk together. I hung back in the separate unasked and unanswerable questions.

22 "Come and walk along with me, Marguerite." I couldn't have refused even if I wanted to. She pronounced my name so nicely. Or more correctly, she spoke each word with such clarity that I was certain a foreigner who didn't understand English could have understood her.

23 "Now no one is going to make you talk—possibly no one can. But bear in mind, language is man's way of communicating with his fellow man and it is language alone which separates him from the lower animals." That was a totally new idea to me, and I would need time to think about it.

24 Your grandmother says you read a lot. Every chance you get. That's good, but not good enough. Words mean more than what is set down on paper. It takes the human voice to infuse them with the shades of deeper meaning."

25 I memorized the part about the human voice infusing words. It seemed so valid and poetic.

26 She said she was going to give me some books and that I not only must read them, I must read them aloud. She suggested that I try to make a sentence sound in as many different ways as possible.

27 "I'll accept no excuse if you return a book to me that has been badly handled." My imagination boggled at the punishment I would deserve if in fact I did abuse a book of Mrs. Flowers's. Death would be too kind and brief.

28 The odors in the house surprised me. Somehow I had never connected Mrs. Flowers with food or eating or any other common experience of common people. There must have been an outhouse, too, but my mind never recorded it.

29 The sweet scent of vanilla had met us as she opened the door.

30 "I made tea cookies this morning. You see, I had planned to invite you for cookies and lemonade so we could have this little chat. The lemonade is in the icebox."

31 It followed that Mrs. Flowers would have ice on an ordinary day, when most families in our town bought ice late on Saturdays only a few times during the summer to be used in the wooden ice-cream freezers.

32 She took the bags from me and disappeared through the kitchen door. I looked around the room that I had never in my wildest fantasies imagined I would see. Browned photographs leered or threatened from the walls and the white, freshly done curtains pushed against themselves and against the wind. I wanted to gobble up the room entire and take it to Bailey, who would help me analyze and enjoy it.

33 "Have a seat, Marguerite. Over there by the table." She carried a platter covered with a tea towel. Although she warned that she hadn't tried her hand at baking sweets for some time, I was certain that like everything else about her the cookies would be perfect.

34 They were flat round wafers, slightly browned on the edges and butter-yellow in the center. With the cold lemonade they were sufficient for childhood's lifelong diet. Remember my manners, I took nice little lady-like bites off the edges. She said she had made them expressly for me and that she had a few in the kitchen that I could take home to my brother. So I jammed one whole cake in my mouth and through crumbs scratched the insides of my jaws, and if I hadn't had to swallow, it would have been a dream come true.

35   As I ate she began the first of what we later called "my lessons in living." She said that I must always be intolerant of ignorance but understanding of illiteracy. That some people, unable to go to school, were more educated and even more intelligent than college professors. She encouraged me to listen carefully to what country people called mother wit. That in those homely sayings was couched the collective wisdom of generations.

36   When I finished the cookies she brushed off the table and brought a thick, small book from the bookcase. I had read *A Tale of Two Cities* and found it up to my standards as a romantic novel. She opened the first page and I heard poetry for the first time in my life.

37   "It was the best of times and the worst of times..." Her voice slid in and curved down through and over the words. She was nearly singing. I wanted to look at the pages. Were they the same that I had read? Or were there notes, music, lined on the pages, as in a hymn book? Her sounds began cascading gently. I knew from listening to a thousand preachers that she was nearing the end of her reading, and I hadn't really heard, heard to understand, a single word.

38   "How do you like that?"

39   It occurred to me that she expected a response. The sweet vanilla flavor was still on my tongue and her reading was a wonder in my ears. I had to speak.

40   I said, "Yes, ma'am." It was the least I could do, but it was the most also.

41   "There's one more thing. Take this book of poems and memorize one for me. Next time you pay me a visit, I want you to recite."

42   I have tried often to search behind the sophistication of years for the enchantment I so easily found in those gifts. The essence escapes but its aura remains. To be allowed, no, invited, into the private lives of strangers, and to share their joys and fears, was a chance to exchange the Southern bitter wornwood for a cup of mead with Beowulf or a hot cup of tea and milk with Oliver Twist. When I said aloud, "It is a far, far better thing that I do, than I have ever done..." tears of love filled my eyes at my selflessness.

43   On that first day, I ran down the hill and into the road (few cars ever came along it) and had the good sense to stop running before I reached the Store.

44   I was liked, and what a difference it made. I was respected not as Mrs. Henderson's grandchild or Bailey's sister but for just being Marguerite Johnson.

45   Childhood's logic never asks to be proved (all conclusions are absolute). I didn't question why Mrs. Flowers had singled me out for attention, nor did it occur to me that Momma might have asked her to give me a little talking to. All I cared about was that she had made tea cookies for me and read to *me* from her favorite book. It was enough to prove that she liked me.

Thinking and Responding to the Reading

1.   Approximately how old is Marguerite in this story? What makes you think this?
2.   How do the opening words of the story "For nearly a year, I sopped around the house, the Store, the school and the church like an old biscuit, dirty and inedible" help you imagine events in Marguerite's past life?
3.   To what do you attribute Marguerite's superior command of English?

4.   Who is Sister Flowers and why does she choose to mentor Marguerite?

5.   Explain "Words mean more than what is set down on paper. It takes the human voice to infuse them with the shades of deeper meaning."

6.   Why does Marguerite admire Sister Flowers?

7.   Sister Flowers tells Marguerite to not tolerate ignorance, but accept illiteracy. Does this wisdom still hold today when educational access is available to most people in our country? Have you met anyone who may not be formally educated, but who is nevertheless wise?

8.   How is being accepted by Sister Flowers a life transforming experience for Marguerite?

Springboard for Composing

In this recollection, Marguerite quickly learned to understand and Sister Flowers's ways, which are quite different. Why do you think this happened? What did she like about this new way of doing things? What needs of hers were met? (Think about what Angelou says about Sister Flowers in paragraph 5.)

GET A KNIFE, GET A DOG, BUT GET RID OF GUNS

Molly Ivins

Vocabulary Words

ricochet, (par. 3)
civil libertarian (par. 4)
infringed (par. 5)
perforating (par. 6)

lethal (par. 8)
wreak (par. 8)
carnage (par. 8)
martial (par. 12)

literally (par. 13)
psychosexual (par. 13)
psyches (par. 14)

1   Guns. Everywhere guns.

2   Let me start this discussion by pointing out that I am not anti-gun. I'm pro-knife. Consider the merits of the knife.

3   In the first place, you have to catch up with someone in order to stab him. A general substitution of knives for guns would promote physical fitness. We'd turn into a whole nation of great runners. Plus, knives don't ricochet. And people are seldom killed while cleaning their knives.

4   As a civil libertarian, I, of course, support the Second Amendment. And I believe it means exactly what it says: *A well-regulated militia being necessary to the security of a free state, the right of the people to keep and bear arms shall not be infringed.* Fourteen-year-old boys are not part of a well-regulated militia. Members of wacky religious cults are not part of a well-regulated militia. Permitting unregulated citizens to have guns is destroying the security of this free state.

5   I am intrigued by the arguments of those who claim to follow the judicial doctrine of original intent. How do they know it was the dearest wish of Thomas Jefferson's heart that teenage drug dealers should cruise the cities of this nation perforating their fellow citizens with assault rifles? Channeling?

6   There is more hooey spread about the Second Amendment. It says quite clearly that guns are for those who form part of a well-regulated militia, that is, the armed forces, including the National Guard. Their reasons for keeping them away from everyone else get clearer by the day.

7   The comparison most often used is that of the automobile, another lethal object that is regularly used to wreak great carnage. Obviously, this society is full of people who haven't enough common sense to use an automobile properly. But we haven't outlawed cars yet.

8   We do, however, license them and their owners, restrict their use to presumably sane and sober adults, and keep track of who sells them to whom. At a minimum, we should do the same with guns.

9   In truth, there is no rational argument for guns in this society. This is no longer a frontier nation in which people hunt their own food. It is a crowded, overwhelmingly urban country in which letting people have access to guns is a continuing disaster. Those who want guns—whether for target shooting, hunting, or potting rattlesnakes (get a hoe) should be subject to the same restrictions placed on gun owners in England, a nation in which liberty has survived nicely without an armed populace.

10 The argument that "guns don't kill people" is patent nonsense. Anyone who has ever worked in a cop shop knows how many family arguments end in murder because there was a gun in the house. Did the gun kill someone? No. But if there had been no gun, no one would have died. At least not without a good foot race first. Guns do kill. Unlike cars, that is all they do.

11 Michael Crichton makes an interesting argument about technology in his thriller *Jurassic Park*. He points out that power without discipline is making this society into a wreckage. By the time someone who studies the martial arts becomes a master—literally able to kill with bare hands—that person has also undergone years of training and discipline. But any fool can pick up a gun and kill with it.

12 "A well-regulated militia" surely implies both long training and long discipline. That is the least, the very least, that should be required of those who are permitted to have guns, because a gun is literally the power to kill. For years I used to enjoy taunting my gun-nut friends about their psychosexual hang-ups—always in a spirit of good cheer, you understand. But letting the noisy minority in the NRA force us to allow this carnage to continue is just plain insane.

13 I do think gun nuts have a power hang-up. I don't know what is missing in their psyches that they need to feel they have the power to kill. But no sane society would allow this to continue.

14 Ban the damn things. Ban them all

15 You want protection? Get a dog.

Thinking and Responding to the Reading

1. Identify the following: Second Amendment, *Jurrasic Park*, and NRA.
2. What is Ivin's claim (argument)?
3. List the major premises in the order in which they are presented.
4. Ivins uses satire to make her argument. Do you think it is effective? Why or why not?
5. Explain why Ivins would compare guns to cars to strengthen her viewpoint.

Springboard for Composing

Is there a moral, ethical, religious, social, political or educational issue that you so believe in that you would join a dedicated group to achieve the advancement of its ideas? If so, what is it and what would you hope to accomplish? If you already belong to such an organization, have you experienced differences of opinion with several members at some point? How did you resolve them?

... OR A CHILDISH ILLUSION OF JUSTICE?

Shelby Steele

Vocabulary Words

plausibly (par. 1)   reparation (par. 3)   inertia (par. 5)
crucible (par. 2)   birthright (par. 3)   stagnated (par. 5)
cuisine (par. 2)   profound (par. 3)   manipulate (par. 6)
scion (par. 3)   esteem (par. 3)   aggrieved (par. 6)
aristocratic (par. 3)   subsidized par. 5)   mark (par. 9)

My father was born in the last year of the 19th century. His father was very likely born into slavery, though there are no official records to confirm this. Still, from family accounts, I can plausibly argue that my grandfather was born a slave.

2   When I tell people this, I worry that I may seem conceited, like someone claiming a connection to royalty. The extreme experience of slavery—its commitment to broken-willed servitude—was so intense a crucible that it must have taken a kind of genius to survive it. In the jaws of slavery and segregation, blacks created a life-sustaining form of worship, rituals for every human initiation from childbirth to death, a rich folk mythology, a world-famous written literature, a complete cuisine, a truth-telling comic sensibility and, of course, some of the most glorious music the world has ever known.

3   Like the scion of an aristocratic family, I mention my grandfather to stand a little in the light of the black American genius. So my first objection to reparation for slavery is that it feels like selling our birthright for a pot of porridge. There is a profound esteem that comes to us from having overcome four centuries of oppression.

4   This esteem is an irreplaceable resource. In Richard Wright's "Black Boy," a black elevator operator makes pocket money by letting white men kick him in the behind for a quarter. Maybe reparations are not quite this degrading, but when you trade on the past victimization of your own people, you trade honor for dollars. And this trading is only uglier when you are a mere descendent of those who suffered but nevertheless prevailed.

5   I believe the greatest problem black America has had over the past 30 years has been precisely a faith in reparational uplift—the idea that all the injustice we endured would somehow translate into the means of uplift. We fought for welfare programs that only subsidized human inertia, for cultural approaches to education that stagnated skill development in our young and for affirmative-action programs that removed the incentive to excellence in our best and brightest.

6   Today 70 percent of all black children are born out of wedlock. Sixty-eight percent of all violent crime is committed by blacks, most often against other blacks. Sixty percent of black fourth graders cannot read at grade level. And so on. When you fight for reparational uplift, you have to fit yourself into a victim-focused, protest identity that is at once angry and needy. You have to locate real transformative power in white society, and then manipulate white guilt by seducing it with neediness and threatening it with anger. And you must nurture in yourself, and pass on to your own children, a sense of ag-

grieved entitlement that sees black success as an impossibility without the intervention of white compassion.

7   The above statistics come far more from this rippling sense of entitlement than from racism. And now the demand for reparations is yet another demand for white responsibility when today's problem is a failure of black responsibility.

8   When you don't know how to go forward, you find an excuse to go backward. You tell yourself that if you an just get a little justice for past suffering, you will find better about the challenges you face. So you make justice a condition of your going forward. But of course, there is no justice for past suffering, and to believe there is only guarantees one's suffering.

9   The worst enemy black America faces today is not white racism but white guilt. This is what encourages us to invent new pleas rather than busy ourselves with the hard work of development. So willing are whites to treat us with deference that they are a hard mark to pass up. The entire civil-rights establishment strategizes to keep us the wards of white guilt. If these groups had to rely on black money rather than white corporate funding, they would all go under tomorrow.

10   An honest black leadership would portray our victimization as only a condition we faced, and nurture a black identity around the ingenuity by which we overcame it. It would see reparations as a childish illusion of perfect justice. I can't be repaid for my grandfather. The point is that I owe him a great effort.

Thinking and Responding to the Reading

1.   After reading the last paragraph of the article, reread the title. Explain the title's significance to Steele's argument.

2.   Why is Steele hesitant to claim a personal connection to slavery through his grandfather?

3.   Define reparations. Look up "black reparations" on the internet and give an example of "black reparations" that you found.

4.   What is Steele's main idea? How does he present it through counter arguments?

5.   What position does Steele want to see advocated by the black leadership?

6.   Explain Steele's reasons for stating, "The worst enemy black America faces today is not white racism but white guilt" (par. 9).

7.   Mikel Johnson's article "Forgiveness" discusses *tashuvah*, the concept that only the person who has been hurt can forgive. Discuss the concept of *tashuvah* as it relates to the last two sentences of paragraph 4.

Springboard for Composing

Have you ever disagreed with someone over a cultural issue? What were the opposing points of view? Were you able to reach some compromise or agreement? Explain how. If not at all, why not?

DO YOU SPEAK MATH?

Lynn Hart

Vocabulary Words

communication (par. 2)   symbols (par. 4)   sly (par. 8)
fumbled (par. 3)   pondered (par. 5)   gratified (par. 8)
intriguing (par. 3)

1   Lynnette finally was getting the chance to sit down and look at her homework. She had known that finding time to study for her class would be difficult, especially with her children and family responsibilities competing for her time. "Boy, here I am, the first day of class, and it's already eight o'clock before I get the chance to start my math," she thought. "I'm glad I'm only taking this one class; otherwise I'd really be in over my head," she added with a sense of relief.

2   Dr. Smith's math class had been different from what Lynnette expected or even remembered from her college days years ago. Dr. Smith had asked the class to respond in writing to the question projected on the overhead screen, a rather unusual question for the first day: How is mathematics communication? Lynnette's first thoughts had been, "What kind of question is that for a math class? Aren't we supposed to be learning algebra?"

3   In a way Lynnette was annoyed. After all, it had taken her many years to decide to come back to college, years of marriage and motherhood. She was in her mid-thirties now, and it was her turn to develop herself. She was impatient to get started on "real college work," and her professor asked her how is mathematics communication! She had sighed and fumbled with her pencil as she began thinking about the question. After a moment her feelings about it had softened, and she found it somewhat intriguing. She'd really never thought about math in this way. Maybe answering that question isn't such a bad idea after all.

4   In thinking back on this first day of being back in a college classroom, Lynnette decided it really hadn't been that bad at all. It was very interesting to listen to how other students answered Dr. Smith's question. Most students had written that math communicates with symbols and formulas. A few said that math is a language—a very foreign one. Another said that math communicates by explaining situations that involve information with numbers. Dr. Smith listed everyone's responses on the board and didn't say which were right or wrong. He just listened and made sure he understood everyone's opinion. Dr. Smith extended this to a homework assignment, asking the class to think more about the question and to give some examples to support their answers. As Dr. Smith went on to teach the lesson, the question and discussion kept coming to Lynnette's mind. They all were good ways of describing math communication. She wondered if there was really one right answer.

5   Now, sitting at home, Lynnette thought about how she should answer the question. How is mathematics communication? She decided to borrow from Webster's. Let's see what the dictionary has to say about communication," she pondered. "Communication,

commune, communicate, okay, communication. It can mean: 'to transmit' or 'a verbal or written message! Oh, here's a good one: "a process by which meanings are exchanged between individuals through a common system of symbols.' Hum, that sounds a lot like what some people were saying in class today" she recalled with a smile. "Okay, here's another: 'a technique for expressing ideas effectively.' Oh, I like that.

6   This is nice too: 'the technology of the transmission of information.'"

7   Lynnette reread the definitions, sat back in her chair, and thought about each one. "Gosh, they really all can apply to math," she realized. "Let's see...doesn't math transmit? It certainly does transmit information. Can math be a verbal or written message?" Lynnette flipped open to a page in her math book. "Sure," she thought. "The example right here, $3x + 5 = 20$, is a written message and could just as well be a verbal one meaning, '3 times some number we call x plus 5 more equals 20.'"

8   She was really beginning to see math in a very different light. She chuckled to herself as she recalled how annoyed she had been by the question at first. Now she realized how sly and clever Dr. Smith had been in giving it to them. It really was making her expand her notions of what math really is about. She continued to think about the other definitions she'd read, "Now, what about math being an exchange of information? Well, that's certainly true. That will happen every time we discuss math homework problems in class. It happened today when Dr. Smith solved a word problem on the board and somebody asked him to explain his steps. Math certainly involves exchanging information," she reasoned. "Hey, this next definition seems to be written just for math because we learn to understand math by using a common system of symbols." Lynnette was amazed when she thought about how much she had learned just by looking up the single word communication. This made her even more eager to get back to math class. "I think being back in school is going to be all right," she thought, feeling gratified. She sat up with a sense of satisfaction and began writing her homework response, remembering that she also had some math problems to complete.

Thinking and Responding to the Reading

1.   What is Lynnette's initial response to the homework question? Why does she feel this way?
2.   At first, in what way or ways does she misunderstand the assignment?
3.   What are the three different definitions Lynnette finds for communication? How do you account for so many definitions for one word?
4.   How does Lynnette eventually answer her math assignment?
5.   Explain how the word "communication" is used both denotatively and connotatively.

Springboard for Composing

Discuss a time you had to explain a difficult idea or situation in a much simpler way to someone. What system did you use? Afterwards, did the concept seem much clearer even to you? Explain this change.

ANGELS ON A PIN

Alexander Calandra

Vocabulary Words

colleague (par. 1)   barometer (par. 2)   scholasticism (par. 12)
arbiter (par. 1)   pedantic (par. 12)   lark (par. 12)

1   Some time ago, I received a call from a colleague who asked if I would be the referee on the grading of an examination question. He was about to give a student a zero for his answer to a physics question while the student claimed he should receive a perfect score and would if the system were not set up against the student. The instructor and the student agreed to an impartial arbiter, and I was selected.

2   I went to my colleague's office and read the examination question: "Show how it is possible to determine the height of a tall building with the aid of a barometer."

3   The student had answered: "Take the barometer to the top of the building, attach a long rope to it, lower the barometer to the street, and then bring it up, measuring the length of the rope. The length of the rope is the height of the building."

4   I pointed out that the student really had a strong case for full credit since he had answered the question completely and correctly. On the other hand, if full credit were given, it could well contribute to a high grade for the student in his physics course. A high grade is supposed to certify competence in physics, but the answer did not confirm this. I suggested that the student have another try at answering the question. I was not surprised that my colleague agreed, but I was somewhat surprised that the student did.

5   I gave the student six minutes to answer the question, with the warning that his answer should show some knowledge of physics. At the end of five minutes, he had not written anything. I asked if he wished to give up, but he said no. He had many answers to this problem, he was just thinking of the best one. I excused myself for interrupting him and asked him to please go on. In the next minute, he dashed off his answer, which read: "Take the barometer to the top of the building and lean over the edge of the roof. Drop the barometer, timing its fall with a stopwatch. Then using the formula $S = \frac{1}{2} gt2$, calculate the height of the building.

6   At this point, I asked my colleague if he would give up. He conceded and gave the student almost full credit.

7   In leaving my colleague's office, I recalled that the student had said he had other answers to the problem, so I asked him what they were. "Oh, yes," said the student, "there are many ways of getting the height of a tall building with the aid of a barometer. For example, you could take the barometer out on a sunny day and measure the height of the barometer, the length of its shadow, and the length of the shadow of the building, and by the use of simple proportion, determine the height of the building."

8   "Fine," I said, "and what are the others?"

9   "Yes," said the student, "There is a very basic measurement method that you will like. In this method, you take the barometer and begin to walk up the stairs. As you climb the stairs, you

mark off the length of the barometer along the wall. You then count the number of marks, and this will give you the height of the building in barometric units. A very direct method.

10   "Of course, if you want a more sophisticated method, you can take the barometer to the end of a string, swing it as a pendulum, and determine the value of "g" at the street level and at the top of the building. From the difference between the two values of "g," the height of the building can, in principle, be calculated.

11   "Finally," he concluded, "there are many other ways of solving this problem. Probably the best," he said, "is to take the barometer to the basement and knock on the superintendent's door. When the superintendent answers, you speak to him as follows: 'Mr. Superintendent, here I have a fine barometer. If you will tell me the height of this building, I will give you this barometer.'"

12   At this point, I asked the student if he really did not know the conventional answer to this question. He admitted that he did, but said that he was fed up with high school and college instructors trying to teach him how to think, to use the "scientific method" and to explore the deep inner logic of the subject in a pedantic way, as is often done in the new mathematics, rather than teaching him the structure of the subject. With this in mind, he decided to revive scholasticism as an academic lark to challenge the Sputnik-panicked classrooms of America.

Thinking and Responding to the Reading

1.   Why does the narrator's colleague need a referee? What is at issue?
2.   Discuss the dilemma of the physics professors. Why are they uncomfortable giving the student full credit?
3.   What is the student's reason for answering the question as he does?
4.   The student uses both divergent and convergent thinking. Diagram both thinking steps.
5.   Give the definition of creative and critical thinking. Did the student successfully solve the problem? Explain your answer.

Springboard for Composing

At times we think we know of a "simpler" or "easier" or even "better" way of fixing something than is generally recommended. Recall an instance in your own experience. How did you arrive at your own method? What mental connections did you have to make to arrive at this idea?

THE MYTH OF DAEDALUS & ICARUS

Vocabulary Words

envy (par. 1)
exiled (par. 1)

labyrinth (par. 2)
heed (par. 4)

1   Daedalus was a highly respected and talented Athenian artisan descendent from the royal family of Cecrops, the mythical first King of Athens. He was known for his skill as an architect, sculptor, and inventor, and he produced many famous works. Despite his self-confidence, Daedalus once committed a crime of envy against Talus, his nephew and apprentice. Talus, who seemed destined to become as great an artisan as his uncle Daedalus, was inspired one day to invent the saw after having seen the way a snake used its jaws. Daedalus, momentarily stricken with jealousy, threw Talus off of the Acropolis. For this crime, Daedalus was exiled to Crete and placed in the service of King Minos, where he eventually had a son, Icarus, with the beautiful Naucrate, a mistress-slave of the King.

2   Minos called on Daedalus to build the famous Labyrinth in order to imprison the dreaded Minotaur. The Minotaur was a monster with the head of a bull and the body of a man. He was the son of Pasiphae, the wife of Minos, and a bull that Poseidon had sent to Minos as a gift. Minos was shamed by the birth of this horrible creature and resolved to imprison the Minotaur in the Labyrinth where it fed on humans, which were taken as "tribute" by Minos and sacrificed to the Minotaur in memory of his fallen son Androgenos.

3   Theseus, the heroic King of Athens, volunteered himself to be sent to the Minotaur in the hopes of killing the beast and ending the "human tribute" that his city was forced to pay Minos. When Theseus arrived to Crete, Ariadne, Minos's daughter, fell in love with him and wished to help him survive the Minotaur. Daedalus revealed the mystery of the Labyrinth to Ariadne who in turn advised Theseus, thus enabling him to slay the Minotaur and escape from the Labyrinth. When Minos found out what Daedalus had done he was so enraged that he imprisoned Daedalus and Icarus in the Labyrinth themselves.

4   Daedalus conceived to escape from the Labyrinth with Icarus from Crete by constructing wings and then flying to safety. He built the wings from feathers and wax, and before the two set off he warned Icarus not to fly too low lest his wings touch the waves and get wet, and not too high lest the sun melt the wax. But the young Icarus, overwhelmed by the thrill of flying, did not heed his father's warning, flew too close to the sun whereupon the wax in his wings melted and he fell into the sea. Daedalus escaped to Sicily and Icarus' body was carried ashore by the current to an island then without a name. Heracles came across the body and recognized it, giving it burial where today there still stands a small rock promontory jutting out into the Aegean Sea, and naming the island and the sea around it after the fallen Icarus.

110

Thinking and Responding to the Reading

1. Define the word myth.
2. Why did Minos have Daedalus imprisoned in the labyrinth that Daedalus built?
3. Why is Minos outraged by Theseus's slaying the Minotaur?
4. How do Daedalus and his son Icarus escape from the labyrinth?
5. What does Icarus do?
6. What is the moral of this story?

Springboard for Composing

Although he had no blueprint to guide him, Daedalus made wings out of feathers with wax to hold them fast yet keep them light because he observed and understood the principle of flight in birds. Think of a project you created or improve upon after you thought about the principles involved. Be sure to include all the details necessary for a reader to understand what you did.

ALLEGORY OF THE CAVE

Plato

Vocabulary Words

allegory (title)   illusion (par. 16)   dazzled (par. 21)
liberated (par. 16)   perplexed (par. 16)   contemplate (par. 25)
compelled (par. 16)   refuge (par. 18)   behold (par. 27)
distress (par. 16)   reluctantly (par. 20)   felicitate (par. 29)
conceive (par. 16)   ascent (par. 20)   endure (par. 32)

1   Is a resident of the cave (a prisoner, as it were) likely to want to make the ascent to the outer world? Why or why not? What does the sun symbolize in the allegory?

2   And now, I said, let me show in a figure how far our nature is enlightened or un-enlightened:--Behold! Human beings living in an underground den, which has a mouth open towards the light and reaching all along the den; here they have been from their childhood, and have their legs and necks chained so that they can not move, and can only see before them, being prevented by the chains from turning round their heads. Above and behind them a fire is blazing at a distance, and between the fire and the prisoners there is a raised way; and you will see, if you look, a low wall built along the way, like the screen which marionette players have in front of them, over which they show the puppets.

3   I see.

4   And do you see, I said, men passing along the wall carrying all sorts of vessels, and statues and figures of animals made of wood and stone and various materials, which appear over the wall? Some of them are talking, others silent.

5   You have shown me a strange image, and they are strange prisoners.

6   Like ourselves, I replied; and they see only their own shadows, or the shadows of one another, which the fire throws on the opposite wall of the cave?

7   True, he said; how could they see anything but the shadows if they were never allowed to move their heads?

8   And of the objects which are being carried in like manner they would only see the shadows?

9   Yes, he said.

10   And if they were able to converse with one another, would they not suppose that they were naming what was actually before them?

11   Very true.

12   And suppose further that the prison had an echo which came from the other side, would they not be sure to fancy when one of the passers-by spoke that the voice which they heard came from the passing shadow?

13   No question, he replied.

14   To them, I said, the truth would be literally nothing but the shadows of the images.

15   That is certain.

[16] And now look again, and see what will naturally follow if the prisoners are released and disabused of their error. At first, when any of them is liberated and compelled suddenly to stand up and turn his neck round and walk and look towards the light, he will suffer sharp pains; the glare will distress him, and he will be unable to see the realities of which in his former state he had seen the shadows; and then conceived some one saying to him, that what he saw before was an illusion, but that now, when he is approaching nearer to being and his eye is turned towards more real existence, he has a clearer vision,--what will be his reply? And you may further imagine that his instructor is pointing to the objects as they pass and requiring him to name them,--will he not be perplexed? Will he not fancy that the shadows which he formerly saw are truer than the objects which are now shown to him?

[17] Far truer.

[18] And if he is compelled to look straight at the light, will he not have a pain in his eyes which will make him turn away to take refuge in the objects of vision which he can see, and which he will conceive to be in reality clearer than the things which are now being shown to him?

[19] True, he said.

[20] And suppose once more, that he is reluctantly dragged up a steep and rugged ascent, and held fast until he is forced into the presence of the sun himself, is he not likely to be pained and irritated? When he approaches the light his eyes will be dazzled, and he will not be able to see anything at all of what are now called realities.

[21] Not all in a moment, he said.

[22] He will require to grow accustomed to the sight of the upper world. And first he will see the shadows best, next the reflections of the men and other objects in the water, and then the objects themselves; then he will gaze upon the light of the moon and the stars and the spangled heaven; and he will see the sky and the stars by night better than the sun or the light of the sun by day?

[23] Certainly.

[24] Last of all he will be able to see the sun, and mere reflections of him in the water, but he will see him in his own proper place, and not in another; and he will contemplate him as he is.

[25] Certainly.

[26] He will then proceed to argue that this is he who gives the season and the years, and is the guardian of all that is in the visible world, and in a certain way the cause of all things which he and his fellows have been accustomed to behold?

[27] Clearly, he said, he would first see the sun and then reason about him.

[28] And when he remembered his old habitation, and the wisdom of the den and his fellow-prisoners, do you not suppose that he would felicitate himself on the change, and pity them?

[29] But then, if I am right, certain professors of education must be wrong when they say that they can put knowledge into the soul which was not there before, like sight into blind eyes.

[30] They undoubtedly say this, he replied.

[31] Whereas, our argument shows that the power and capacity of learning exists in the soul already; and that just as the eye was unable to turn from darkness to light without the whole body, so too the instrument of knowledge can only by the movement of the whole

soul be turned from the world of becoming into that of being, and learn by degrees to endure the sight of being, and of the brightest and best of being, or in other words, of the good.

32   Very true.

Thinking and Responding to the Reading

1.   Before reading the remaining questions, draw a cave, fire and prisoners.
2.   Reread the first paragraph and then summarize what Plato is telling his student. Make sure you answer in the summary what he "sees." What is his argument?
3.   In paragraphs 3-11 he describes what the prisoners "see" and "hear." Restate what is said in your own words.
4.   In paragraph 13 he says, "to them, I said, the truth would be literally nothing but the shadow images." What does it mean to only see the "shadow images"?
5.   In paragraph 14, Plato tells us that if the prisoners are released, they will see something else. What will they see?
6.   He continues to describe that the prisoners must look directly into the sun. In paragraphs 17-26 he describes what will happen to the prisoners. Paraphrase or summarize this section of the reading.
7.   Paragraphs 27-31 state Plato's argument about learning. Restate the thesis (argument).

Springboard to Composing

Plato uses the allegory of the cave to teach how we learn. Each aspect of learning is connected to another one, so the learning builds upon itself. Think of something that you learned how to do by connecting it to something else you already knew how to do. Be specific when conveying your ideas.

MAORI CREATION STORY

New Zealand

Vocabulary Words

primal (par. 7)	hurled (par.7)	cosmos (par. 14)
exerted (par. 7)	placid (par. 11)	mantle (par. 16)

1   In the beginning was Te Kore, the Void, the Nothing, and from Te Kore came Te Poo, the Dark, the Night. Ranginui, the Sky Father, and Papatuanuku, the Earth Mother lay in each other's arms so closely that the world did not have light.

2   Papatuanuku gave birth to many children, but the children, the gods, were stuck between Papatuanuku and Ranginui's clinging bodies. The children longed for freedom—for the wind blowing over sharp hilltops and steep valleys, for light to warm their pale bodies.

3   "What can we do?" they asked. "We need to get out."

4   One of them, Taane-muhuta, mighty father of the forest, father of all living things that love light and freedom, said, "We must force them apart."

5   All the children agreed that this was a good idea. One by one they tried to push their parents apart. They did not succeed. Finally Taane-muhuta rose.

6   For as long as a man can hold his breath, Taane-muhuta stood, silent and unmoving, summoning all his strength. He pressed his hands against the body of his mother and turning upside-down he planted his feet firmly on his father. He straightened his back and pushed.

7   The primal parents clung to each other. Taane-muhuta exerted all his strength, straining back and limbs. He pushed for hours, he pushed for days, he pushed for weeks, he pushed for years and years. And very, very slowly Taane managed to uncurl his body, straighten himself, until at last the mighty bodies of earth and sky were forced apart. The fierce continuous thrust of Taane tore the heaven from the earth. Ranginui was hurled far away while angry winds screamed through the space between earth and sky. Light came into the world, and for the first time since the world was created, plants started to grow.

8   Taane and his brothers looked at the soft curves of their mother. As the light crept across the land, they saw a veil of silver mist that hung over her naked shoulders—the mist of grief for her lost husband. Tears dropped fast from Rangi's eyes. His tears ran into rivers and they became a sea. The showers of rain ran together in pools and streams across the body of Papa. The water threatened to become a flood. Something had to be done. The children turned Papa over so that Rangi could not see her face. Now he doesn't cry so much. But his tears are still there in the dewdrops on the grass every morning and his sighs are the mists that rise from the ground.

9   Taane still loved his parents greatly even though he so forcibly separated them. He set to work to wrap his mother in beauty that had not been dreamed of in the dark world. He brought his own children, the trees, and set them in the earth. But Taane was like a child, learning by trial and error the wisdom that had not yet been born. He planted the trees upside down. Their heads were buried in the soil, while the bare white roots remained stiff and unmoving in the breeze.

10   There was no place for his other children—the birds and the insects. He pulled up a giant kauri tree, shook the soil from its branches, set the roots firmly in the ground, and proudly surveyed the spreading crown set above the clean, straight trunk. The earth lay still and beautiful, wrapped in a dressing of living green. The ocean lapped Papa's body. The birds and the insects ran and fluttered in the fresh breeze. The breeze played with the leaves, singing the song of a new world.

11   The gods frolicked under the leaves of the garden of Taane. Each had his own job. Rango-maa-taane preserved the fertility of the growing things. Haumia-tiketike tended the humble fernroot. Tuu-matauenga was the god of war. Tangaroa controlled the waves. Only one of the seventy brothers left the placid shelter of his mother to follow his father: Taawhiri-maatea, the god of all the winds that blow between earth and sky.

12   Taane-muhuta raised his eyes to where Rangi lay, cold and gray and unlovely in the vast spaces above the earth and was sorry for the unhappiness of his father. He took the bright sun and placed it on Rangi's back with the silver moon in front. He found a blue cloak and placed it across his shoulders. He traveled through the heavens until he found a cloth of glowing red. After that he rested for seven days and then spread the cloth across the sky from east to west and from north to south.

13   But Taane was not satisfied. He decided that the gift was not enough for his father and he stripped off the red cloth. A small piece remained, a fragment of the garment men still see at the time of the setting sun.

14   "Great father," Taane cried, "in the long dark nights when Marama the moon shines on your breast in all things sorrow, I will journey to the very ends of the cosmos to find beauty for you."

15   Somewhere in the silence he heard an answering sigh. He passed swiftly to the very end of the world, into the darkness, until he reached Mauganui, the Great Mountain, where the Shining Ones lived. They were the children of Uru, Taane-mahuta's brother. The two brothers watched them playing at the foot of the mountain.

16   Taane begged Uru to give him some of the shining lights to fasten on the mantle of the sky. Uru rose to his feet and gave a great shout. The Shining Ones heard and came rolling up the slope to their father. Uru placed a basket in front of Taane. He plunged his arms into the glowing mass of lights and piled the Shining Ones into the basket.

17   Taane placed the flowing lights onto the breast of Rangi and sprinkled the dark blue robe with the Children of Light. The basket he hung in the wide heavens. Sometimes Uru's children tumble and fall swiftly towards the earth, but for the most part they remain like fireflies on the blanket of the night sky.

Thinking and Responding to the Reading

1.   Why do the children want to separate from their parents? What does this involve?
2.   How did Heaven and Earth separate? Explain each character's action.
3.   What is the effect of Rangi's tears? Where can we still see his tears?
4.   Find three of your favorite metaphors or similes and explain what they mean.
5.   Compare and contrast this version of creation with the Judeo-Christian story of creation.

116

Springboard for Composing

All known cultures have a creation story. Speculate why humans compose stories about the world's beginning. Recall where and when you first heard or read about the origins of our world.

THE JUDEO-CHRISTIAN CREATION STORY

Vocabulary Words

void (par. 1)	reason (par. 7)	toil (par. 8)
bounds (par. 3)	brute (par. 7)	reverence (par. 10)
instinct (par. 7)	tending (par. 8)	taint (par.10)

1   There was a time, long years ago, when this earth on which we live was not, when neither sun nor moon shone for it, when the space it now fills was void and dark.

2   God, who is without beginning or end, who makes all and rules all, spoke, and His voice sounded the note of creation. On the first creative day, He called forth light, and the darkness fled away in the presence of the light, and hid itself in night.

3   On the second creative day, God made the air, or clear blue sky. On the third day, He gave bounds to the seas and caused the dry land to appear; and He made the earth to bring forth grass, and flowers, and fruits, and trees.

4   On the fourth day, He set the sun and moon and stars in the sky, so as to tell the days, the nights, the seasons and the years. On the fifth day, he made the air to bring forth its winged birds, and the seas to swarm, with fishes, great and small.

5   On the sixth day, He made the animals of the land, wild and tame, fierce and harmless, beasts, insects and reptiles. And to crown this last creative day, He made man, after His own image, and gave him power over all the other creatures, in the air, in the waters and upon the land. And when God had completed His work of creation, He blessed it, and rested for a day.

6   And His day of rest, which was the seventh, is the day which came to be the Sabbath, by His own command, "Remember the Sabbath day to keep it holy."

7   Thus God made this world and the things around it and the things upon it, everything beautiful and useful in its way. To all the living things he gave a wonderful power, which is called instinct, by means of which they feed, and protect and multiply themselves. But to mankind He gave a much higher power, called reason, by means of which it is lifted above the brute, and is filled with knowledge, and lofty desires, and worshipful spirit. He also gave to man a soul, which is immortal.

8   The first man whom God created was named Adam, which name means that he was of earth, or, as the Bible says, of dust. He was given a pleasant place to live in, the Garden of Eden, where grass and fruits and flowers grew without tending, where animals played without harm to each other, and where Adam had no need of shelter, nor toil, nor even clothing. This was Paradise, because it was all so beautiful and free from sin.

9   Only one thing was wanting. Adam needed a companion, because he was lonely. So God gave him a help mate. He caused a sleep to fall on Adam, during which He took one of his ribs, of which He made a creature called woman, because she was of the bone and flesh of Adam. The woman became Adam's wife. He called her Eve, which word means that in her the human race would find motherhood.

10   Eve was gifted, just as Adam was, with beauty of body, with reason, with love, with reverence. They were happy in the Garden, where care came not. So pure was all the creation about them, and so innocent were they in their hearts, that their nakedness was not a source of shame. They loved their Creator, and they moved about their beautiful dwelling-place singing His praises. They were untouched by any sorrow, or pain, or fear, and they were visited by God, who talked with them and told them what they should do in order to appear pleasing in His eye, and forever keep their dwelling-place free from the taint of sin.

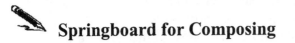

Thinking and Responding to the Reading

1.   How is God portrayed in this creation story? Find examples to support your answer.
2.   Cite some phrases and/or words that appear "old fashioned." How do they influence the tone of the story?
3.   What does it mean when the narrator says "to crown his last creative day" in paragraph 5? How is this related to man being created "in His own image"?
4.   What is the difference between instinct and reason?
5.   Compare and contrast this version of creation to the "Maori Creation Story."

Springboard for Composing

What is your version of the world's beginnings? Do you remember when you first heard or read about it? Do you know someone who believes in what you do? Do you feel more, less or the same comfort level with this person because of this? Conversely, do you know someone who believes a different creation story? Do you feel more, less or the same comfort level with this person because of this difference?

CINDERELLA

A Folktale of China

Vocabulary Words

hemp (par. 2)   consciousness (par. 14)   console (par. 16)
quandary (par. 9)   smallpox (par. 15)   innumerable (par. 18)
fishmonger (par. 9)   delicacies (par. 15)   entrails (par. 20)

1 There were once two sisters. The elder was very beautiful, and everyone called her Beauty. But the younger had a face covered with pock marks, so that everyone called her Pock Face. She was the daughter of the second wife, and was so spoiled that she was a very unpleasant girl. Beauty's real mother had died when Beauty was very young. After her death she turned into a yellow cow and lived in the garden. Beauty adored the yellow cow, but it had a miserable existence because the stepmother treated it so badly.

2 One day the stepmother took the ugly daughter to the theater and left Beauty at home. Beauty wanted to accompany them, but the stepmother said, "I will take you tomorrow if you straighten the hemp in my room."

3 Beauty went off and sat down in front of the stack of hemp, but after a long time she had only divided half of it. Bursting into tears, she took it off to the yellow cow, who swallowed the whole mass and then spat it out again all neatly arranged piece by piece. Beauty dried her tears, and gave the hemp to her mother on her return home. "Mother, here is the hemp. I can go to the theater tomorrow, can't I?"

4 When the next day came, her stepmother again refused to take her saying, "You can go when you have separated the sesame seeds from the beans."

5 The poor girl had to divide them seed by seed, until the exhausting task made her eyes ache. Again she went to the yellow cow, who said to her, "You stupid girl? You must separate them with a fan." Now she understood, and the sesame and beans were soon divided. When she brought the seeds all nicely separated, her stepmother knew that she could no longer prevent her going to the theatre. However, she asked her, "How can a servant girl be so clever? Who helped you?"

6 Beauty had to admit that the yellow cow had advised her, which made the stepmother very angry. Therefore, without saying a word, she killed and ate the cow. Beauty had loved the cow so dearly that she could not eat its flesh. Instead, she put the bones in an earthenware pot and hid them in her bedroom.

7 Day after day, the stepmother would still not take Beauty to the theater. One evening, when the stepmother had gone to the theater with Pock Face, Beauty was so cross that she smashed everything in the house, including the earthenware pot containing the cow's bones. Whereupon there was a loud crackling sound, and a white horse, a new dress, and a pair of embroidered shoes came out. The sudden appearance of these things gave Beauty a terrible start, but she soon saw that they were real objects. Quickly pulling on the new dress and the shoes, she jumped on the horse and rode out of the gate.

120

8   While she was riding along, one of her shoes slipped off and fell into the ditch. She wanted to dismount and pick it up, but could not do so; at the same time she did not want to leave it lying there.

9   She was in a real quandary, when a fishmonger appeared. "Brother fishmonger, please pick up my shoe," she said to him. He answered with a grin, "With great pleasure, if you will marry me." "Who could marry you?" she said crossly. "Fishmongers always stink." Seeing that he had no chance, the fishmonger went on his way.

10   Next, a clerk from a rice shop went by, and she said to him, "Brother rice broker, please give me my shoe." "Certainly, if you will marry me," said the young man. "Marry a rice broker! Their bodies are all covered with dust."

11   The rice broker departed, and soon an oil merchant came by, whom she also asked to pick up her shoe. "I will pick it up if you consent to marry me," he replied. "Who could want to marry you?" Beauty said with a sigh. "Oil merchants are always so greasy."

12   Shortly a scholar came by, whom she also asked to pick up her shoe. The scholar turned to look at her, and then said, "I will do so at once if you promise to marry me." The scholar was very handsome, and so she nodded her head in agreement. He picked up the shoe and put it on her foot. Then he took her back to his house and made her his wife.

13   Three days later, Beauty went with her husband to pay the necessary respects to her parents. Her stepmother and sister had quite changed their manner, and treated them both in the most friendly and attentive fashion. In the evening they wanted to keep Beauty at home, and she, thinking they meant it kindly, agreed to stay and to follow her husband in a few days.

14   The next morning her sister took her by the hand and said to her with a laugh, "Sister, come and look into the well. We will see which of us is the most beautiful." Suspecting nothing, Beauty went to the well and leaned over to look down. At this moment her sister gave her a shove and pushed her into the well; then she quickly covered the well with a basket. Poor Beauty lost consciousness and was drowned.

15   After ten days the scholar began to wonder why his wife had still not returned. He sent a messenger to inquire, and the stepmother sent back a message that his wife was suffering from a bad attack of smallpox and would not be well enough to return for some time. The scholar believed this, and every day he sent salted eggs and other sickbed delicacies, all of which found their way into the stomach of the ugly sister.

16   After two months the stepmother was irritated by the continual messages from the scholar, and decided to deceive him by sending back her own daughter as his wife. The scholar was horrified when he saw Pock Face, and said, "Goodness! How changed you are! Surely you are not Beauty. My wife was never such a monster. Good Heavens!" Pock Face replied seriously, "If I am not Beauty, who do you think I am then? You know perfectly well I was very ill with smallpox, and now you want to disown me. I shall die! I shall die!" She began to howl. The tender-hearted scholar could not bear to see her weeping, and although he still had some doubts he begged her forgiveness and tried to console her. Gradually she stopped weeping.

17   Beauty, however, had been transformed into a sparrow, and she used to come and call out when Pock Face was combing her hair, "Comb once, peep; comb twice, peep; comb thrice, up to the spine of Pock Face." The wicked wife answered, "Comb once,

comb twice, comb thrice, to the spine of Beauty." The scholar was very mystified by this conversation, and he said to the sparrow, "Why do you sing like that? Are you by any chance my wife? If you are, call three times, and I will put you in a golden cage and keep you as a pet." The sparrow called out three times, and the scholar brought a golden cage to keep it in.

18   The ugly sister was very angry when she saw that her husband was keeping the sparrow, and so she secretly killed it and threw it into the garden. It was at once transformed into a bamboo with many shoots. When Pock Face ate the bamboo shoots, an ulcer formed on her tongue, but the scholar found them excellent. The wicked woman became suspicious again, and had the bamboo cut down and made into a bed. When she lay on it, innumerable needles pricked her, but the scholar found it extremely comfortable. Again she became very cross and threw the bed away.

19   Next door to the scholar lived an old woman who sold money bags. One day on her way home she saw the bed and thought to herself, "No one has died here; why have they thrown the bed away? I shall take it." She took the bed into her house and had a very comfortable night.

20   The next day she saw that the food in the kitchen was already cooked. She ate it up, but naturally she felt a little nervous, not having any idea who could have prepared it. For several days she found she could have dinner the moment she came home. Finally, being no longer able to contain her anxiety, she came back early one afternoon and went into the kitchen, where she saw a dark shadow washing rice. She ran up quickly and clasped the shadow round the waist. "Who are you?" she asked, "and why do you cook food for me?" The shadow replied, "I will tell you everything. I am the wife of your neighbor the scholar and am called Beauty. My sister threw me into the well; I was drowned, but my soul was not destroyed. Please give me a rice pot as head, a stick as hand, a dish cloth as entrails, and firehooks as feet, and then I can assume my former shape again."

21   The old woman gave her what she asked for, and in a moment a beautiful girl appeared. The old woman was delighted at seeing such a charming girl, and she questioned her very closely about who she was and what had happened to her. She told the old woman everything, and then said, "Old woman, I have a bag which you must offer for sale outside the scholar's house. If he comes out, you must sell it to him." And she gave her an embroidered bag.

22   The next day the old woman stood outside the scholar's house and shouted that she had a bag for sale. Maddened by the noise, he came out to ask what kind of bags she sold, and she showed him Beauty's embroidered bag. "Where did you get this bag?" he asked, "I once gave it to my wife." The old woman then told the whole story to the scholar, who was overjoyed to hear that his wife was still alive. He arranged everything with the old woman, put a red cloth on the ground, and brought Beauty back to his house.

23   When Pock Face saw her sister return, she gave her no peace. She began to grumble and say that the woman was only pretending to be Beauty, and that actually she was a spirit. She wanted to have a trial to see which was the genuine wife. Beauty, of course, knew that she herself was the real bride. She said, "Good. We will have a test." Pock Face suggested that they should walk on eggs, and whoever broke the shells would be the loser. Although Pock Face broke all the eggs, and Beauty none, Pock Face refused to admit her loss and insisted on another trial.

[24] This time they were to walk up a ladder made of knives. Beauty went up and down first without receiving the tiniest scratch, but before Pock Face had gone two steps her feet were cut to the bone. Although she had lost again, she insisted on another test—that of jumping into a caldron of hot oil. She hoped that Beauty, who would have to jump first, would be burned. Beauty, however, was quite unharmed by the boiling oil, but the wicked sister jumped into it and did not come up again.

[25] Beauty put the roasted bones of the wicked sister into a box and sent them over to her stepmother by a stuttering old servant woman, who was told to say, "Your daughter's flesh." But the stepmother loved carp and understood "carp flesh" instead of "your daughter's flesh." She thought her daughter had sent her over some carp, and opened the box in a state of great excitement; but when she saw the charred bones of her daughter lying inside, she let out a piercing scream and fell down dead.

Thinking and Responding to the Reading

1. Look up the definition of a folktale. How does this story fit the definition?
2. How do the names in this story reveal the personalities of the characters and advance the plot?
3. List the signs that the scholar receives after Beauty is drowned. What does each sign symbolize?
4. Describe each competition between the two sisters and explain their symbolism. Why do they compete to their deaths?
5. What is the moral of this story?

Springboard for Composing

Remember a time when a relative, teacher, parent, coworker or friend told you a tale about anything or anyone. When and where did this take place? What was the tale about and why was it told to you? What did the two of you share in this telling?

DISCOVERY OF A FATHER

Sherwood Anderson

Vocabulary Words

dignified (par. 1)	windbag (par. 7)	immaculate (par. 23)	dignity (par. 43)
livery (par. 4)	intimate (par. 13)	glimpse (par. 39)	

1   You hear it said that fathers want their sons to be what they feel they cannot themselves be, but I tell you it also works the other way. A boy wants something very special from his father. I know that as a small boy I wanted my father to be a certain thing he was not. I wanted him to be a proud, silent, dignified father. When I was with other boys and he passed along the street, I wanted to feel a flow of pride. "There he is. That is my father."

2   But he wasn't such a one. He couldn't be. It seemed to me then that he was always showing off. Let's say someone in our town had got up a show. They were always doing it. The druggist would be in it, the shoestore clerk, the horse doctor, and a lot of women and girls. My father would manage to get the chief comedy part. It was, let's say a Civil War play and he was a comic Irish soldier. He had to do the most absurd things. They thought he was funny, but I didn't.

3   I thought he was terrible. I didn't see how mother could stand it. She even laughed with the others. Maybe I would have laughed if it hadn't been my father.

4   Or there was a parade, the Fourth of July or Decoration Day. He'd be in that, too, right at the front of it, as Grand Marshal or something, on a white horse hired from a livery stable.

5   He couldn't ride for shucks. He fell off the horse and everyone hooted with laughter, but he didn't care. He even seemed to like it. I remember once when he had done something ridiculous, and right out on Main Street, too. I was with some other boys and they were laughing and shouting at him and he was shouting back and having as good a time as they were. I ran down an alley back of some stores and there in the Presbyterian Church sheds I had a good long cry.

6   Or I would be in bed at night and father would come home a little lit up and bring some men with him. He was a man who was never alone. Before he went broke, running a harness shop, there were always a lot of men loafing in the shop. He went broke, of course, because he gave too much credit. He couldn't refuse it and I thought he was a fool. I had got to hating him.

7   There'd be men I didn't think would want to be fooling around with him. There might even be the superintendent of our schools and a quiet man who ran the hardware store. Once I remember there was a white haired man who was a cashier of the bank. It was a wonder to me they'd want to be seen with such a windbag. That's what I thought he was. I know now what it was that attracted them. It was because life in our town, as in all small towns, was at times pretty dull and he livened it up. He made them laugh. He could tell stories. He'd even get them to sing.

8   If they didn't come to our house they'd go off, say at night, to where there was a grassy place by a creek. They'd cook food there and drink beer and sit about listening to his stories.

124

9 He was always telling stories about himself. He'd say this or that wonderful thing had happened to him. It might be something that made him look like a fool. He didn't care.

10 If an Irishman came to our house, right away father would say he was Irish. He'd tell what county in Ireland he was born in. He'd tell things that happened there when he was a boy. He'd make it seem so real that, if I hadn't known he was born in southern Ohio, I'd have believed him myself.

11 If it was a Scotchman the same thing happened. He'd get a burr into his speech. Or he was a German or a Swede. He'd be anything the other man was. I think they all knew he was lying, but they seemed to like him just the same. As a boy that was what I couldn't understand.

12 And there was mother. How could she stand it? I wanted to ask but never did. She was not the kind you asked such questions.

13 I'd be upstairs in my bed, in my room above the porch, and father would be telling some of his tales. A lot of father's stories were about the Civil War. To hear him tell it he'd been in about every battle. He'd known Grant, Sherman, Sheridan and I don't know how many others. He'd been particularly intimate with General Grant so that when Grant went East to take charge of all the armies, he took father along.

14 "I was an orderly at headquarters and Sim Grant said to me, 'Irve' he said, I'm going to take you along with me."

15 It seems he and Grant used to slip off sometimes and have a quiet drink together. That's what my father said. He'd tell about the day Lee surrendered and how, when the great moment came, they couldn't find Grant.

16 "You know," my father said, "about General Grant's book, his memoirs. You've read of how he said he had a headache and how, when he got word that Lee was ready to call it quits, he was suddenly and miraculously cured."

17 "Huh," said father. "He was in the woods with me.

18 "I was in there with my back against a tree. I was pretty well corned. I had got hold of a bottle of pretty good stuff.

19 "They were looking for Grant. He had got off his horse and come into the woods. He found me. He was covered with mud.

20 "I had the bottle in my hand. What'd I care? The war was over. I knew we had them licked."

21 My father said that he was the one who told Grant about Lee. An orderly riding by had told him, because the orderly knew how thick he was with Grant. Grant was embarrassed.

22 "But, Irve, look at me. I'm all covered with mud," he said to father.

23 And then, my father said, he and Grant decided to have a drink together. They took a couple of shots and then, because he didn't want Grant to show up potted before the immaculate Lee, he smashed the bottle against the tree.

24 "Sim Grant's dead now and I wouldn't want it to get out on him," my father said.

25 That's just one of the kinds of things he'd tell. Of course the men knew he was lying, but they seemed to like it just the same.

26 When we got broke, down and out, do you think he ever brought anything home? Not he. If there wasn't anything to eat in the house, he'd go off visiting around at farmhouses. They all wanted him. Sometimes he'd stay away for weeks, mother working to keep us fed, and then home he'd come bringing, let's say, a ham. He'd got it from some farmer friend. He'd slap it on the table in the kitchen. "You bet I'm going to see that my kids have something to eat," he'd say, and mother would just stand smiling at him. She'd never say a word about all the weeks and

months he'd been away, not leaving us a cent for food. Once I heard her speaking to a woman in our street. Maybe the woman had dared to sympathize with her. "Oh," she said, "it's all right. He isn't ever dull like most of the men in this street. Life is never dull when my man is about."

27   But often I was filled with bitterness, and sometimes I wished he wasn't my father. I'd even invent another man as my father. To protect my mother I'd make up stories of a secret marriage that for some strange reason never got known. As though some man, say the president of a railroad company or maybe a Congressman, had married my mother, thinking his wife was dead and then it turned out she wasn't.

28   So they had to hush it up but I got born just the same. I wasn't really the son of my father. Somewhere in the world there was a very dignified, quite wonderful man who was really my father. I even made myself half believe these fancies.

29   And then there came a certain night. He'd been off somewhere for two or three weeks. He found me alone in the house, reading by the kitchen table.

30   It had been raining and he was very wet. He sat and looked at me for along time, not saying a word. I was startled, for there was on his face the saddest look I had ever seen. He sat for a time, his clothes dripping. Then he got up.

31   "Come on with me," he said.

32   I got up and went with him out of the house. I was filled with wonder but I wasn't afraid. We went along a dirt road that led down into a valley, about a mile out of town, where there was a pond. We walked in silence. The man who was always talking had stopped his talking.

33   I didn't know what was up and had the queer feeling that I was with a stranger. I don't know whether my father intended it so. I don't think he did.

34   The pond was quite large. It was still raining hard and there were flashes of lightning followed by thunder. We were on a grassy bank at the pond's edge when my father spoke, and in the darkness and rain his voice sounded strange.

35   "Take off your clothes," he said. Still filled with wonder, I began to undress. There was a flash of lightning and I saw that he was already naked.

36   Naked, we went into the pond. Taking my hand he pulled me in. It may be that I was too frightened, too full of a feeling of strangeness, to speak. Before that night my father had never seemed to pay any attention to me.

37   "And what is he up to now?" I kept asking myself. I did not swim very well, but he put my hand on his shoulder and struck out into the darkness.

38   He was a man with big shoulders, a powerful swimmer. In the darkness I could feel the movement of his muscles. We swam to the far edge of the pond and then back to where we had left our clothes. The rain continued and the wind blew. Sometimes my father swam on his back and when he did he took my hand in his large powerful one and moved it over so that it rested always on his shoulder. Sometimes there would be a flash of lightning and I could see his face clearly.

39   It was as it was earlier, in the kitchen, a face filled with sadness. There would be a momentary glimpse of his face and then again the darkness, the wind, and the rain. In me there was a feeling I had never known before.

40   It was a feeling of closeness. It was something strange. It was as though there were only we two in the world. It was as though I had been jerked suddenly out of myself, out of my world of the schoolboy, out of a world in which I was ashamed of my father.

⁴¹   He had become blood of my blood; he the strong swimmer and I the boy clinging to him in the darkness. We swam in silence and in silence we dressed in our wet clothes, and went home.

⁴²   There was a lamp lighted in the kitchen and when we came in, the water dripping from us, there was my mother. She smiled at us. I remember that she called us "boys."

⁴³   "What have you boys been up to," she asked, but my father did not answer. As he had begun the evening's experience with me in silence, so he ended it. He turned and looked at me. Then he went, I thought, with a new and strange dignity out of the room.

⁴⁴   I climbed the stairs of my own room, undressed in the darkness and got into bed. I couldn't sleep and did not want to sleep. For the first time I knew that I was the son of my father. He was a story teller as I was to be. It may be that I even laughed a little softly there in the darkness. If I did, I laughed knowing that I would never again be wanting another father.

Thinking and Responding to the Reading

1.   Find specific phrases or words that Anderson uses to describe his father's traits. Which show his father's humor and which show his irresponsibility?
2.   Why does Anderson's father tell stories?
3.   What did his father do particularly well when he told stories? Give some examples.
4.   What do you infer when you read that the father abandoned the family for weeks at a time? Do you think the boy was justified in fantasizing that this wasn't his real father?
5.   What does the boy realize when he and his father go swimming together? What is the significance of the light in the kitchen, and why is the mother both waiting and pleased?
6.   What does Anderson mean by "He had become blood of my blood…."? (par. 41)
7.   This is a coming-of-age story, an end of innocence. Describe how Anderson changes his perception of both himself and his father.

Springboard for Composing

Make a list of reasons why we both tell and listen to stories. Now think of someone you know who is a good story teller. What makes his/her stories interesting to hear?

AUNT JIM

Noreen Duncan

Vocabulary Words

tinkly (par. 1)	vexed (par. 2)	fete (par. 4)	plantains (par. 5)
guavas (par. 1)	wooing (par. 2)	fortnight (par. 5)	wafted (par. 5)

1   She wore brown canvas and rubber-soled half boots; you know the ones the older children called gym boots. That's how she got her name: Aunt Jim. She lived with Aunt Lil in Aunt Lil's house, and the children loved Aunt Lil and her house, and they loved spending the August holidays with Aunt Lil. They loved waking up early to Aunt Lil's humming and singing, her tinkly little laugh, the smell of breakfast, salt fish and fried bakes and fresh chocolaty cocoa tea, with cinnamon and frothy milk. They spent the mornings catching lizards, sometimes *batty mamselles*, or the nasty little ravine fish, *guabines*. While Aunt Lil did the ladies' hair and cooked lunch, Aunt Jim cleaned the yard, picked green mangoes and ceries and guavas for them, and drew perfect circles in the dirt for them to pitch marbles. Then she sat in the gallery and watched; she didn't watch Aunt Lil or the ladies or the children or anybody really, she just watched. She didn't say anything. After lunch, breadfruit, zaboca, shrimp or fish, Aunt Lil and Aunt Jim went into the bedroom, and they closed the door.

2   The children, tired and full of country food, would fall asleep, dreaming about the sea or the river, or Tarzan and Jane. In the afternoons, Aunt Jim walked behind the children, with a stick, as they went, single file, down the road and to the beach, and she sat on the beach and watched. She never said anything, but the children enforced her rules. If one pushed another's head underwater and held him, he would come up red-eyed and spitting salt: "Don't do that, boy. You want Aunt Jim to get vexed or what?" Then, as it grew dark, Aunt Lil and Aunt Jim sat in the gallery, and the children would doze off to the sounds of their voices, swirling and darting and swooping around as the moths and candle flies, chasing and wooing around the lamp flame.

3   Aunt Lil's tinkly little laugh and her sweet smell filled the children's days and their night sleep. She smiled and sang and wore an apron with flowers, and a hibiscus over her ear in her hair, which curled a little around her neck. She talked and laughed with everybody – the ladies whose hair she did in the drawing room, and the fish sellers, and the hops bread man. On Sundays, she took the children and many of the neighbour children to church. Aunt Jim did not go to church. She sat in the gallery and waited until they came back, and after Aunt Lil had taken off her hat, her high heels, her pretty dress, she and Aunt Jim ate breakfast then, and drank strong country coffee together. In the afternoon, they went to a matinee, Aunt Lil and Aunt Jim.

4   Aunt Jim's face and features were perfect, perfectly oval eyes, neat little nose and mouth, but she did something with the muscles of her face, something that didn't make her look pretty at all, at all. Her forearms were large and well-developed, one could imagine, if she and Aunt Lil went to a carnival fete, Aunt Jim would put her arm around

128

Aunt Lil's small waist, pulling her to her, hard, and dance close, one arm around Aunt Lil, the other hanging down. But that never happened. It could never happen.

5   The husband of Aunt Jim's sister died suddenly, and Aunt Jim went to see about her. She never came back. Nobody asked where she was or when she was coming back. Nobody said anything about her. And the children grew big and couldn't spend all of their August holidays at Aunt Lil's, but they still loved her and she them; they always came to spend a week or a fortnight or so, bringing their friends from their high schools. Aunt Lil baked and iced cakes and made jams and sweets then; she didn't do hair anymore. The children woke late to the smell of her breakfasts, the plantains fried, the new sweet bread, the coconut bake and the sounds of her singing and humming as she boiled fudge and made sugar cakes, and boiled the country coffee. All day people came by to pick up black cakes and bottles of guava jam, and Aunt Lil's tinkly little laugh and her sweet smell wafted through the house.

6   The children and their friends went down to the beach by themselves when they felt like it. But every now and then, when one would shove another's head under water, and he would come up red-eyed and salt spitting, he would say, "Don't do that, boy. You want Aunt Jim to get vexed or what?" Then one of the friends would ask, "Who is Aunt Jim?" And one of the children would say, "*Cheups*. Don't bother with him. He is always bringing up old jokes."

Thinking and Responding to the Reading

1.   Describe Aunt Lil and Aunt Jim physically. How do these descriptions imply a difference in their personalities? Could Lil and Jim have switched names? Explain why or why not.

2.   Duncan hints at a deeper relationship between the two women. What is this relationship? Where in the reading did you find this implication?

3.   In paragraph 4, the narrator says, "It could never happen." To what is the narrator referring? Why could this never happen at the place and time? Do you think it could happen now? Why or why not?

4.   At the end of the story a boy says, "Don't do that, boy. You want Aunt Jim to get vexed or what?" Knowing that Aunt Jim left many years back, why would he say this?

5.   What is implied by another child's response: "He is always bringing up old jokes"?

Springboard for Composing

What elements of interpersonal relationships concerning people who are different from you did you understand more sharply after reading this story? Think of a story you've been told or read that made part of the world clearer to you after hearing the story.

THE ROAD NOT TAKEN

Robert Frost

Vocabulary Words

diverged (line 1)   undergrowth (line 5)   trodden (line 12)

1   Two roads diverged in a yellow wood,
2   And sorry I could not travel both
3   And be one traveler, long I stood
4   And looked down one as far as I could
5   To where it bent in the undergrowth;

6   Then took the other, as just as fair,
7   And having perhaps the better claim,
8   Because it was grassy and wanted wear;
9   Though as for that the passing there
10 Had worn them really about the same,

11 And both that morning equally lay
12 In leaves no step had trodden black,
13 Oh, I kept the first for another day!
14 Yet knowing how way leads on to way,
15 I doubted if I should ever come back.

16 I shall be telling this with a sigh
17 Somewhere ages and ages hence:
18 Two roads diverged in a wood, and I—
19 I took the one less traveled by,
20 And that has made all the difference.

Thinking and Responding to the Reading

1. Frost uses the word "diverged" in the first line of this poem. Relate his use of "diverged" to "divergent thinking" in the creative thinking process.
2. List the narrator's options.
3. The narrator settles on a choice. Which lines in the poem show his convergent thinking?

4. Explain in your own words the meaning of the following figurative phrases:
   a. "it bent in the undergrowth"
   b. "it was grassy and wanted wear"
   c. "in leaves no step had trodden black"
5. What happens literally when two roads diverge? What is the figurative meaning of two roads diverging?
6. In line 15, the speaker says, "I doubted if I should ever come back." Why do you think he says this?
7. Explain lines 19 and 20 "I took the one less traveled by,/ And that has made all the difference."

Springboard for Composing

The speaker in this poem chose the road "less traveled by,/ And that has made all the difference." We all have to make choices in life. Which road will you take? What are the advantages and disadvantages of this road (choice)?

I CREATE ART WHICH CREATES ME

Joseph Eschenberg

Vocabulary Words

replete (par. 1)	abstract (par. 4)	consciousness (par. 5)
predator (par. 1)	unfettered (par. 4)	vortex (par. 6)
roiling (par. 2)	altered (par. 5)	shaman (par. 7)
exotic (par. 3)		

1   The five-part painting that I call "Religion, Sex, and TV," based on John Lennon's "Working Class Hero," a track of the *John Lennon/Plastic Ono Band* album, is about teen runaways. Each piece in the set first directs the viewer to the mixed messages a teen receives from television; then the action transfers the viewer to street scenes replete with sexual predators, and finally it ends with a look at home scenes.

2   As I listen to Lennon's music, roiling emotion emerges from my inner being, and in my mind's eye each scene becomes personal. I'm driven to think about runaway teens; how and why do they leave their homes to live their life on the streets? Where do they sleep? Where do they bathe? How do they eat? Underaged, they can't legally earn a living, so they're forced to sell their body for money. In great part, the shame they feel for doing this leads to drug and alcohol abuse or perhaps, the drug and/or alcohol addiction leads to prostitution. As I consider these questions and situations, I find myself needing to show teens that running away from home can turn into a dirty, ugly picture, far from the glamorous, safe, and "fun" images that they are presented with on television. I do this through art.

3   In this series, I first painted the background colors; then I added pieces of heavy paper on which I'd sprayed the word EXOTIC. I continued to add new elements to represent the raw emotions of the situation. I used printers' plates, needles, photography, razor blades, acrylic paint, chalk, markers, construction tape and any other material that seemed appropriate. The creation was finished when I felt a relationship with the piece's message. Only then did I name it.

4   Though my resulting art may be thought-provoking, creating it is not necessarily a conscious process for me. Since I am an abstract artist, I rely on an unfettered response to drive my hands to create. As an artist, I believe the process of creating is an endless journey. I never know quite where a piece will take me and how it will end up. Sometimes I don't know at all where I'm going with the piece I'm working on, and for others I think I know exactly where I'm going only to change direction halfway through. In either case, I end up at an unknown place.

5   Music has a very strong influence on my emotional state and effect on my art. Besides Lennon, the musicians John Cale, Lou Reed, Robbie Robertson, Tom Waits and Carol Orff also influence my art. However, the biggest impact comes from Native American tribal music. Music produces in me a state of excitement and energy that transports me to another state of being where I connect with the "creative spiritual force." So once I've allowed the music into my soul, I can journey far and discover many things,

132

and the creative process starts to rush like a stream down from the mountains. Most of my art contains a deep emotional meaning brought on by these inner journeys which are not always obvious to the viewer. While I'm in an altered state of consciousness, I create what I feel from inside myself. What does not change is my need to create. Though my flights are mostly brought on by music, events in my life may have the same effect.

6   At a recent art opening, someone asked me if I use drugs to help create my art. I laughed. "No," I said, and explained that my art starts with a visit to the vortex of my being. It would be easier if drugs could produce the same result for me, but they can't. I must deliberately put myself into an altered state yet remain conscious of my real surrounds. Just so that the reader can relate to this process: Imagine yourself playing air guitar to your favorite guitarist. Can you feel yourself standing on stage, bending the strings of the guitar? Or perhaps you are standing alone in your room lip-synching to your favorite R&B artist? Don't you feel as if you're there, on stage?

7   I feel my work needs a reason for being created. I don't create art to sell it. Rather, I create art because I'm led to do so. My journey is similar to a shaman's "…who changes her or his state of consciousness at will in order to contact and/or travel to another reality to obtain power and knowledge. Mission accomplished, the shaman journeys home to use this power and knowledge to help either himself or others."

 Thinking and Responding to the Reading

1.   Why has the artist chosen to name his essay "I Create Art Which Creates Me"? Does he mean, literally, that his art creates him? Or is the title figurative?
2.   How does he use music to help him create his art? What does he mean by "altered state of consciousness" and "can journey far and discover many things"?
3.   What is the process that Eschenberg uses to create a piece of art?
4.   Explain the quote at the end of the essay. How does it symbolize the thesis?
5.   Look at Eschenberg's art pieces, *Religion, Sex & TV #3* and Religion, *Sex & TV #5*. What assumptions can you make about them? Do you consider his works of art a descriptive or prescriptive argument? Explain.

Springboard to Composing

Think about the last time you created something (a poem, a custom design, a new look to a room, a song, a drawing). What was it and what was your purpose? Before you began, did you have to prepare yourself in any way? Did you use some form of props or inspiration? Music? A special place? Silence? A particular time of day or night? A recollection? Did the creation process go smoothly or did it have to be revised as you went along? Did you take pleasure in your creation after it was completed?

Religion Sex & TV #3

Mixed Media on Paper, 28" x 38"

By Joseph Eschenberg © 2000 jeschenberg@artonthestreet.net

Religion Sex & TV #5

Mixed Media on Paper, 28" x 38"

By Joseph Eschenberg © 2000 jeschenberg@artonthestreet.net

THE EIFFEL TOWER

Lieut.-Com. R. T. Gould

Vocabulary Words

centime (par. 2)	inevitably (par. 5)	Seine (par. 6)
stupendous (par. 3)	campanile (par. 5)	caissons (par. 7)
unquenchable (par. 3)	surmounted (par. 5)	box girders (par. 8)
vanguard (par. 3)	stratum (par. 6)	deviated (par. 10)

The work of a brilliant and imaginative French engineer, the Eiffel Tower stands to-day, a predominant landmark of Paris, towering nearly 1,000 feet above the banks of the Seine. The story of its conception and construction is unique in the history of engineering.

1   Surely, M. Eiffel," said the Minister of Commerce and Industry, "you cannot be serious!"

2   "But yes, M. le Ministre. The proposal which I have just had the honour of outlining to you is of the very greatest seriousness. Only grant your authorization, and I swear to you—I, Gustave Eiffel—that I will crown your Exhibition with the tallest structure ever built by man. And I will execute the work under strict guarantees and from my own resources, not asking the Government of the Republic to fund a single centime of the cost!"

3   Such a stupendous tower as M. Eiffel proposed, with calm confidence, to build in time for the opening of the exhibition in May 1889 was a thing which—excluding what might or might not have been done at Babel long ago—the world had never seen before. It would form, Lockroy reflected, a monument to French genius and to the unquenchable spirit of the French people and a proof that France was still, as ever, to be found in the vanguard of the world's progress. Before long, Lockroy's mind was made up. He told Eiffel to go ahead.

4   In a short time Eiffel had completed his detailed plans and was laying out his foundations. His design, bold and fantastic in outline, has long been recognized as being in its way a masterpiece—a work of real genius. To-day his tower still stands as the crowning achievement of a career which up to then had been uniformly successful.

5   He was therefore led, naturally and almost inevitably, to design his great tower as a tall pyramid with curved edges, these edges being composed of four huge built-up columns, leaving the ground independently of one another, connected (at various levels) by horizontal girder frames, and ultimately merging (about half-way up) into a tapering, diagonally-braced shaft of square section. His final design provided for two intermediate platforms, whose floors were to be respectively 189 and 39 feet from the ground. The tower itself was to end at a height of 896 feet. On the top there would be an observation platform 53 feet square; from this would rise a campanile surmounted by a dome and lantern, bringing the total height of the structure to 984 feet. Such was the plan for the Eiffel Tower, and such are its dimensions to-day. The flagstaff above the lantern rises slightly beyond the 1,000-feet mark.

Mai 1888

Juillet 1888

Septembre 1888

Mai 1889

6   Work on the foundations began immediately, the four sets of piers being located at the corners of a square, with their centers some 330 feet apart. Preliminary borings showed that under the sites of all four piers was a bed of hard, compact clay, more than 50 feet thick and able to bear a loading of from 3 to 4 tons per square foot. Overlaying this was a stratum of hard gravel—which, for the two piers remote from the Seine, came to within 23 feet of the surface. Here there was no great difficulty in excavating down to the gravel and forming concrete foundations for the stonework of the piers. But with the two piers nearest the Seine (about 300 feet away) conditions were not so favourable.

7   Here the gravel was struck at a depth of 40 feet, that is, 16 feet below the mean level of the river. On top of the gravel were soft deposits through which water persistently oozed; and there was the possibility of similar deposits occurring between the gravel and the clay. Eiffel could not afford to take chances; so he pushed his caissons through the gravel and found, to his great relief, that, lying between the gravel and clay was a thick stratum of hard, fine sand—better, for load-bearing, than even the clay itself.

8   When the concrete foundations had been carried high enough the masonry work began. Each "edge" of the huge iron pyramid—each "leg" of the tower—was to be composed of four huge iron box girders, connected by lattice girders to form, in effect, a skeleton tube of square section abut 50 feet each way. Each of the four enormous box girders composing one "leg" of the tower had its own pier, so that there were sixteen piers in all to be built. These were arranged in groups of four, in small squares, and each of these four squares was situated at one corner of a large square.

9   The stone used for the piers was capable of supporting a load of over 1,600 lb. per square inch—roughly, four times the maximum stress which the weight of the tower could impose on it.

10   Iron bolts 20 feet long were built into each pier to hold the lower ends of the girders. Although the completed tower's weight (rather over 7,000 tons) would make it perfectly stable without any such anchorage, Eiffel kept to his policy of taking, during the building of the tower, no risk that he could possibly avoid. A gale might strike the tower before it was half finished, or a sudden emergency might necessitate bringing a heavy load on the structure a long way from its axis; in either event, neglect to "anchor" it might have fatal consequences. Eiffel even went so far as to provide, at each pier, a permanent hydraulic press, forming part of the anchorage, by means of which the whole gigantic structure, once completed, could be tilted bodily if it deviated measurably from the perpendicular. This deviation never occurred.

11   Above the piers came the beginnings of the ironwork; and the Parisians, for the first time, began to catch a glimpse of the huge iron monster which was so soon to tower above their beloved city and to form, in after years, their most familiar landmark.

Thinking and Responding to the Reading

1.   Gustave Eiffel won the prize for the 1889 Exhibition. What was his purpose in designing the Tower?
2.   Based on the reasons to build the Eiffel Tower, give evidence which supports that it is a work of art.

138

3.	The description of building the tower is a pattern or organization known as process. Rephrase or draw the tower as it is described in paragraphs 5-10.
4.	List some other man-made landmarks around the world. Why do we create such landmarks? What does the landmark say about its society and the evolution or technology of man?

Springboard for Composing

Gustave Eiffel went about designing and building the Eiffel Tower as a scientist, taking no chances it might not turn out perfectly. But it began as an artistic concept, a "bold and fantastic" concept, a vision of beauty and uniqueness to be enjoyed by the whole world. Would it have detracted from the masterpiece if it had ended up with a small flaw, perhaps not quite perpendicular as the *Leaning Tower of Pisa*? Does art have to be perfect to be admirable and enjoyable? What does perfect mean? Have you ever created something that turned out less than perfect or not quite as you first imagined it, yet you were pleased with the results despite the imperfections?

SONNET 18

William Shakespeare

Vocabulary Words

temperate (line 2)   lease (line 4)   untrimmed (line 8)   eternal (line 9)

1   Shall I compare thee to a summer's day?
2   Thou art more lovely and more temperate.
3   Rough winds do shake the darling buds of May,
4   And summer's lease hath all too short a date.
5   Sometime too hot the eye of heaven shines,
6   And often is his gold complexion dimmed.
7   And every fair from fair sometime declines,
8   By chance or nature's changing course untrimmed.
9   But thy eternal summer shall not fade,
10 Nor lose possession of that fair thou ow'st,
11 Nor shall Death brag thou wander'st in his shade
12 When in eternal lines to time thou grow'st.
13 So long as men can breathe, or eyes can see,
14 So long lives this, and this gives life to thee.

Thinking and Responding to the Reading

1. In the opening line, the speaker asks a woman if he should compare her to a summer's day. What does he decide to do?
2. How does the speaker describe summer?
3. How does the speaker feel towards the woman? How do you know this?
4. What do the lines "So long as men can breathe, or eyes can see, /So long lives this, and this gives life to thee" mean?
5. Compare this poem to Sonnet 130. How are they similar? Different?

Springboard for Composing

At some point in time many of us are moved to write a poem, lyrics to a song, or love letter or create a piece of art to or about someone as Shakespeare did in this poem. If you did create such a piece, please share with your classmates how many versions you created and changes you made before you were satisfied. If you made no corrections, does this mean that it turned out perfectly on your initial try? How was this possible?

SONNET 130

William Shakespeare

Vocabulary Words

mistress (line 1)   damasked (line 5)   reeks (line 8)   belied (line 14)
dun (line 3)

1   My mistress' eyes are nothing like the sun;
2   Coral is far more red than her lips' red;
3   If snow be white, why then her breasts are dun;
4   If hairs be wires, black wires grow on her head.
5   I have seen roses damasked, red and white,
6   But no such roses see I in her cheeks;
7   And in some perfumes is there more delight
8   Than in the breath that from my mistress reeks.
9   I love to hear her speak, yet well I know
10 That music hath a far more pleasing sound;
11 I grant I never saw a goddess go;
12 My mistress, when she walks, treads on the ground:
13 And yet, by heaven, I think my love as rare
14 As any she belied with false compare.

Thinking and Responding to the Reading

1. Describe the speaker's mistress. You may want to draw a picture as well.
2. Do you think the speaker loves his mistress? Why or why not? Give evidence from the poem.
3. Explain the lines "And yet, by heaven, I think my love as rare/As any she belied wish false compare."
4. Compare this poem to Sonnet 18 by William Shakespeare. In what ways are they alike? How are they dissimilar?

Springboard for Composing

At some point in time many of us are moved to write a poem, lyrics to a song, or love letter or create a piece of art to or about someone as Shakespeare did in the this poem. If you did create such a piece, please share with your classmates how many versions you created a nd c hanges you m ade b efore you w ere s atisfied. If you m ade n o c orrections, does this mean that it turned out perfectly on your initial try? How was this possible?

THE POWER OF FORGIVENESS

Student Author

Vocabulary Words

prejudice (par. 1)   coincidentally (par. 7)   malice (par. 8)
haven (par. 3)   fashion (par. 8)   immensely (par. 9)

1   It was 12:37 a.m. as the bus pulled from the terminal at Bowling Green, Kentucky. The streets were silent and the night was cool. I'd gotten my sister on her way to Ft. Knox after a weekend visit. At this time, I wanted nothing more than to go back to the dorm and get some rest. I never thought that a trip to the bus station could be so dramatic, that I would face death because of other's prejudice. Later on, I would need to overcome the effects of that prejudice.

2   After giving my sister spending money, I couldn't afford to take a cab back to the dorm. So I decided to get a little exercise and run to the dorm, about four miles away. When I had gone about two blocks, I noticed a truck slowly following me. When I turned around to see who it was, the driver sped up, went to the next block, and turned right. After I'd run another couple blocks, I noticed the truck in front of me. A guy on the passenger side started yelling at me, "Hey, bootlip, rug head, nigger." However, I continued running, pretending to ignore him.

3   The guys took the next left as I continued jogging up the hill to the campus. Three blocks further on, they appeared again. This time, the driver had three other guys sitting in the back of the truck. "Nigger, we're going to kill you," they yelled as they threw cans and bottles at me. Trying not to show any fear, I continued my uphill journey to Western Kentucky University. By this time, I feared for my life and started praying silently to God. I knew that each step would bring me closer to a safe haven.

4   When the guys in the pickup took the next left, I passed them by, and I didn't see or hear from them for three more blocks. However, as I approached the corner of the fourth block, they surprised me. Five white guys jumped from the corner and surrounded me. One guy wearing a University of Louisville baseball cap said to me, "Where ya' goin', Niggah?" and pushed me into a guy behind me. "Where'd ya steal that sweat suit?" Petrified beyond response, I bounced from one guy to another. Then the guy wearing the U of L hat hit me in the stomach. As I folded over, another guy kicked me in the side. Immediately after that blow, another kicked me hard in the rear, and then blows came from everywhere.

5   As I fell to the sidewalk, I felt a stick break on my back. There were more kicks to my face and ribs and then, I felt nothing.

6   When I awakened, my mother was sitting beside my bed. When she saw me move my head, she simply said, "Thank God." It took me three weeks to get out of the hospital, and seven more to recover from four broken ribs, a broken collar bone and arm, fractured skull, and severely beaten face. Physically, I did recover.

142

7   As people came to see me, I felt the tension between the blacks and whites. Coincidentally, the police reported that I was "assaulted by five unknown assailants," and left it at that. They failed to investigate either the vehicle or the license plate number that a witness reported.

8   When I got better, I purchased a .38 caliber handgun and walked the street every night for at least a month. I didn't speak to, eat with, or associate with white people in any form or fashion. One night, as I was walking away from the bus stop, I saw the pickup. As I waited for the driver to come out of the convenience store, the anger and hatred rose within me. All the malice I've ever felt transferred to the index finger of my right hand on the trigger of my .38.

9   When the guy came out of the store, I grabbed him from behind and jammed the gun in his side. I dragged him behind the building and put the gun to this throat. "Do you remember me?" I asked. "Uh...yeah," he answered. "Before I blow your brains out, I want to know why you all did that to me that night." When this man started to cry and plead for his life, I felt immensely powerful. However, he said, "I really am sorry, and I came to see you in the hospital. I'm the one who sent the card. 'Don't hate the whole white race for the mistakes of the few...I wrote that.'"

10   I remembered the card. As I looked at that man again, I saw the pain he had been carrying for four months. As I let up on the trigger, I looked at him and said, "I forgive you," and walked away. Then I took the bullets out of the gun and threw them to the ground.

11   As I walked up the hill to Western Kentucky University, each step gave me a new freedom. When I got to the top of the hill, I was a brand new man. I was not only free of malice and prejudice; I had become a man who could forgive the prejudice of others. I had decided that night to walk in a new power, the power of forgiveness.

Thinking and Responding to the Reading

1.   Characterize the narrator from clues given in the first three paragraphs.
2.   Explain the line, "As people came to see me, I felt the tension between the blacks and whites."
3.   Do you think Lewis would have pulled the trigger had the man not pleaded for his life? Is it a false or honest plea? What in the story makes you think this?
4.   The narrator says at the end of paragraph 11, "I had become a man who could forgive the prejudice of others. I had decided that night to walk in a new power, the power of forgiveness." How do you account for his ability to change after almost being beaten to death?
5.   Compare this story with "Forgiveness" by Mykel C. Johnson.

Springboard for Composing

Write down the harmful consequences that may result from holding a grudge, anger or resentment towards someone whom, theoretically, you could forgive. Have you ever been in this situation? How did you resolve it?

FORGIVENESS

Mykel C. Johnson

Vocabulary Words

foibles (par. 2)
riled up (2)
jockeying (par. 2)
sacredness (par. 2)
sanctity (par. 5)
trespasses (par. 5)

reconciliation (par. 6)
remorse (par. 10)
atonement (par. 13)
apartheid (par. 16)
amnesty (par. 16)

perpetrators (par. 16)
retributive (par. 18)
redress (par. 18)
askew (par. 18)
atrocity (par. 20)

1   Conflict is all around us. It is as local as a morning person and a night person trying to live in the same house. It is as world shaking as the struggle between Israelis and Palestinians trying to share the same piece of land in the Middle East. Forgiveness is one of the tools we have for making peace.

2   Forgiveness is a form of love. It has its roots in a belief that persons are connected. When we care about cultivating and nurturing those bonds, we are more gentle with the foibles and limitations of others. We hold in our hearts a cooperative spirit. At the opposite extreme is to see others as separate and apart. Then it is easy for them to become competitors or enemies, to be a source of irritation. Driving a car in Boston was often an experience of such a disconnected perspective. With people yelling and honking and jockeying for position, I would start to feel tense and riled up, ready to snap at the next driver who slowed down to turn left. No wonder it explodes into the violence now identified as road rage. Forgiveness begins in small compassions, in overlooking the imperfections of others, to focus on their essential okay-ness: their sacredness.

3   Unitarian Universalists have always been liberal in our belief in the essential goodness of people and generous in our bestowal of forgiveness. There was a comic expression of this benevolence in a newspaper cartoon, Doug Marlett's "Kudzu." The first frame is a picture of the Holy Roller preacher at bat in the interfaith baseball game. The umpire calls out, "Strike Three." In the next frames, the preacher is still at bat, as the ump shouts, "Strike Four, Strike Five." The preacher finally comments: "Unitarians—ya gotta love 'em."

4   It was the Universalists who imagined a God so full of love that he would ultimately forgive everyone. In a time when most believed in divine judgment and eternal punishment, the Universalists declared that all would be restored: everyone would go to heaven. God was too loving to send any of his children to hell.

5   For me, growing up in a Catholic environment, forgiveness was associated with great holiness. We learned the story of Saint Maria Goretti, a twelve-year-old Italian girl who was stabbed to death when she refused the sexual advances of a young man in her neighborhood. Part of the evidence of her sanctity was that on her deathbed she forgave her murderer. In this, she was following the example of Jesus, who prayed for his executioners from the cross: "Father forgive them, for they know not what they do." Jesus had taught his disciples to pray, "Forgive us our trespasses, as we forgive those who trespass against us." And when asked how often one must forgive a wrongdoer who apologized, he answered "seventy times seven times."

144

⁶ But forgiveness got more complicated for me, when I learned about the problem of domestic violence. When battered women began to speak up and seek out shelter, one of the issues that emerged was that the cycle of battering included apology and regret. Women were being urged by their priests and pastors to forgive their battering husbands as part of their Christian duty. But after the apologies and tearful reconciliations, the cycle of control and violence would only get worse. Forgiveness was not helping. Leaving the abuser was often the only option for breaking the cycle. And so I began to try to understand the limits of forgiveness.

⁷ Resolving conflict requires all of us to acknowledge and deal with aggression and abuse. Otherwise, we are leaving the vulnerable in danger. As liberals we don't like to talk about evil or sin. But to be peacemakers we must be able to recognize when a line has been crossed beyond human faults and limitations and into abusive behavior. We must know when to forgive, and when forgiveness would be a mask for fear or weakness. When facing aggression, we must have the strength to confront and contain.

⁸ The great teacher of non-violence, Mahatma Gandhi, said, "Forgiveness is a virtue of the brave. He alone who is strong enough to avenge a wrong knows how to love and forgive. There is no question of the mouse forgiving the cat. It is not forgiveness if the mouse allows itself to be torn to pieces by her."

⁹ Simon Wiesenthal was a Jewish prisoner in a concentration camp in Poland. All around him, Jews were being killed everyday. One day, on a work detail at a nearby hospital, he was brought by a nurse to the bed of a dying Nazi soldier. Once they were alone, the soldier painfully told him a long story of how he had participated in the horrible killing of Jewish families. The families had been herded into a building, and the building was set on fire. When they began to jump out the windows, the soldiers were ordered to shoot them. This young Nazi soldier had shot a father and his small son.

¹⁰ He grabbed onto Simon's hand, full of remorse. "I know that what I have told you is terrible. In the long nights while I have been waiting for death, time and time again I have longed to talk about it to a Jew and beg forgiveness from him. I know that what I am asking is almost too much for you, but without your answer I cannot die in peace."

¹¹ Simon chose to remain silent….

¹² Afterward, he was haunted by the incident. If you were Simon, what would you have done? Should he have forgiven the Nazi soldier? He raised the question again and again during and after the war. Eventually he created a book from the story and the responses he received from others. [The Sunflower: On the Possibilities and the Limits of Forgiveness.]

¹³ According to a Jewish understanding, reconciliation can only happen between the wrongdoer and the one who was wronged. Teshuvah is the practice of repentance and comes from the Hebrew word "to return." There are three steps to a complete Teshuvah. First, one must ask forgiveness of the person you have wronged. Judaism believes that it is only through human interaction that the victim can best be healed and the wrongdoer most profoundly changed. Second, one turns to God to confess one's wrongs, expressing shame and regret for having committed this act, and resolving never to act that way again. Third, when confronted with the same situation one chooses not to repeat the act. Judaism also distinguishes between repentance and atonement. Atonement only comes after one bears the consequences of one's acts. Only after bearing the consequences of a wrongful act is one restored to right relationship with God and one's fellow humans.

¹⁴ With this understanding of forgiveness, most Jews expressed the belief that Simon had no power to forgive the Nazi because he was not the person who had been killed. In fact, murder is

an unforgivable sin because there is no opportunity for apology to the victim. Simon Wiesenthal survived the camps and went on to work for the prosecution of Nazi war criminals. This was his way of trying to bring about atonement.

[15] My questions about forgiveness and reconciliation brought me to Martha Minow's book *Between Vengeance and Forgiveness: Facing History After Genocide and Mass Violence*. She addresses the question of how people can break the cycle of revenge. I was especially moved by her account of the work of the Truth and Reconciliation Commission in South Africa.

[16] The Commission was created as part of the compromise that brought an end to apartheid. South Africans concluded that to achieve unity and morally acceptable reconciliation, it was necessary that the truth about gross violations of human rights be established by an official investigation. The price for achieving this full disclosure was to offer amnesty to perpetrators. It was a conditional amnesty: it was only available to those who personally applied for it, and who disclosed fully the facts of misdeeds that could be characterized as having a political objective.

[17] The primary focus of the Commission was on hearing the testimony of victims. Pumla Gobodo-Madikizela, a psychologist serving on the human rights committee, reported that many victims conceive of justice in terms of revalidating oneself, and of affirming the sense that you're right, you were damaged, and it was wrong. The Commission offered such validation as it heard testimony from survivors and family members of those who were tortured and murdered.

[18] For Archbishop Desmond Tutu, the convener of the Commission, forgiveness and reconciliation were an important part of the process. He said, "Retributive justice is largely Western. The African understanding is far more restorative—not so much to punish as to redress or restore a balance that has been knocked askew. The justice we hope for is restorative of the dignity of the people."

[19] What role did forgiveness play in the Truth and Reconciliation Commission? Forgiveness was a refusal by the victim to dehumanize the perpetrators as they had been dehumanized. Forgiveness was an act of personal power that put the perpetrator and victim back on an equal level. Forgiveness was a commitment to the future, which was rooted deeper than the betrayals of the past. It has been in the hope and exhilaration of being full participants in creating a new country, that many have found the strength to bear the painful process of examining the wounds of the past.

[20] The essence of forgiveness is that it cannot be required. And yet, to witness forgiveness in the hearts of those who have faced atrocity renews our sense of hope and faith in humanity. In a great injury, something is broken, psychologically or spiritually. The break erodes our sense of living in a fair world; it corrupts our experience of our own worth, and fragments our control over our own lives and emotions. But deeper than that, it also fundamentally damages our faith in the worthiness of others. Forgiveness somehow absorbs those losses and transforms them. To witness great forgiveness is to renew our experience of the sacredness of all people.

Thinking and Responding to the Reading

1. How would you define the word sacred or sacredness? What does Johnson mean by people's "…essential okayness: their sacredness"?

2. In this essay, forgiveness is examined as a tool for making peace (par. 1), a form of love (par. 2), something associated with great holiness (par. 5), a virtue of the brave (par. 8),

146

and an act of personal power (par. 19). Which seems to you to be the most important point and why?

3. As Johnson considers the limits of forgiveness, she refers to several scenarios. Add further examples of your own to her list.

4. Paraphrase "Forgiveness is a virtue of the brave. He alone who is strong enough to avenge a wrong knows how to love and forgive." Do you agree with this statement? Why or why not?

5. How would you answer the question: "If you were Simon Wiesenthal, what would you have done?"

6. What is "*Teshuvah*"?

7. Explain the African perspective on forgiveness.

8. What is meant by "forgiveness was an act of personal power that put the perpetrator and victim back on an equal level"? Be sure to explain "equal level."

9. What role did the Truth and Reconciliation Commission play in helping both perpetrator and victim?

10. Paraphrase paragraph 20. Explain your own definition of forgiveness after thinking about this essay.

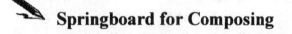 **Springboard for Composing**

Johnson writes, "In a great injury, something is broken, psychologically or spiritually. The break erodes our sense of living in a fair world...it fundamentally damages our faith in the worthiness of others." Think back to a situation in which you either suffered or inflicted a great injury. Do you recall feeling that the world was indeed unjust and that this particular person was not as worthy as you thought? If you were the perpetrator, did you feel less worthy? What other emotions and thoughts did you experience at the time and later on? How was the situation reconciled?

from *THE ILIAD*

HOMER

Vocabulary Words

seizes (line 12)	borne (line 54)	wrath (line 105)	aides-in-arms (line 121)
flees (line 13)	wretched (line 62)	venture (line 113)	anoint (line 131)
plague (line 21)	dispenses (line 68)	suppliant (line 118)	bier (line 141)
realm (line 27)	stalking (line 71)	flanked (line 121)	

1   …The old king went straight up to the lodge
       where Achilles dear to Zeus would always sit.
       Priam found the warrior there inside…
       many captains sitting some way off, but two,
5   veteran Automedon and the fine fighter Alcimus
       were busy serving him. He had just finished dinner,
       eating, drinking, and the table still stood near.
       The majestic king of Troy slipped past the rest
       and kneeling down beside Achilles, clasped his knees
10   and kissed his hands, those terrible, man-killing hands
       that had slaughtered Priam's many sons in battle.
       Awesome—as when the grip of madness seizes one
       who murders a man in his own fatherland and flees
       abroad to foreign shores, to a wealthy, noble host,
15   and a sense of marvel runs through all who see him—so
       Achilles marveled, beholding majestic Priam.
       His men marveled too, trading startled glances.
       But Priam prayed his heart out to Achilles:
       "Remember your own father, great godlike Achilles—as
20   old as I am, past the threshold of deadly old age!
       No doubt the countrymen round about him plague him now,
       with no one there to defend him, beat away disaster.
       No one—but at least he hears you're still alive
       and his old heart rejoices, hopes rising, day by day,
25   to see his beloved son come sailing home from Troy.
       But I—dear god, my life so cursed by fate…
       I fathered hero sons in the wide realm of Troy
       and now not a single one is left, I tell you.
       Fifty sons I had when the sons of Achaea came,
30   nineteen born to me from a single mother's womb
       and the rest by other women in the palace. Many,
       most of them violent Ares cut the knees from under.
       But one, one was left me, to guard my walls, my people—the
       one you killed the other day, defending his fatherland,

148

35   my Hector! It's all for him I've come to the ships now,
to win him back from you—I bring a priceless ransom.
Revere the gods, Achilles! Pity me in my own right,
remember your own father! I deserve more pity…
I have endured what no one on earth has ever done before—I
40   put to my lips the hands of the man who killed my son."

Those words stirred within Achilles a deep desire
to grieve for his own father. Taking the old man's
hand he gently moved him back. And overpowered by memory
both men gave way to grief. Priam wept freely
45   for man-killing Hector, throbbing, crouching
before Achilles' feet as Achilles wept himself,
now for his father, now for Patroclus once again,
and their sobbing rose and fell throughout the house.
Then, when brilliant Achilles had his fill of tears
50   and the longing for it had left his mind and body,
he rose from his seat, raised the old man by the hand
and filled with pity now for his gray head and gray beard,
he spoke out winging words, flying straight to the heart
"Poor man, how much you've borne—pain to break the spirit!
55   What daring brought you down to the ships, all alone,
to face the glance of the man who killed your sons,
so many fine brave boys! You have a heart of iron.
Come, please, sit down on this chair here…
Let us put our griefs to rest in our own hearts,
60   rake them up no more, raw as we are with mourning.
What good's to be won from tears that chill the spirit?
So the immortals spun our lives that we, we wretched men
live on to bear such torments—the gods live free of sorrows.
There are two great jars that stand on the floor of Zeus's halls
65   and hold his gifts, our miseries one, the other blessings.
When Zeus who loves the lightning mixes gifts for a man,
now he meets with misfortune, now good times in turn.
When Zeus dispenses gifts from the jar of sorrows only,
he makes a man an outcast—brutal, ravenous hunger
70   drives him down the face of the shining earth,
stalking far and wide, cursed by gods and men.
So with my father, Peleus. What glittering gifts
the gods rained down from the day that he was born!
He excelled all men in wealth and pride of place,
75   he lorded the Myrmidons, and mortal that he was,
they gave the man an immortal goddess for a wife.
Yes, even on him the Father piled hardships,
no powerful race of princes born in his royal halls,
only a single son he fathered, doomed at birth,

80 cut off in the spring of life—and I,
    I give the man no care as he grows old
    since here I sit in Troy, far from my fatherland,
    a grief to you, a grief to all your children.
    And you too, old man, we hear you prospered once:
85 as far as Lesbox, Macar's kingdom, bounds to seaward,
    Phrygia east and upland, the Hellespont vast and north—that
    entire realm, they say, you lorded over once,
    you excelled all men, old king, in sons and wealth.
    But then the gods of heaven brought this agony on you—
90 ceaseless battles around your walls, your armies slaughtered.
    You must bear up now. Enough of endless tears,
    the pain that breaks the spirit.
    Grief for your son will do no good at all.
    You will never bring him back to life—
95 Sooner you must suffer something worse."

    But the old and noble Priam protested strongly:
    "Don't make me sit on a chair, Achilles, Prince,
    not while Hector lies uncared-for in your camp!
    Give him back to me, now, no more delay—I
100 must see my son with my own eyes.
    Accept the ransom I bring you, a king's ransom!
    Enjoy it, all of it—return to your own native land,
    safe and sound...since now you've spared my life."

    A dark glance—and the headstrong runner answered,
105 "No more, old man, don't tempt my wrath, not now!
    My own mind's made up to give you back your son.
    A messenger brought me word from Zeus—my mother,
    Thetis who bore me, the Old Man of the Sea's daughter.
    And what's more, I can see through you, Priam—no
110 hiding the fact from me: one of the gods
    has led you down to Achaea's fast ships.
    No man alive, not even a rugged young fighter,
    would dare to venture into our camp. Never—how
    could he slip past the sentries unchallenged?
115 Or shoot back the bolt of my gate with so much ease?
    So don't anger me now. Don't stir my raging heart still more.
    Or under my own roof I may not spare your life, old man—
    suppliant that you are--may break the laws of Zeus!"

    The old man was terrified. He obeyed the order.
120 But Achilles bounded out of doors like a lion—not
    alone but flanked by his two aides-in-arms,
    veteran Automedon and Alcimus, steady comrades,

150

Achilles' favorites next to the dead Patroclus.
They loosed from harness the horses and the mules,
125 they led the herald in, the old king's crier,
and sat him down on a bench. From the polished wagon
they lifted the priceless ransome brought for Hector's corpse
but they left behind two capes and a finely-woven shirt
to shroud the body well when Priam bore him home.
130 Then Achilles called the serving-women out:
"Bathe and anoint the body—bear
it aside first. Priam must not see his son."
He feared that, overwhelmed by the sight of Hector,
wild with grief, Priam might let his anger flare
135 and Achilles might fly into fresh rage himself,
cut the old man down and break the laws of Zeus.
So when the maids had bathed and anointed the body
sleek with olive oil and wrapped it round and round
in a braided battle-shirt and handsome battle-cape,
140 then Achilles lifted Hector up in his own arms
and laid him down on a bier, and comrades helped him
raise the bier and body onto the sturdy wagon…

Thinking and Responding to the Reading

1. What is an epic poem?
2. Why does old king Priam want to slip past the guards? To whom does he "pray out his heart"?
3. Who did Achilles kill in battle? Why?
4. Characterize a person who says, "Grief for your son will do no good at all. You will never bring him back to life" but also states, "Those words stirred within Achilles a deep desire to grieve for his own father."
5. Explain Priam's emotions towards Achilles.
6. Define the following: *grief, fortitude, pity* and *forgiveness*.
7. What light does this excerpt shed on the theme of forgiveness?
8. Compare lines 42-65 to Abraham Lincoln's *Gettysburg Address*. What message is addressed in both? How can reading this literary epic help us to understand loss by wars?

Springboard to Composing

Think of a loss you had to reconcile. What were the circumstances? How did you reconcile it, or did you?

OBSERVATIONS ON MUSIC'S PLACE IN LIFE: EXCERPTS FROM A RADIO TALK

Edward Johnson

Vocabulary Words

manifestation (par. 1)	bereft (par. 3)	persistence (par. 5)	poignancy (par. 9)
audible (par. 1)	avail (par. 3)	profound (par. 7)	despair (par. 9)
facets (par. 2)	renders (par. 4)	conception (par. 7)	gamut (par. 9)
afflicted (par. 2)	requisites (par. 5)	irrespective (par. 9)	constitutes (par. 9)

1   Let us consider the singer's medium of communication—the voice. Has it ever occurred to you how important a factor the voice is as a manifestation of life? Do you realize what it would mean to you, if you were unable to express through your voice the joy and sorrow in your heart? Voice is the audible expression of our reactions through the emotional channels: the senses.

2   Let me quote a few lines from an article in *The Atlantic Monthly*, by Helen Keller, one of the great women of our time. She says:—"Use your eyes as if tomorrow you would be stricken blind. Hear the music of voices, the song of a bird, the mighty strains of an orchestra, as if tomorrow you would be stricken deaf. Touch each object. Smell the perfume of flowers. Make the most of every sense. Glory in all the facets of pleasure and beauty which the world reveals to you through the several means of contact which nature provides." What a significant message, from one so sorely afflicted.

3   Fortunately, we are not faced with so hopeless an alternative, but I cannot imagine a more unhappy state than suddenly to be bereft of hearing. What a world of sound and color, of rhythm and accent, and of imagination, would be forever closed! Is our consciousness awake then, to the tremendous capacity of our sense of hearing, and are we alive to the natural alliance between the voice and the auditory nerve? For one who sings, the voice is the natural instrument, but without well-trained ears, it is of little avail.

4   Of all the arts, none is so universal in its appeal as music—none so simple. Music not only mirrors the emotions and quickens and enriches our feeling for life, but renders us more deeply responsive to what is best and finest within us—to beauty—to love—and to religion. Music has been called the language of the universe, and its function in life is as normal and natural as speech itself.

5   The student who starts on a professional career spends the early years of his life in preparation of music—of poetry—of languages, and other requisites that are necessary to produce a serious and well-cultured artist. Besides his vocal equipment, he must be physically strong and mentally alert—for the road is long and difficult. With persistence, discipline and patience, there comes the day when what he has accomplished must be presented to the public. Then comes the crucial test—the debut! No one who has not had such an experience can estimate adequately what it means to the young singer.

[6] Personally, I well remember that terrible ordeal! It was just before the war, in Padua, the city of St. Anthony, and the opera was "Andrea Chenier" by Umberto Giordano. The role of the ill-fated poet of the French Revolution was assigned me, and though it had all the qualities that appealed to me—the romance and poetry and though the music in its broad, melodic phrases and declamatory style, seemed to suit my voice, nevertheless, fear was in my heart. The Italian language was new to me, and though I had translated my name from Edward Johnson to Eduardo Di Giovanni, that is to say—Edward, son of John—a certain self-consciousness was upon me. The change of name might fool some of the public, but it did not fool me!

[7] As my great moment in the first act arrived—there arose within me the profound emotion which brings sincerity and conviction, and through which is acquired assurance and authority—an emotion, which, by its force, not only released me from myself, but gave me power to translate the true meaning and feeling of the librettist and the composer. That, I believe, is the test of the real artist. If he can conquer the preconceived emotion of his auditors, and project his own interpretation and his mood upon the listener—if he can impose his conception upon the audience, he is master of the situation.

[8] The artist, by offering the best he has, elevates the public to his own level, and the public should feel a sincere and profound enjoyment in upholding the artist in his efforts. In any matter relating to art, only the best is good enough for the public. The most vital difference between an artist and an amateur is more a matter of perfection in technique than the capacity to feel and understand.

[9] Great music brings us together—irrespective of birth, position, culture, or ability. It humanizes and refines, and above all other arts, it reflects our feelings and our emotions—the joy of life—the surge of passion—the tenderness of love—the poignancy of despair—in fact, that whole gamut of human emotion which constitutes so large a part of our conscious life. Translated into music, these feelings assume a heightened beauty and dignity. It is the only art worthy to reveal the Infinite.

Thinking and Responding to the Reading

1. Explain the thesis statement, "Voice is the audible expression of our reactions through the emotional channels: the senses."
2. Johnson uses a quote by Helen Keller in paragraph 2. What is the message in this quote? Sum it up in one sentence.
3. List the emotions the author describes that are testaments to "a real artist's ability to communicate his concepts to the audience."
4. Explain the conclusion in par. 9. Does it adequately support/extend his thesis?
5. Compare Johnson's explanation of art to Joseph Eschenberg's explanation of art.

Springboard for Compositing

"Of all the arts, none is so universal in its appeal as music--none so simple," writes Johnson. He ends his article by saying, "It is the only art worthy to reveal the Infinite." What does he mean by these lines, and do you agree? Explain your answer.

AARON COPLAND: AN INTIMATE SKETCH

Leonard Bernstein

Vocabulary Words

seared (par. 1)	bewail (par. 9)	syndrome (par. 12)	retrograde (par. 14)
patriarchal (par. 2)	plight (par. 9)	impetus (par. 12)	inversion (par. 14)
avant-garde (par. 2)	sternness (par. 9)	transient (par. 12)	forsaking (par. 15)
provincial (par. 6)	glower (par. 9)	serialism (par. 14)	hiatus (par. 15)
transcription (par. 8)	beacon (par. 11)	sabbatical (par. 14)	

1   On November 14, [1970] Aaron Copland will be seventy years old. November 14—it's a date seared into my mind. Two of the most important events of my life occurred on that day, the first in 1937, the second in 1943—and so I never forgot Aaron's birthday.

2   In the fall of 1937 I had just begun my junior year at Harvard. Although I had never seen Copland, I had long adored him through his music. He was the composer who would lead American music out of the wilderness, and I pictured him as a cross between Walt Whitman and an Old Testament prophet, bearded and patriarchal. I had dug up and learned as much of his music as I could find; the *Piano Variations* had virtually become my trademark. I was crazy about them then—and I still find them marvelous today—but in those days, I especially enjoyed disrupting parties with the work. It was the furthest you could go in avant-garde "noise," and I could be relied upon to empty any room in Boston within three minutes by sitting down at the piano and starting it.

3   At the time, one of my close friends was a fellow student who went by the name of I.B. Cohen. (He's now known as I. Bernard Cohen, Professor of History of Science at Harvard, but nobody yet knows what the I. stands for.) He was way beyond me—a graduate student who knew everything about anything—but we did have two things in common: the name Bernstein (his mother's maiden name) and a great crush on Anna Sokolow.

4   Anna Sokolow was a young and very striking dancer whose recital in Boston I.B. and I had attended. We both promptly fell in love with her. When we learned that her Boston performance was in effect a pre-Broadway tryout for her New York debut, we determined that nothing in the world would stop us from going down to catch that recital.

5   I.B. acquired tickets through a friend of his, the poetess Muriel Rukeyser and on magical November 14, we came to New York, met Muriel, and went with her to the Guild Theater on Broadway for the recital. Our seats happened to be in the first row of the balcony; I made my way through, followed by Muriel and I.B. Already in his seat on my right was an odd-looking man in his thirties, a pair of glasses resting on his great hooked nose and a mouth filled with teeth flashing a wide grin at Muriel. She leaned across to greet him, then introduced us: "Aaron Copland...Leonard." I almost fell out of the balcony.

154

⁶ At the end of the recital, Copland announced that it was his birthday, that he was having a few people up to his "loft" (Aaron Copland's famous loft!) and would we care to join them. It was indeed a loft, above a candy factory on Sixty-Third Street, where Lincoln Center now stands. (He worked in the loft, lived down the block at the Empire Hotel, still standing at Sixty-Third Street and Broadway.) As was my shameless wont, I gravitated to the piano. Naturally, I began with the *Variations*. It must have startled everybody that this last-minute guest, whom nobody knew—a provincial college boy from Boston who had been to New York only once or twice before and who was now obviously thrilled to be in a loft!...with artists!!—was playing their host's ferocious work. I was so excited to be the center of such a party that I followed the *Variations* with every piece I could remember; I recall to my shame that I must have stayed at the piano for hours.

⁷ From that time on, Aaron and I were fast friends. He seemed to be terribly taken by the conviction with which I played his music and even made such extravagant remarks as, "I wish I could play it like that." And thereafter, whenever I came to New York I went to Aaron's. I would arrive in the morning and we'd have breakfast at his hotel, then wander around and sometimes go to a concert. And all during those years I would bring him my own music for his criticism. I remember that I was writing a violin sonata during those Harvard days, and a two-piano piece, and a four-hand piece, and a string quartet. I even completed a trio. I would show Aaron the bits and pieces and he would say, "All that has to go...This is just pure Scriabin. You've got to get that out of your head and start fresh...This is good; these two bars are good. Take these two bars and start from there." And in these sessions he taught me a tremendous amount about taste, style, and consistency in music. I had never really studied composition with anybody before: at Harvard I had taken advanced harmony and fugue with Walter Piston and orchestration with Edward Burlingame Hill, but these were all theoretical elements of composition. Through his critical analyses of whatever I happened to be working on at the moment, Aaron became the closest thing to a composition teacher I ever had.

⁸ We of course played other music than mine at these sessions. We played his. Not while he was composing it though: Aaron was very jealous of the music he was working on and would never show anything before it reached its reasonably final form. But then would come that glorious day when he would pull something out and we would play it, four-hand, from the score. I learned such works as *Billy the Kid* and *An Outdoor Overture*—later, the Piano Sonata and Third Symphony—that way before they were ever performed publicly, and the scores to *Quiet City*, *Of Mice and Men*, and *Our Town* before Hollywood got them. *El Salon Mexico* had already been composed—and first performed by Carlos Chavez in Mexico City a few months before I met Aaron—but the published piano transcription was made by me.

⁹ During those years, I was also very much concerned about my own future and I'd bring all my problems to Aaron. He became a surrogate father to me. Even after I developed the close relationship to Koussevitzky that made me his official (according to the press) substitute son, it was always Aaron to whom I would turn with my worries. I was quite a whiner in those days and I would constantly bewail my plight to him: "When is anybody ever going to play my music?" Or, in later years, "Oh Lord, how does anybody ever get to conduct an orchestra?" He would always giggle first—the infectious giggle is his most common reaction to anything—then, with an attempt at sternness,

glower. "Stop complaining. You are destined for success. Nobody's worried about you. You are the one person worried about you," and I would get very angry and insist upon being worried about.

10   Then on Sunday, November 14 (again), 1943—his forty-third birthday—I was awakened at nine in the morning by a phone call from the New York Philharmonic, of which I was then the assistant conductor. Bruno Walter was sick and I would have to conduct the concert, scheduled for national broadcast, at three that afternoon. There was no time for a rehearsal and barely time to shake my hangover. That concert, of course, changed my life. It was a dramatic success, all the more so for me since Aaron's words seemed to come providentially true on his birthday. When the review, incredibly, made the front page of the *New York Times* the following morning, Aaron's response was, "Oh, it's only what everybody expected," and I, of course, got twice as furious with him as ever.

11   I was not, certainly, the only young musician for whom Aaron was a beacon. In America he was The Leader, the one to whom the young always came with their compositions. Every premiere of a new Copland work found the concert hall filled with young composers and musicians. And from all over the world young composers would come to study with him at Tanglewood. (Aaron and I used to spend our summers there— we opened the first Tanglewood season together in 1940—he as administrative head of the school, I as a student.)

12   But then, after the war, the Schoenberg syndrome took hold and was heartily embraced by the young, who gradually stopped flocking to Aaron: the effect on him— and therefore on American music—was heartbreaking. He is, after all, one of the most important composers of our century. I am not thinking historically now, but musically. In fact he became an impetus to subsequent American music only because his own music is so important. It contains a rare combination of spontaneity and care: his creative material is purely instinctive and his crafting of it extremely professional. Unlike much of the past decade's transient works, Aaron's music has always contained the basic values of art, not the least of which is communicativeness.

13   As these virtues became unfashionable, so did Aaron's music. One of the sadnesses, I recall in recent years occurred at the premiere of his *Inscape*, when he said to me, "Do you realize there isn't one young composer here, there isn't one young musician who seems to be at all interested in this piece, a brand-new piece I've labored over?" The truth is that when the musical winds blew past him, he tried to catch up—with twelve-tone music, just as it too was becoming old-fashioned to the young.

14   When he started writing twelve-tone I figured that it was inevitable—everybody has to fool with serialism. God knows I spent my whole sabbatical in 1964 in a desperate attempt at it: I've actually thrown away more twelve-tone pieces than I had written otherwise. But still I asked him, "Of all people, why you—you who are so instinctive, so spontaneous? Why are you bothering with tone rows and with the rules of retrograde and inversion, and all that?" and he answered me. "Because I need more chords. I've run out of chords."* And that lasted for four more pieces and then he didn't write any more. How sad for him. How awful for us.

15   Of course, as Aaron himself pointed out when I complained to him about his forsaking composition for the stage (he's become quite an excellent conductor, by the way, and has always been a marvelous lecturer), how many composers have lived into

their late sixties still writing? We know the obvious example of Verdi, who at sixty thought he was through as an operatic composer, struggling halfheartedly with *King Lear*, only to emerge after a fifteen-year hiatus, in his mid-seventies, with his two masterpieces *Otello* and *Falstaff*. Perhaps, we can hope, this will happen to Aaron. All it will take, it seems to me, is another musical turn, this time to a rediscovery of the basic simplicities of art, in which Copland will once more be looked to as a leader, will once again feel wanted as a composer.

[16]   Happy Birthday, Aaron. We miss your music.

[17]   *This reminds me that Paul Simon (of Garfunkel fame) told me the summer before last that upon meeting Bob Dylan for the first time Dylan's first sentence had been, "Hey, you got any new chords? *I've run out of chords*."

Thinking and Responding to the Reading

1.   Who is Leonard Bernstein? Who is Aaron Copland? For what are they famous?
2.   Why was Bernstein so excited to meet Aaron Copland? What does this tell you about admiring someone? Is the admiration mutual?
3.   Who went to Tanglewood, and what happened there?
4.   What were some of Bernstein's worries?
5.   Why did Copland's music become unfashionable?
6.   Why do Copland and Bob Dylan say, "I've run out of chords"? Explain what you think the composers meant by this.

Springboard for Composing

Bernstein's musical understanding and composition was greatly enriched by Copland's guiding comments. Has someone ever helped you to understand a new type of music or the meaning behind some lyrics? What was your initial reaction? Did your reaction to the music or lyrics change after the guiding comments? If so, how, or in what ways? If not, why don't you think it changed?

HOW WE LISTEN TO MUSIC

Aaron Copland

Vocabulary Words

planes (par. 1)   digress (par. 6)   arpeggios (par. 17)
sensuous (par. 1)   commensurate (par. 6)   staccatos (par. 17)
sheerly (par. 1)   intransigent (par. 7)   layman (par. 17)
hypothetical (par. 1)   exuberance (par. 10)   correlate (par. 20)
engendered (par. 2)   subtle (par. 10)   analogous (par. 22)
mere (par. 2)   manipulation (par. 16)   subjective (par. 25)
deride (par. 3)   engrossed (par. 17)   objective (par. 25)
usurp (par. 5)

1   We all listen to music according to our separate capacities. But, for the sake of analysis, the whole listening process may become clearer if we break it up into its component parts, so to speak. In a certain sense we all listen to music on three separate planes. For lack of a better terminology, one might name these: (1) the sensuous plane, (2) the expressive plane, (3) the sheerly musical plane. The only advantage to be gained from mechanically splitting up the listening process into these hypothetical planes is the clearer view to be had of the way in which we listen.

2   The simplest way of listening to music is to listen for the sheer pleasure of the musical sound itself. That is the sensuous plane. It is the plane on which we hear music without thinking, without considering it in any way. One turns on the radio while doing something else and absent-mindedly bathes in the sound. A kind of brainless but attractive state of mind is engendered by the mere sound appeal of the music.

3   You may be sitting in a room reading this book. Imagine one note struck on the piano. Immediately that one note is enough to change the atmosphere of the room--proving that the sound element in music is a powerful and mysterious agent, which it would be foolish to deride or belittle.

4   The surprising thing is that many people who consider themselves qualified music lovers abuse that plane in listening. They go to concerts in order to lose themselves. They use music as a consolation or an escape. They enter an ideal world where one doesn't have to think of the realities of everyday life. Of course they aren't thinking about the music either. Music allows them to leave it, and they go off to a place to dream, dreaming because of and apropos of the music yet never quite listening to it.

5   Yes, the sound appeal of music is a potent and primitive force, but you must not allow it to usurp a disproportionate share of your interest. The sensuous plane is an important one in music, a very important one, but it does not constitute the whole story.

6   There is no need to digress further on the sensuous plane. Its appeal to every normal human being is self-evident. There is, however, such a thing as becoming more sensitive to the different kinds of sound stuff as used by various composers.   For all composers do not use that sound stuff in the same way. Don't get the idea that the value of music is commensurate with its sensuous appeal or that the loveliest sounding music is

158

made by the greatest composers. If that were so, Ravel would be a greater creator than Beethoven. The point is that the sound forms an integral part of his style and must be taken into account when listening. The reader can see, therefore, that a more conscious approach is valuable even on this primary plane of music listening.

7   The second plane on which music exists is what I have called the expressive one. Here, immediately, we tread on controversial ground. Composers have a way of shying away from any discussion of music's expressive side. Did not Stravinsky himself proclaim that his music was an "object," a "thing," with a life of its own, and with no other meaning than its own purely musical existence? This intransigent attitude of Stravinsky's may be due to the fact that so many people have tried to read different meanings into so many pieces. Heavens knows it is difficult enough to say precisely what it is that a piece of music means, to say it definitely, to say it finally so that everyone is satisfied with your explanation. But that should not lead one to the other extreme of denying to music the right to be "expressive."

8   My own belief is that all music has an expressive power, some more and some less, but that all music has a certain meaning behind the notes and that that meaning behind the notes constitutes, after all, what the piece is saying, what the piece is about. This whole problem can be stated quite simply by asking, "Is there a meaning to music?" My answer to that would be, "Yes." And "Can you state in so many words what the meaning is?" My answer to that would be, "No." Therein lies the difficulty.

9   Simple-minded souls will never be satisfied with the answer to the second of these questions. They always want music to have a meaning, and the more concrete it is the better they like it. The more the music reminds them of a train, a storm, a funeral, or any other familiar conception the more expressive it appears to be to them. This popular idea of music's meaning—stimulated and abetted by the usual run of music commentator—should be discouraged wherever and whenever it is met. One timid lady once confessed to me that she suspected something seriously lacking in her appreciation of music because of her inability to connect it with anything definite. That is getting the whole thing backward of course.

10   Still, the question remains: How close should the intelligent music lover wish to come to pinning a definite meaning to any particular work? No closer than a general concept, I should say. Music expresses, at different moments, serenity or exuberance, regret or triumph, fury or delight. It expresses each of these moods, and many others, in a numberless variety of subtle shadings and differences. It may even express a state of meaning for which there exists no adequate word in any language. In that case, musicians often like to say that it has only a purely musical meaning. They sometimes go farther and say that *all* music has only a purely musical meaning. What they really mean is that no appropriate word can be found to express the music's meaning and that, even if it could, they do not feel the need of finding it.

11   But whatever the professional musician may hold, most musical novices still search for specific words with which to pin down their musical reactions. That is why they always find Tschaikovsky easier to "understand" than Beethoven. In the first place, it is easier to pin a meaning-word on a Tschaikovsky piece than on a Beethoven one. Much easier. Moreover, with the Russian composer, every time you co me back to a piece of his it almost always says the same thing to you, whereas with Beethoven it is often quite difficult to put your finger right on what he is saying. And any musician will tell you that

that is why Beethoven is the greater composer. Because music which always says the same thing to you will necessarily soon become dull music, but music whose meaning is slightly different with each hearing has a greater chance of remaining alive.

¹² Listen, if you can, to the forty-eight fugue themes of Bach's *Well Tempered Clavichord*. Listen to each theme, one after another. You will soon realize that each theme mirrors a different world of feeling. You will also soon realize that the more beautiful a theme seems to you the harder it is to find any word that will describe it to your complete satisfaction. Yes, you will certainly know whether it is a gay theme or a sad one. You will be able, in other works, in your own mind, to draw a frame of emotional feeling around your theme. Now study the sad one a little closer. Try to pin down the exact quality of its sadness. It is pessimistically sad or resignedly sad; it is fatefully sad or smilingly sad?

¹³ Let us suppose that you are fortunate and can describe to your own satisfaction in so many words the exact meaning of your chosen theme. There is still no guarantee that anyone else will be satisfied. Nor need they be. The important thing is that each one feel for himself the specific expressive quality of a theme or, similarly, an entire piece of music. And if it is a great work of art, don't expect it to mean exactly the same thing to you each time you return to it.

¹⁴ Themes or pieces need not express only one emotion, of course. Take such a theme as the first main one of the *Ninth Symphony*, for example. It is clearly made up of different elements. It does not say only one thing. Yet anyone hearing it immediately gets a feeling of strength, a feeling of power. It isn't a power that comes simply because the theme is played loudly. It is a power inherent in the theme itself. The extraordinary strength and vigor of the theme results in the listener's receiving an impression that a forceful statement has been made. But one should never try to boil it down to "the fateful hammer of life," etc. That is where the trouble begins. The musician, in his exasperation, says it means nothing but the notes themselves, whereas the nonprofessional is only too anxious to hang on to any explanation that gives him the illusion of getting closer to the music's meaning.

¹⁵ Now, perhaps, the reader will know better what I mean when I say that music does have an expressive meaning but that we cannot say in so many words what that meaning is.

¹⁶ The third plane on which music exists is the sheerly musical plane. Besides the pleasurable sound of music and the expressive feeling that it gives off, music does exist in terms of the notes themselves and of their manipulation. Most listeners are not sufficiently conscious of this third plane.

¹⁷ Professional musicians, on the other hand, are, if anything, too conscious of the mere notes themselves. They often fall into the error of becoming so engrossed with their arpeggios and staccatos that they forget the deeper aspects of the music they are performing. But from the layman's standpoint, it is not so much a matter of getting over bad habits on the sheerly musical plane as of increasing one's awareness of what is going on, in so far as the notes are concerned.

¹⁸ When the man in the street listens to the "notes themselves" with any degree of concentration, he is most likely to make some mention of the melody. Either he hears a pretty melody or he does not, and he generally lets it go at that. Rhythm is likely to gain his attention next, particularly if it seems exciting. But harmony and tone color are gen-

erally taken for granted, if they are thought of consciously at all. As for music's having a definite form of some kind, that idea seems never to have occurred to him.

[19]   It is very important for all of us to become more alive to music on its sheerly musical plane. After all, an actual musical material is being used. The intelligent listener must be prepared to increase his awareness of the musical material and what happens to it. He must hear the melodies, the rhythms, the harmonies, the tone colors in a more conscious fashion. But above all he must, in order to follow the line of the composer's thought, know something of the principles of musical form. Listening to all of these elements is listening on the sheerly musical plane.

[20]   Let me repeat that I have split up mechanically the three separate planes on which we listen merely for the sake of greater clarity. Actually, we never listen on one or the other of these planes. What we do is to correlate them—listening in all three ways at the same time. It takes no mental effort, for we do it instinctively.

[21]   Perhaps an analogy with what happens to us when we visit the theater will make this instinctive correlation clearer. In the theater, you are aware of the actors and actresses, costumes and sets, sounds and movement. All these give one the sense that the theater is a pleasant place to be in. They constitute the sensuous plane in our theatrical reactions.

[22]   The expressive plane in the theater would be derived from the feeling that you get from what is happening on the stage. You are moved to pity, excitement, or gayety. It is this general feeling, generated aside from the particular words being spoken, a certain emotional something which exists on the stage, that is analogous to the expressive quality in music.

[23]   The plot and plot development is equivalent to our sheerly musical plane. The playwright creates and develops a character in just the same way that a composer creates and develops a theme. According to the degree of your awareness of the way in which the artist in either field handles his material will you become a more intelligent listener.

[24]   It is easy enough to see that the theatergoer never is conscious of any of these elements separately. He is aware of them all at the same time. The same is true of music listening. We simultaneously and without thinking listen on all three planes.

[25]   In a sense, the ideal listener is both inside and outside the music at the same moment, judging it and enjoying it, wishing it would go one way and watching it go another—almost like the composer at the moment he composes it; because in order to write his music, the composer must also be inside and outside his music, carried away by it and yet coldly critical of it. A subjective and objective attitude is implied in both creating and listening to music.

[26]   What the reader should strive for, then, is a more *active* kind of listening. Whether you listen to Mozart or Duke Ellington, you can deepen your understanding of music only by being a more conscious and aware listener—not someone who is just listening, but someone who is listening *for* something.

Thinking and Responding to the Reading

1. Who is Aaron Copland? For what is he famous?
2. List and explain the three hypothetical listening planes that Copeland discusses.
3. Think about the sensual level of listening and what is meant by "music allows them to leave it [everyday life]." What kind of music do you listen to achieve this effect for yourself? On what plane(s) do you listen to your music?
4. Are you an "active" listener, one who listens "for something"?
5. Examine on what level of listening you are concentrating when you dislike a piece of music. What would it take to get you to call upon the other levels as well? What might you achieve?
6. Find where Copland describes the "ideal listener." Paraphrase this description.

Springboard for Composing

According to Copland, all music has meaning attached to it. List two or three of your favorite pieces of music and describe the meaning you sense lies behind them. Now think of two or three specific pieces of music (not generalized categories) that you dislike. Do these musical pieces still have meaning? Is this what you object to or is it something else?

HOMEMADE EDUCATION
from *The Autobiography of Malcolm X*

MALCOLM X

Vocabulary Words

convey (par. 2)   functional (par. 2)   emulate (par. 4)
articulate (par. 2)   envy (par. 4)   inevitable (par. 11)

1   It was because of my letters to the Elijah Mohammad that I happened to stumble upon starting to acquire some kind of homemade education.

2   I became increasingly frustrated at not being able to express what I wanted to convey in letters that I wrote, especially those to Mr. Elijah Muhammad. In the street, I had been the most articulate hustler out there—I had commanded attention when I said something. But now, trying to write simple English, I not only wasn't articulate, I wasn't even functional. How would I sound writing in slang, the way I would *say* it, something such as "Look, daddy, let me pull your coat about a cat, Elijah Muhammad—"

3   Many who today hear me somewhere in person, or on television, or those who read something I've said, will think I went to school far beyond the eighth grade. This impression is due entirely to my prison studies.

4   It had really begun back in Charlestown Prison, when Bimbi first made me feel envy of his stock of knowledge. Bimbi had always taken charge of any conversation he was in, and I had tried to emulate him. But every book I picked up had few sentences which didn't contain anywhere from one to nearly all of the words that might as well have been in Chinese. When I just skipped those words, of course, I really ended up with little idea of what the book said. So I had come to the Norfolk Prison Colony still going through only book-reading motions. Pretty soon, I would have quit even these motions unless I had received the motivation that I did.

5   I saw that the best thing I could do was get hold of a dictionary—to study to learn some words. I was lucky enough to reason also that I should try to improve my penmanship. It was sad. I couldn't even write in a straight line. It was both ideas together that moved me to request a dictionary along with some tablets and pencils from the Norfolk Prison Colony school.

6   I spent two days just riffling uncertainly through the dictionary's pages. I'd never realized so many words existed! I didn't know *which* words I needed to learn. Finally, just to start some kind of action, I began copying.

7   In my slow, painstaking, ragged handwriting, I copied into my tablet everything printed on that first page, down to the punctuation marks.

8   I believe it took me a day. Then, aloud, I read back, to myself, everything I'd written on the tablet. Over and over, aloud, to myself, I read my own handwriting.

9   I woke up the next morning, thinking about those words—immensely proud to realize that not only had I written so much at one time, but I'd written words that I never knew were in the world. Moreover, with a little effort, I also could remember what many

of these words meant. I reviewed the words whose meanings I didn't remember. Funny thing, from the dictionary's first page right now, that "aardvark" springs to my mind. The dictionary had a picture of it, a long-tailed, long-eared, burrowing African mammal, which lives off termites caught by sticking out its tongue as an anteater does for ants.

10 I was so fascinated that I went on—I copied the dictionary's next page. And the same experience came when I studied that. With every succeeding page, I also learned of people and places and events from history. Actually the dictionary is like a miniature encyclopedia. Finally the dictionary's A section had filled a whole tablet—and I went on into the B's. That was the way I started copying what eventually became the entire dictionary. It went a lot faster after so much practice helped me to pick up handwriting speed. Between what I wrote in my tablet, and writing letters, during the rest of my time in prison I would guess I wrote a million words.

11 I suppose it was inevitable that as my word-based broadened, I could for the first time pick up a book and read and now begin to understand what the book was saying. Anyone who has read a great deal can imagine the new world that opened. Let me tell you something: from then until I left that prison, in every free moment I had, if I was not reading in the library, I was reading on my bunk. You couldn't have gotten me out of books with a wedge. Between Mr. Muhammad's teachings, my correspondence, my visitors—usually Ella and Reginald—and my reading of books, months passed without my even thinking about being imprisoned. In fact, up to then, I had never been so truly free in my life.

Thinking and Responding to the Reading

1. What did Malcolm X realize when he read books while in prison?
2. What method did he use to remedy his reading comprehension problems?
3. What did Malcolm X learn from the dictionary? Is the learning of words helpful to you in your reading comprehension? Explain.
4. In paragraph 11, Malcolm X says, "In fact, up to then, I had never been so truly free in my life," and "Anyone who has read a great deal can imagine the new world that opened." Based on your own experience how has reading changed your life? If you haven't read something yet where your life has been changed, explain what impediments get in your way while reading; explain your struggle with reading as Malcolm X did.

Springboard for Composing

Indirectly, Bimbi in Charleston Prison and his command of words motivated Malcolm X to begin his own education. Suppose that Bimbi actually had told Malcolm X how to acquire "his stock of knowledge." Do you think he would have recommended the dictionary method? Discuss a time when you learned some information or how to do something indirectly. Who influenced or taught you? What did you learn?

HOW I LEARNED TO READ AND WRITE
from *The Autobiography of Frederick Douglass*

Frederick Douglass

Vocabulary Words

perceiving (par. 1)	deeming (par. 2)	persevere (par. 5)	revelation (par. 7)
intolerable (par. 1)	impudent (par. 2)	precursor (par. 6)	dispelling (par. 7)
ventured (par. 1)	exalted (par. 3)	human chattels (par. 6)	to wit (par. 7)
disposition (par. 2)	transient (par. 3)	forbade (par. 6)	perpetuate (par. 7)
supercilious (par. 2)	perverted (par. 4)	disconsolate (par. 6)	assented (par. 7)
contempt (par. 2)	roused (par. 5)	oracular (par. 7)	underrated (par. 7)
petulance (par. 2)	emboldened (par. 5)	exposition (par. 7)	rendered (par. 7)
preservation (par. 2)	consented (par. 5)	discourse (par. 7)	resolute (par. 7)
bated (par. 2)	exultingly (par. 5)	transitory (par. 7)	amiable (par. 7)
scorn (par. 2)	aptness (par. 5)	allayed (par. 7)	

1   Established in my new home in Baltimore, I was not very long in perceiving that in picturing to myself what was to be my life there, my imagination had painted only the bright side; and that the reality had its dark shades as well as its light ones. The open country which had been so much to me, was all shut out. Walled in on every side by towering brick buildings, the heat of the summer was intolerable to me, and the hard brick pavements almost blistered my feet. If I ventured out onto the streets, new and strange objects glared upon me at every step, and startling sounds greeted my ears from all directions. My country eyes and ears were confused and bewildered. Troops of hostile boys pounded upon me at every corner. They chased me, and called me "Eastern Shore man," till really I almost wished myself back on the Eastern Shore.

2   My new mistress happily proved to be all she had seemed, and in her presence I easily forgot all outside annoyances. Mrs. Sophia was naturally of an excellent disposition—kind, gentle, and cheerful. The supercilious contempt for the rights and feelings of others, and the petulance and bad humor which generally characterized slaveholding ladies, were all quite absent from her manner and bearing toward me. She had never been a slaveholder—a thing then quite unusual at the South—but had depended almost entirely upon her own industry for a living. To this fact the dear lady no doubt owed the excellent preservation of her natural goodness of heart, for slavery could change a saint into a sinner, and an angel into a demon. I hardly knew how to behave toward "Miss Sopha," as I used to call Mrs. Hugh Auld. I could not approach her even as I had formerly approached Mrs. Thomas Auld. Why should I hang down my head, and speak with bated breath, when there was no pride to scorn me, no coldness to repel me, and no hatred to inspire me with fear? I therefore soon came to regard her as something more akin to a mother

than a slaveholding mistress. So far from deeming it impudent in a slave to look her straight in the face, she seemed ever to say, "Look up, child; don't be afraid."

³   The sailors belonging to the sloop esteemed it a great privilege to be the bearers of parcels or messages to her, for whenever they came, they were sure of a most kind and pleasant reception. If little Thomas was her son, and her most dearly loved child, she made me something like his half-brother in her affections. If dear Tommy was exalted to a place on his mother's knee, "Freddy" was honored by a place at the mother's side. Nor did the slave boy lack the caressing strokes of her gentle hand, soothing him into the consciousness that, though motherless, he was not friendless. Mrs. Auld was not only kind-hearted, but remarkably pious; frequent in her attendance of public workshop, much given to reading the Bible, and to chanting hymns of praise when alone. Mr. Hugh was altogether a different character. He cared very little about religion; knew more of the world and was more a part of the world than his wife. He set out doubtless to be, as the world goes, a respectable man, and to get on by becoming a successful shipbuilder, in that city of shipbuilding. This was his ambition, and it fully occupied him. I was of course of very little consequence to him, and when he smiled upon me, as he sometimes did, the smile was borrowed from his lovely wife, and like all borrowed light, was transient, and vanished with the source whence it was derived. Though I must in truth characterize Master Hugh as a sour man of forbidding appearance, it is due to him to acknowledge that he was never cruel to me, according to the notion of cruelty in Maryland. During the first year or two, he left me, almost exclusively to the management of his wife. He was my lawgiver.

⁴   In hands so tender as hers, and in the absence of the cruelties of the plantation, I became both physically and mentally much more sensitive, and a frown from my mistress caused me far more suffering than had Aunt Katy's hardest cuffs. Instead of the cold, damp floor of my old master's kitchen, I was on carpets; for the corn bag in winter, I had a good straw bed, well furnished with covers; for the coarse cornmeal in the morning, I had good bread and mush occasionally; for my old torn-linen shirt, I had good clean clothes. I was really well off. My employment was to run errands, and to take care of Tommy, to prevent his getting in the way of carriages, and to keep him out of harm's way generally. So for a time everything went well. I say for a time, because the fatal poison of irresponsible power, and the natural influence of slave customs, were not very long in making their impression on the gentle and loving disposition of my excellent mistress. She regarded me at first as a child, like any other. This was the natural and spontaneous thought; afterwards, when she came to consider me as property, our relations to each other were changed, but a nature so noble as hers could not instantly become perverted, and it took several years before the sweetness of her temper was wholly lost.

⁵   The frequent hearing of my mistress reading the Bible aloud, for she often read aloud when her husband was absent, awakened my curiosity in respect to this mystery of reading, and roused in me the desire to learn. Up to this time I had known nothing whatever of this wonderful art, and my ignorance and inexperience of what it could do for me, as well as my confidence in my mistress, emboldened me to ask her to teach me to read. With an unconsciousness and inexperience equal to my own, she readily consented, and in an incredibly short time, by her kind assistance, I had mastered the alphabet and could spell words of three or four letters. My mistress seemed almost as proud of my progress as if I had been her own child, and supposing that her husband would be as well pleased,

she made no secret of what she was doing for me. Indeed, she exultingly told him of the aptness of her pupil, and of her intention to persevere in teaching me, as she felt her duty to do, at least to read the Bible.

[6] And here arose the first dark cloud over my Baltimore prospects, the precursor of chilling blasts and drenching storms. Master Hugh was astounded beyond measure, and probably for the first time proceeded to unfold to his wife the true philosophy of the slave system, and the peculiar rules necessary in the nature of the case to be observed in the management of human chattels. Of course he forbade her to give me any further instruction, telling her in the first place that to do so was unlawful, as it was also unsafe; "for," said he, "if you give a nigger an inch he will take an ell. Learning will spoil the best nigger in the world. If he learns to read the Bible it will forever unfit him to be a slave. He should know nothing but the will of his master, and learn to obey it. As to himself, learning will do him no good, but a great deal of harm, making him disconsolate and unhappy. If you teach him how to read, he'll want to know how to write, and this accomplished, he'll be running away with himself."

[7] Such was the tenor of Master Hugh's oracular exposition and it must be confessed that he very clearly comprehended the nature and the requirements of the relation of a master and slave. His discourse was the first decidedly antislavery lecture to which it had been my lot to listen. Mrs. Auld evidently felt the force of what he said, and like an obedient wife, began to shape her course in the direction indicated by him. The effect of his words on me was neither slight nor transitory. His iron sentences, cold and harsh, sunk like heavy weights deep into my heart, and stirred up within me a rebellion not soon to be allayed. This was a new and special revelation dispelling a painful mystery against which my youthful understanding had struggled, and struggled in vain, to wit, the white man's power to perpetuate the enslavement of the black man. "Very well," thought I. "Knowledge unfits a child to be a slave." I instinctively assented to the proposition, and from that moment I understood the direct pathway from slavery to freedom. It was just what I needed, and it came to me at a time and from a source whence I least expected it. Of course I was greatly saddened at the thought of losing the assistance of my kind mistress, but the information so instantly derived to some extent compensated me for the loss I had sustained in this direction. Wise as Mr. Auld was, he underrated my comprehension, and had little idea of the use to which I was capable of putting the impressive lesson he was giving to his wife. He wanted me to be a slave; I had already voted against that on the home plantation of Colonel Lloyd. That which he most loved I most hated; and the very determination which he expressed to keep me in ignorance only rendered me the more resolute to seek intelligence. In learning to read, therefore, I am not sure that I do not owe quite as much to the opposition of my master as to the kindly assistance of my amiable mistress. I acknowledge the benefit rendered me by the one, and by the other, believing that but for my mistress I might have grown up in ignorance.

Thinking and Responding to the Reading

1. How does Douglass's mistress, Mrs. Sophia, treat him? List examples from the text to support.
2. Frederick Douglass was taught how to read by his mistress, Mrs. Sophia. What reasons did she give her husband for giving him reading instruction?
3. What was Master Hugh Auld's reaction to this news? Quote the lines which indicate his position towards teaching slaves to read.
4. What was Frederick's resolution after hearing Master Auld? Find the lines in the text to support your answer.
5. What did he realize he must do to gain his freedom?
6. What connections can you make today about reading and freedom? Do you have the relative freedom you need based on your desire to read or could you have more? Explain why.
7. Do you think it is human nature to strive for some goal we wish to attain more when there are impediments standing in our way, or do we attain our goals more easily when opportunities are given to us without any impediments?
8. Frederick Douglass uses many metaphors and similes. Find three and explain their meanings.

Springboard to Composing

Can you think of a time when someone discouraged you from trying or doing something but you did it anyway? What was it? Why do you think you were discouraged? What was the result? What did you gain or lose from the experience?

from MY TEACHER'S GENIUS

Helen Keller

Vocabulary Words

immeasurable (par. 1)	plummet (par. 3)	traversed (par. 15)
unconsciously (par. 2)	sentiment (par. 6)	amenities (par. 31)
languor (par. 2)	confounding (pa. 6)	placid (par. 39)
tangible (par. 3)	repentance (par. 8)	innate (par. 41)

1   The most important day I remember in all my life is the one on which my teacher, Anne Mansfield Sullivan, came to me. I am filled with wonder when I consider the immeasurable contrasts between the two lives which it connects. It was the third of March, 1887, three months before I was seven years old.

2   On the afternoon of that eventful day, I stood on the porch, dumb, expectant. I guessed vaguely from my mother's signs and from the hurrying to and fro in the house that something unusual was about to happen, so I went to the door and waited on the steps. The afternoon sun penetrated the mass of honey-suckle that covered the porch, and fell on my upturned face. My fingers lingered almost unconsciously on the familiar leaves and blossoms which had just come forth to greet the sweet southern spring. I did not know what the future held of marvel or surprise for me. Anger and bitterness had preyed upon me continually for weeks and a deep languor had succeeded this passionate struggle.

3   Have you ever been at sea in a dense fog, when it seemed as if a tangible white darkness shut you in, and the great ship, tense and anxious, groped her way toward the shore with plummet and sounding-line, and you waited with beating heart for something to happen? I was like that ship before my education began, only I was without compass or sounding-line, and had no way of knowing how near the harbour was. "Light!" was the wordless cry of my soul, and the light of love shone on me in that very hour.

4   I felt approaching footsteps. I stretched out my hand as I supposed to my mother. Someone took it, and I was caught up and held close in the arms of her who had come to reveal all things to me, and, more than all things else, to love me.

5   The morning after my teacher came she led me into her room and gave me a doll. The little blind children at the Perkins Institution had sent it and Laura Bridgman had dressed it; but I did not know this until afterward. When I had played with it a little while, Miss Sullivan slowly spelled into my hand the word "d-o-l-l." I was at once interested in this finger play and tried to imitate it. When I finally succeeded in making the letters correctly I was flushed with childish pleasure and pride. Running downstairs to my mother I held up my hand and made the letters for doll. I did not know that I was spelling a word or even that words existed; I was simply making my fingers go in monkey-like imitation.   In the days that followed I learned to spell in this uncomprehending way a great many words, among them *pin*, *bat*, *cup* and a few verbs like *sit*, *stand* and *walk*. But my teacher had been with me several weeks before I understood that everything has a name.

6   One day, while I was playing with my new doll, Miss Sullivan put my big rag doll into my lap also, and spelled "d-o-l-l" and tried to make me understand that "d-o-l-l" applied to both. Earlier in the day we had had a tussle over the words "m-u-g" and "w-a-t-e-r." Miss Sullivan had tried to impress it upon me that "m-u-g" is mug and that "w-a-t-e-r" is water, but I persisted in confounding the two. In despair she had dropped the subject for the time, only to renew it at the first opportunity. I became impatient at her repeated attempts and, seizing the new doll, I dashed it upon the floor. I was keenly delighted when I felt the fragments of the broken doll at my feet. Neither sorrow nor regret followed my passionate out-burst. I had not loved the doll. In the still, dark world in which I lived there was no strong sentiment of tenderness. I felt my teacher sweep the fragments to one side of the hearth, and I had a sense of satisfaction that the cause of my discomfort was removed. This thought, if a wordless sensation may be called a thought, made me hop and skip with pleasure.

7   We walked down the path to the well-house, attracted by the fragrance of the honeysuckle with which it was covered. Someone was drawing water and my teacher placed my hand under the spout. As the cool stream gushed over one hand she spelled into the other the word water, first slowly, then rapidly. She stood still, my whole attention fixed upon the motions of her fingers. Suddenly I felt a misty consciousness as of something forgotten—a thrill of returning thought; and somehow the mystery of language was revealed to me. I knew then that "w-a-t-e-r" meant the wonderful cool something that was flowing over my hand. That living word awakened my soul, gave it light, hope, joy, set it free! There were barriers still, it is true, but barriers that could in time be swept away.

8   I left the well-house eager to learn. Everything had a name, and each name gave birth to a new thought. As we returned to the house every object which I touched seemed to quiver with life. That was because I saw everything with the strange, new sight that had come to me. On entering the door I remembered the doll I had broken. I felt my way to the hearth and picked up the pieces. I tried vainly to put them together. Then my eyes filled with tears; for I realized what I had done, and for the first time I felt repentance and sorrow.

9   I learned a great many new words that day. I do not remember what they all were; but I do know that mother, father, sister, teacher were among them – words that were to make the world blossom for me, "like Aaron's rod, with flowers." It would have been difficult to find a happier child than I was as I lay in my crib at the close of that eventful day and lived over the joys it had brought me, and for the first time longed for a new day to come.

10   I recall many incidents of the summer of 1887 that followed my soul's sudden awakening. I did nothing but explore with my hands and learn the name of every object that I touched; and the more I handled things and learned their names and uses, the more joyous and confident grew my sense of kinship with the rest of the world.

11   In the Spring, I had my first lessons in the beneficence of nature. I learned how the sun and the rain make to grow out of the ground every tree that is pleasant to the sight and good for food, how birds build their nests and live and thrive from land to land, how the squirrel, the deer, the lion and every other creature finds food and shelter. As my knowledge of things grew I felt more and more the delight of the world I was in.

[12] But about this time I had an experience which taught me that nature is not always kind. One day my teacher and I were returning from a long ramble. The morning had been fine, but it was growing warm and sultry when at last we turned our faces homeward. Two or three times we stopped to rest under a tree by the wayside. Our last halt was under a wild cherry tree a short distance from the house. The shade was grateful, and the tree was so easy to climb that with my teacher's assistance I was able to scramble to a seat in the branches. It was so cool up in the tree that Miss Sullivan proposed that we have our luncheon there. I promised to keep still while she went to the house to fetch it.

[13] Suddenly a change passed over the tree. All the sun's warmth left the air. I knew the sky was black, because all the heat, which meant light to me, had died out of the atmosphere. A strange odour came up from the earth. I knew it, it was the odour that always precedes a thunderstorm and a nameless fear clutched at my heart. I felt absolutely alone, cut off from my friends and the firm earth. The immense, the unknown, enfolded me. I remained still and expectant; a chilling terror crept over me. I longed for my teacher's return; but above all things I wanted to get down from that tree.

[14] It worked my suspense up the highest point, and just as I was thinking the tree and I should fall together, my teacher seized my hand and helped me down. I clung to her, trembling with joy to feel the earth under my feet once more. I had learned a new lesson—that nature "wages open war against her children, and under softest touch hides treacherous claws."

[15] I had now the key to all language, and I was eager to use it. Children who hear acquire language without any particular effort; the words that fall from others' lips they catch on the wing, as it were, delightedly, while the little deaf child must trap them by a slow and often painful process. But whatever the process, the result is wonderful. Gradually from naming an object we advance step by step until we have traversed the vast distance between our first stammered syllable and the sweep of thought in a line of Shakespeare.

[16] At first, when my teacher told me about a new thing I asked very few questions. My ideas were vague, and my vocabulary was inadequate; but as my knowledge of things grew, and I learned more and more words, my field of inquiry broadened, and I would return again and again to the same subject, eager for further information. Sometimes a new word revived an image that some earlier experience had engraved on my brain.

[17] I remember the morning that I first asked the meaning of the word "love." This was before I knew many words. I had found a few early violets in the garden and brought them to my teacher. She tried to kiss me: but at that time I did not like to have anyone kiss me except my mother. Miss Sullivan put her arm gently round me and spelled into my hand, "I love Helen."

[18] "What is love?" I asked.

[19] She drew me closer to her and said, "It is here," pointing to my heart, whose beats I was conscious of for the first time. Her words puzzled me very much because I did not then understand anything unless I touched it.

[20] I smelt the violets in her hand and asked, half in words, half in signs, a question which meant, "Is love the sweetness of flowers?"

[21] "No," said my teacher.

[22] Again I thought. The warm sun was shining on us.

23   "Is this not love?" I asked, pointing in the direction from which the heat came. "Is this not love?"

24   It seemed to me that there could be nothing more beautiful than the sun, whose warmth makes all things grow. But Miss Sullivan shook her head, and I was greatly puzzled and disappointed. I thought it strange that my teacher could not show me love.

25   A day or two afterward I was stringing beads of different sizes in symmetrical groups—two large beads, three small ones, and so on. I had made many mistakes, and Miss Sullivan had pointed them out again and again with gentle patience. Finally I noticed a very obvious error in the sequence and for an instant I concentrated my attention on the lesson and tried to think how I should have arranged the beads. Miss Sullivan touched my forehead and spelled with decided emphasis, "Think."

26   In a flash I knew that the word was the name of the process that was going on in my head. This was my first conscious perception of an abstract idea.

27   For a long time I was still—I was not thinking of the beads in my lap, but trying to find a meaning for "love" in the light of this new idea. The sun had been under a cloud all day, and there had been brief showers; but suddenly the sun broke forth in all its southern splendour.

28   Again I asked my teacher, "Is this not love?"

29   "Love is something like the clouds that were in the sky before the sun came out," she replied. Then in simpler words than these, which at that time I could not have understood, she explained: "You cannot touch the clouds, you know; but you feel the rain and know how glad the flowers and the thirsty earth are to have it after a hot day. You cannot touch love either; but you feel the sweetness that it pours into everything. Without love you would not be happy or want to play."

30   The beautiful truth burst upon my mind—I felt that there were invisible lines stretched between my spirit and the spirits of others.

31   The deaf and the blind find it very difficult to acquire the amenities of conversation. How much more this difficulty must be augmented in the case of those who are both deaf and blind! They cannot distinguish the tone of the voice or, without assistance, go up and down the gamut of tones that give significance to words; nor can they watch the expression of the speaker's face, and a look is often the very soul of what one says.

32   The next important step in my education was learning to read.

33   As soon as I could spell a few words my teacher gave me slips of cardboard on which were printed words in raised letters. I quickly learned that each printed word stood for an object, an act, or a quality. I had a frame in which I could arrange the words in little sentences; but before I ever put sentences in the frame I used to make them in objects. I found the slips of paper which represented, for example, "doll," "is," "on," "bed" and placed each name on its object; then I put my doll on the bed with the words *is, on bed* arranged beside the doll, thus making a sentence of the words, and at the same time carrying out the idea of the sentence with the things themselves.

34   One day, Miss Sullivan tells me, I pinned the word *girl* on my pinafore and stood in the wardrobe. On the shelf I arranged the words, *is, in, wardrobe*. Nothing delighted me so much as this game. My teacher and I played it for hours at a time. Often everything in the room was arranged in object sentences.

35   From the printed slip it was but a step to the printed book. I took my "Reader for Beginners" and hunted for the words I knew; when I found them my joy was like that of a game of hide-and-seek. Thus I began to read.

36   For a long time I had no regular lessons. Even when I studied most earnestly it seemed more like play than work. Everything Miss Sullivan taught me she illustrated by a beautiful story or a poem. Whenever anything delighted or interested me she talked it over with me just as if she were a little girl herself. What many children think of with dread, as a painful plodding through grammar, hard sums and harder definitions, is to-day one of my most precious memories.

37   I cannot explain the peculiar sympathy Miss Sullivan had with my pleasures and desires. Perhaps it was the result of long association with the blind. Added to this she had a wonderful faculty for description. She went quickly over uninteresting details, and never nagged me with questions to see if I remembered the day-before-yesterday's lesson. She introduced dry technicalities of science little by little, making every subject so real that I could not help remembering what she taught.

38   Thus I learned... At the beginning I was only a little mass of possibilities. It was my teacher who unfolded and developed them. When she came, everything about me breathed of love and joy and was full of meaning. She has never since let pass an opportunity to point out the beauty that is in everything, nor has she ceased trying in thought and action and example to make my life sweet and useful.

39   It was my teacher's genius, her quick sympathy, her loving tact which made the first years of my education so beautiful. It was because she seized the right moment to impart knowledge that made it so pleasant and acceptable to me. She realized that a child's mind is like a shallow brook which ripples and dances merrily over the stony course of its education and reflects here a flower, there a bush, yonder a fleecy cloud; and she attempted to guide my mind on its way, knowing that like a brook it should be fed by mountain streams and hidden springs, until it broadened out into a deep river, capable of reflecting in its placid surface, billowy hills, the luminous shadows of trees and the blue heavens, as well as the sweet face of a little flower.

40   Any teacher can take a child to the classroom, but not every teacher can make him learn. He will not work joyously unless he feels that liberty is his, whether he is busy or at rest; he must feel the flush of victory and the heart-sinking of disappointment before he takes with a will the tasks distasteful to him and resolves to dance his way bravely through a dull routine of textbooks.

41   My teacher is so near to me that I scarcely think of myself apart from her. How much of my delight in all beautiful things is innate, and how much is due to her influence, I can never tell. I feel that her being is inseparable from my own, and that the footsteps of my life are in hers. All the best of me belongs to her – there is not a talent, or an aspiration or a joy in me that has not been awakened by her loving touch.

173

Thinking and Responding to the Reading

1.   What methods did Anne Sullivan use to teach Keller the meaning of words? How does schema building relate to Helen's learning the meanings of words?
2.   When did Keller first link words with objects? What were Keller's feelings and behavior immediately after she made the association between words and things? What was her reaction in the following months?
3.   Why did Keller have difficulty learning abstract ideas, such as love and thought?
4.   In paragraph 31, Keller says, "The deaf and blind find it very difficult to acquire the amenities of conversation." What does she say they lack?
5.   Keller refers to nature throughout this article. What is her attitude towards nature? Cite specific examples to support your opinion.
6.   Keller refers to Sullivan's "genius" in paragraph 39. Why does she use this word? Do you agree with her? Explain.

Springboard for Composing

Conveying the concept of an abstract idea to Helen must have been very challenging to Ms. Sullivan. In such a case, she couldn't just single out an object and spell out its name. In fact, all of us have to make our own meaning about an abstraction, possibly with some help from a teacher of sorts. Pick an abstract idea such as *happiness*, *air*, *faith*, or *democracy* and try to express its meaning in words of your own. Now look up the dictionary definition. How do your definitions compare? (Though different words may have been used, do they convey the same meaning?)

LIFE UNDER THE CHIEF DOUBLESPEAK OFFICER

William Lutz

Vocabulary Words

buzzwords (par. 2)   persistency (par. 6)   redundancies (par. 10)
kickbacks (par. 3)   lefty (par. 9)   indefinite (par. 12)
merger (par. 6)

1   If there's one product American business can produce in large amounts, it's doublespeak. Doublespeak is language that only pretends to say something; it's language that hides, evades or misleads.

2   Doublespeak comes in many forms, from the popular buzzwords that everyone uses but no one really understands – "glocalization," "competitive dynamics," "re-equitizing" and "empowerment" – to language that tries to hide meaning: "re-engineering," "synergy," "adjustment," "restructure" and "force management program."

3   With doublespeak, no truck driver is the worst driver, just the "least-best" driver, and bribes and kickbacks are called "rebates" or "fees for produce testing" Even robbery can be magically transformed with doublespeak, as a bank in Texas did when it declared a robbery of an ATM to be an "unauthorized transaction." Willie Sutton would have loved to have heard that.

4   Automobile junkyards, junk and used car parts have become "auto dismantlers and recyclers" who sell "predismantled, previously owned parts." Don't want people to know you're in the business of disposing of radioactive and chemical wastes? Then call your company "U.S. Ecology Inc."

5   Wages may not be increasing, but the doublespeak of job titles sure has increased. These days, your job title has to have the word "chief" in it. How many kinds of "chiefs" are there? Try these titles on for size: Chief Nuclear Officer, Chief Procurement Officer, Chief Information Officer, Chief Learning Officer, Chief Transformation Officer, Chief Cultural Officer, Chief People Officer, Chief Ethics Officer, Chief Turnaround Officer, Chief Technology Officer, and Chief Creative Officer. After all the "operations improvement" corporations have undergone, you have to wonder who all those "chiefs" are leading. Never before have so few been led by so many.

6   These days, a travel agent may be called a "travel counselor," "vacation specialist," "destination counselor" or "reservation specialist." As part of their merger, Chase Manhattan Bank and Chemical Bank decided that the position of "Relationship Manager" would be divided between executives of both banks. What is a "Relationship Manager"? Once upon a time this person was called a salesman. And if you're late in paying your bill after buying something from one of these "Relationship Managers," you'll be called by the "Persistency Specialist," or bill collector. If you're "downsized," the "Outplacement Consultant" or unemployment counselor will help you with "re-employment engineering," or how to find another job.

[7] With doublespeak, banks don't have "bad loans" or "bad debts"; they have "nonperforming assets" or "nonperforming credits" which are "rolled over" or "rescheduled." Corporations never lose money; they just experience "negative cash flow," "deficit enhancement," "net profit revenue deficiencies," or "negative contributions to profits."

[8] No one gets fired these days, and no one gets laid off. If you're high enough in the corporation pecking order, you "resign for personal reasons." (And then you're never unemployed; you're just in an "orderly transition between career changes.")

[9] But even those far below the lofty heights of corporate power are not fired or laid off. Firing workers is such big business in these days of "re-engineering," "restructuring" and "downsizing" that there are companies whose business is helping other companies fire their workers. (Think about that for a minute.) These companies provide "termination and outplacement consulting" for corporations involved in "reduction activities." In other words, they teach companies how to fire or lay off workers. During these days of "cost rationalization," companies fire or lay off workers many different ways. How do I fire thee? Let me count the ways.

[10] Companies make "workforce adjustments," "headcount reductions," "census reductions," or institute a program of "negative employee retention." Corporations offer workers "vocational relocation," "career assignment and relocation," a "career change opportunity," or "voluntary termination." Workers are "dehired," "deselected," "selected out," "repositioned," "surplussed," "rightsized," "correct sized," "excessed," or "uninstalled." Some companies "initiate operations improvements," "assign candidates to a mobility pool," "implement a skills mix adjustment," or "eliminate redundancies in the human resource area."

[11] One company denied it was laying off 500 people at its headquarters. "We don't characterize it as a layoff," said the corporate doublespeaker (sometimes called a spin doctor). "We're managing our staff resources. Sometimes you manage them up, and sometimes you manage them down." Congratulations. You've just been managed down, you staff resource you.

[12] An automobile company announced the closing of an entire assembly plant and the elimination of over 8,000 jobs by announcing "a volume-related production schedule adjustment." Not to be outdone by its rival, another car company "initiated a career alternative enhancement program" that enhanced over 5,000 workers out of their jobs. By calling the permanent shutdown of a steel plant an "indefinite idling," a corporation thought that it wouldn't have to pay severance or pension benefits to the workers who were left without jobs.

[13] Doublsepeak can pay for the company, but usually not for the workers who lose their jobs.

[14] As Pogo said, "We have met the enemy, and he is us." Or maybe Dilbert got it better: "Do we really get paid for writing this stuff?"

176

Thinking and Responding to the Reading

1. Define connotation and denotation.
2. List ten connotative words from the article and give each denotative meaning.
3. Discuss how language influences our critical and creative thinking.
4. What Doublespeak do we hear from companies and politicians today? List some of the connotative phrases you have heard and explain their meaning.
5. Look at the section on slang in your textbook. Is slang a form of connotation? Explain.

Springboard for Composing

According to Lutz, "Doublespeak is language that pretends to say something; it is language that hides, evades, or misleads." In fact, Lutz makes the point that "no one knows what anyone's saying anymore." As a professor of English, he is trying to make the reader aware of this danger. Since no solution is proposed in this portion of the essay, you are left to reach conclusions on your own, and you must be your own teacher. What is the danger lurking behind all this misleading language? What are your thoughts on how some of the mentioned terms might negatively affect you and others? Do you know of any solutions?

HYDROPLANING

Vocabulary Words

channel (par. 1)   ripe (2)   antilock (par. 3)
hydroplaning (par. 1)   tread (par. 2)   straddling (par. 4)
maneuver (par. 2)   traction (par. 2) mishap (par. 5)

1   Losing control of your car and hydroplaning uncontrollably across the road is every driver's nightmare. Hydroplaning is a major source of traffic accidents on wet roads and under rainy conditions. Hydroplaning is the result of the car's tires moving fast across a wet surface—so fast that they don't have sufficient time to channel that moisture away from the center of the tire. The result is that the tire is lifted by the water away from the road and all traction is lost. The tires lose contact with the road and ride on the layer of water on the road.

2   Hydroplaning is most easily recognized by the loss of steering. The tug on the steering wheel disappears. It is as if the steering wheel has been disconnected. You may not even realize it is happening until you try to maneuver and find you are not in control of the vehicle. Hydroplaning is affected by a combination of six circumstances:

1.   **Water volume**. Although hydroplaning is more likely with half an inch or more of water on the road, even moisture from dew or fog can create conditions ripe for hydroplaning. Water on the roads deep enough to cause hydroplaning may not be obviously visible, so you must use caution on any wet roads.

2.   **Speed**. Partial hydroplaning can occur at speeds above 30 mph. At speeds above 55 mph, tires may lose all contact with the road. If the road is wet, you should limit your speed.

3.   **Tires**. Poor tire tread can increase the chances of hydroplaning. Tread grooves should be at least 1/16 of an inch deep. You should check your tires periodically by placing a penny with Lincoln's head upside down in a tread groove. If the top of his head shows, it's time to get new tires.

4.   **Vehicle Weight**. A lighter vehicle gets less traction, which increases the risks of hydroplaning. Also, if too much weight is concentrated in the front or rear of the vehicle, the car is more likely to hydroplane.

5.   **Road Surface**. A smooth surface or road that accumulates a lot of water creates ideal hydroplaning conditions. You should maneuver near the center line or near the right edge of the roadway. Over the years car tires create grooves in the roadway. This will be where the build up of the water occurs. You should avoid that groove by driving to the left or right of it. If you are following a car, follow in its tracks.

6.   **Heavy Rain**. The risk of hydroplaning is greatly increased after heavy rains when water has had time to accumulate on the road. Be especially cautious after a heavy rain.

178

3   If your car starts to hydroplane, there are some simple things you can do to help maintain control:

- Remain calm, ease off the gas, and avoid sharp braking.
- Steer straight. If you do skid, steer in the direction of the skid.
- If you must brake, do so once your vehicle regains contact with the road. Pump your brakes to avoid skidding or brake lockup. For cars with antilock brakes, keep continuous pressure on the brake pedal.
- If there is a car in front of you, try to follow the tire tracks of that car. However, continue to slow down and increase your following distance.

4   There is also a simple maneuver that can help you to maintain control of your vehicle at high speeds when there is standing water on the road. By shifting the vehicle's position from the center of the lane to one side of the lane, and straddling the puddles, the tires will have better traction on the higher road surface.

5   A cool head, common sense, and knowing what to do can help you react properly, preventing a disastrous mishap.

 **Thinking and Responding to the Reading**

1.   Define hydroplaning in one sentence using your own words.
2.   Why is hydroplaning dangerous?
3.   Were any of suggestions for avoiding hydroplaning new to you? If so which ones? Did you find this information helpful? If you knew all the suggestions already, where did you learn them?

Springboard for Composing

Few drivers have given close thought to the precise causes of hydroplaning and how to cope with them should hydroplaning occur. Yet such knowledge might save their life. Think back to a time when you found yourself driving or as a passenger under dangerous natural conditions. Describe precisely what you felt happening to your car, what your reaction was, and how you handled the situation. Were you scared or calm? How did you react right after the incident? What had you learned from the experience?

THE DIRE CALAMITY AND THE GREATER SAN FRANCISCO EARTHQUAKE

Jack London

Vocabulary Words

dire (title)	entombed (par. 13)	gratuitous (par. 33)
calamity (title)	conflagration (par. 17)	adverse (par. 36)
seismic (par. 4)	cyclones (par. 28)	ascertained (par. 37)
metropolis (par. 4)	unabated (par. 30)	annals (par. 38)
temblor (par. 7)	profuse (par. 33)	fraught (par. 39)

1   Pioneer San Francisco received a rude awakening Wednesday morning, April 18, 1906.

2   The awful call came without warning like a mysterious bolt of lightening, rushing through the upper strata of the earth, causing devastation, terror and death at the hour of thirteen minutes past five o'clock in the morning, when a large majority of the city's people were still asleep in their homes.

3   It seems as if all-wise Providence had chosen the most fortunate hour for the appalling catastrophe.

4   If the seismic disturbance had occurred in the daytime when the busy thoroughfares of the metropolis were lined with people, or in the evening when the theatres were crowded, there would have been a still more horrifying chapter in the world's history than the one which the city by the Golden Gate has just contributed.

5   Terrible as the distress and the calamity appear, the people of San Francisco and California have ample cause for genuine and deep-felt gratitude.

6   The earthquake shock did much damage.

7   There is little use in denying this fact as there is in exaggerating the results of the temblor.

8   The first heavy shock, a few minutes after five in the morning struck terror to the bravest and the coolest of the city's sleeping populace. In a few seconds the streets in the residence districts were lined with people who rushed out of their apartments and homes in night attire. Furniture, pianos, bookcases danced through the rooms as if possessed with demons; crockery and china ware dashed out of their snug closets on the floors; chimneys toppled over and houses cracked, crushed and caved in.

9   The lower portions of the city, and particularly where the buildings were resting on "filled" ground, seemed to have fared the worst.

10   Most of the old buildings along Montgomery street and east along the waterfront were badly cracked by the shock.

[11] The Valencia Hotel near Eighteenth Street, caved in, and in the fall killed a number of lodgers and injured others.

[12] The large five-story Brunswick Hotel on Sixth and Howard streets, with its three hundred rooms which are all reported to have been occupied, collapsed to the ground.

[13] The Portland House, on Sixth street, between Mission and Market, collapsed, and it is stated that about sixty persons were entombed among the crashing ruins. Their heart-rendering cries for help were heard a block away. A large number of these, however, were saved before the fire overtook them and taken to the emergency hospital established at the Mechanics' Pavilion.

[14] Nearly all the lodging-houses south of Market street met the same fate.

[15] But although the damage from the earthquake was great, San Francisco would have recovered from the shock in a marvelously short space of time.

[16] It was not the earthquake, but the fire—the great terrible fire—that destroyed pioneer San Francisco.

[17] For three days and three nights that awful conflagration swept the stricken city, devouring half a century's fruition of human energy, skill and ingenuity.

[18] Fires broke out in a half dozen places shortly after the earthquake and although our excellent fire-fighters responded promptly to the call of duty, they were greatly handicapped at the very start by the lack of water, many of the mains having been broken by the temblor. Despite the fireman's heroic efforts the fire spread.

[19] The old buildings south of Market and east of Seventh burned like so many boxes of matches, and the people fled before the ravaging elements to the nearest place of safety.

[20] Men, women and children, most of them poorly clad, clutching a family picture, carrying some relic, a bundle of bed clothes, a grip or dragging a truck, hurried away from the scorching flames to what destinations they knew not.

[21] They were motivated by but one thought—to get away from the terrible fire.

[22] The gloomy tide of humanity rolled on, out through the Mission Road to the cemeteries, over the hills to Golden Gate Park and on to the beach. It was one mighty surging wave of human faces of living grief and throbbing despair.

[23] Wednesday afternoon the fire broke out in Hayes Valley and swept on towards the St. Ignatious College, on Van Ness Avenue, totally destroying that noble structure.

[24] The fire made short work of the Franklin Hotel; it blazed in a few minutes and fell into Market Street.

[25] The Mechanics' Pavilion was an easy prey to the flames, but the sick and injured were rushed out to other improvised hospitals before the fire reached the pavilion.

[26] East and west, north and south, the terrible conflagration ate its way.

[27] On Wednesday night and Thursday morning the lower portion of Market Street, Chinatown and Nob Hill was one seething furnace.

[28] Thousands of angry flames shot high into the sky, and the cracking timbers, the falling buildings and the terrific roar of the fire sounded like a dozen cyclones.

[29] Thursday morning dawned on the dire calamity, but it brought additional terror to the stricken people. The fire was still raging worse than on Wednesday and the black smoke hung over the doomed city like a shroud of death.

[30] Thursday, Thursday night, Friday, Friday night and Saturday the all destructive fire continued its work of devastation unabated.

31   It was a panorama that people who saw it will never forget and never wish to see again, but through it all for three days and three nights the brave fire laddies fought the merciless element. Many of them dropped utterly exhausted at their post of duty, which was quickly taken up by one of their comrades. They stood in the smoke of the roaring furnaces to fight the flames and cases are on record where police officers and volunteer firemen had to continually apply a stream of water on the regular firemen on duty in order to keep them from being burned or scorched.

32   Dynamiting of buildings was resorted to in order to confine the fire, but the flames were no sooner subdued in one place before they broke out in another.

33   As is usual in all cases of extraordinary emergency those who knew it all were profuse in their gratuitous advice of how things ought to be done and the great San Francisco fire produced a few fire experts who were brim full of good ideas and wonderful theories, but they all kept a very safe distance from the fire.

34   Expressions were frequently heard from all sides to the effect that if the late Chief Sullivan had been well and alive the fire would have been confined within a very limited area. No doubt there was considerable truth in these statements. Fire fighting was the chosen profession of the late chief, and he had made a life study of the conditions presented by a big fire in San Francisco. In fact, he had often stated that San Francisco could not always escape a big conflagration, and he predicted on more than one occasion the great fire with its causes and terrible results which we have just passed through, but which he was not permitted to combat.

35   Time and again had he asked the ex-Board of Supervisors to provide an adequate water supply for the protection of the city against the fire, and as often did he ask in vain.

36   But regardless of the various and adverse comments both during the progress of the fire and afterward, the fact remains that every member of the San Francisco Fire Department battled for days and nights with the raging elements as men never fought before. They were also ably assisted by the Police Department and the Federal troops.

37   It is stated that the edge of the fire limit is over twenty-nine miles long and the burnt area is composed as being over eight square miles. The property loss is variously estimated between $200,000,000 and $400,000,000. The exact loss of life has not yet, and never will be ascertained, but Coroner Walsh estimates it not less than fifteen hundred.

38   Compared with the Chicago fire in 1871 the burned district in San Francisco is six times the size of the one laid bare in Chicago, and the property loss and loss of life comes very nearly in the same proportion. The dire calamity is the greatest and most distressing event of its kind not only in the history of our country, but within the annals of the world.

39   Terrible as the disaster still appears before our eyes, it has already been fraught with many and wonderful blessings, and San Francisco's sad misfortune will in time prove to have been her best fortune.

Thinking and Responding to the Reading

1.   Who is Jack London and for what is he known?

182

2. What day and time did the earthquake occur? What subsequently happened to the city? How much of San Francisco was destroyed?
3. What is the author's tone in paragraph 33? Explain your answer.
4. What was the primary reason for the great conflagration (fire)?
5. Paragraph 39 states, "Terrible as the disaster still appears before our eyes, it has already been fraught with many and wonderful blessings, and San Francisco's sad misfortune will in time prove to have been her best fortune." What are the "many blessings" and "her best fortune" that have come out of the calamity?
6. Have you ever lived through a natural disaster (hurricane, flood, tornado or earthquake)? How do you view nature since having lived through a natural disaster?

 Springboard for Composing

London does not explain scientifically the causes or results of the earthquake. However, he paints such a vivid anecdotal picture of the event that the reader is well informed what to expect of such a cataclysmic natural force. In similar fashion, recall and describe all that was to be seen, heard and felt when you were caught in some natural disaster, such as a storm, blizzard, windstorm, undertow, mudslide, or icy road.

A BRIEF HISTORY OF THE 1889 JOHNSTOWN FLOOD

Edwin Hutcheson

Vocabulary Words

peripheral (par. 1)	marooned (par. 4)	feat (par. 15)
watershed (par. 1)	debris (par. 5)	submerged (par. 20)
scurry (par. 1)	torrents (par. 8)	contingent (par. 22)
dam (par. 3)	restrain (par. 9)	legislation (par. 23)
prestigious (par. 3)	plunged (par. 9)	nuisance (par. 24)
entrepreneurs (par. 3)		

1   Johnstown had been built into a river valley on the Appalachian Plateau. The Little Conemaugh and the Stony Creek Rivers which ran along the peripheral of the town and merged to form the Conemaugh River at the western end, drained a 657 square mile watershed which dropped down into the rivers from mountains 500 feet above. At least once a year, one or both of the rivers overflowed into the streets sending the town's residents into a scurry to protect what they could of their homes and belongings.

2   Some of the floods were caused when heavy snows melted too quickly in the spring. And, others at any season of the year, when a heavy rain fell over the area. Whichever, floods were a fact of life to the nineteenth century residents of this industrial community in south Pennsylvania. And, in the late afternoon of May 31, 1889, people were gathered in the upper stories of their homes, waiting out the worst of it, just as they had done many times before.

3   Even as the residents of Johnstown prepared for their long wait, activity at the South Fork dam, just 14 miles above the city was frantic. The South Fork dam held back Lake Conemaugh, the pleasure lake of the South Fork Fishing and Hunting Club, a prestigious club which included such famed entrepreneurs as Andrew Carnegie and Henry Clay Frick on its membership rolls. Officials there feared the dam would fail. Since midmorning, they'd worked to avoid this, because they feared the consequences. (The lake was a little over two miles long, a little over a mile wide at its widest spot, and 60 feet deep at the dam itself.)

4   Among the attempts were efforts to add height to the dam, then to dig a second spillway to relieve pressure from the breast, and finally to release the heavy screens placed on the overflows to keep the stocked fish from escaping into the streams below. By a little after 3 p.m., when most people in Johnstown were settling in to be marooned for the evening, club officials and the laborers they recruited, as well as a good sized audience from the little community of South Fork just below the dam, watched in dumbfounded horror as the dam "just moved away."

5   Within the hour, a body of water which engineers at the time estimated moved into the valley with the force of Niagara Falls, rolled into Johnstown with 14 miles of accumulated debris, which included houses, barns, animals, people, dead and alive.

184

6   Those who saw it coming described it as a rolling hill of debris about 40 feet high and a half mile wide. But most only heard the thunderous rumble as it swept into the city to add Johnstown to a wake that already included bits and pieces of the communities of South Fork, Mineral Point, Woodvale and East Conemaugh.

7   Some continued to wait out the disaster in their houses, others were picked up by the flood wave for a wild ride through the town to the Pennsylvania Railroad Company's Stone Bridge where debris piled up 40 feet high and over 30 acres, then caught fire. Still others were shot down the Conemaugh River to die or be rescued at Nineveh, Bolivar or other communities downstream.

8   Six-year-old Gertrude Quinn Slattery was one of those caught in the flood wave. Years later she would write about her experience as she was hurled through the torrents on what she described as a "raft with a wet muddy mattress and bedding."

9   "I had great faith that I would not be abandoned," she wrote. "While my thoughts were thus engaged, a large roof came floating toward me with about twenty people on it. I cried and called across the water to them to help me. This, of course they could not do. The roof was big, and they were all holding on for dear life, feeling every minute that they would be tossed to death. While I watched I kept praying, calling, and begging someone to save me. Then I saw a man come to the edge, the others holding him and talking excitedly. I could see they were trying to restrain him but he kept pulling to get away which he finally did, and plunged into the swirling waters and disappeared.

10   Then his head appeared and I could see he was looking in my direction and I called, cried, and begged him to come to me. He kept going down and coming up, sometimes lost to my sight entirely, only to come up next time much closer to my raft. The water was now between fifteen and twenty feet deep.

11   "As I sat watching this man struggling in the water my mind was firmly fixed on the fact that he was my saviour. At last he reached me, drew himself up and over the side of the mattress and lifted me up. I put both arms around his neck and held on to him like grim death. Together we went downstream with the ebb and flow of the reflex to the accompaniment of crunching, grinding, gurgling, splashing and crying and moaning of many. After drifting about we saw a little white building, standing at the edge of the water, apparently where the hill began. At the window were two men with poles helping to rescue people floating by. I was too far out for the poles, so the men called:

12   'Throw that baby over to us.'

13   "My hero said: 'Do you think you can catch her?'"

14   "They said: 'We can try.'"

15   So Maxwell McAchren threw me across the water (some say twenty feet, others fifteen. I could never find out, so I leave it to your imagination. It was considered a great feat in the town, I know.)"

16   The response to the disaster was immediate as over 100 newspapers and magazines sent writers and illustrators to Johnstown to recount the story for the world.

17   Although not noted for their accuracy, the reports touched the hearts of the readers. People sent money, clothing, and food. Medial societies and doctors and hospitals sent medicines and bandages. Doctors left their practices and hurried to Johnstown to assist. Lumber was sent for rebuilding houses and businesses.

18   The dead were lined up in the morgues throughout the city and in the communities further down the Conemaugh River until some survivor in search of a loved one came to identify them.

[19] Although damaged itself, the Presbyterian Church on Main Street was the site of one of the morgues. A reporter from the New York *Evening Post* described the scene there.

[20] "The first floor has been washed out completely and the second, while submerged, was badly damaged, but not ruined. The walls, floors, and pews were drenched and the mud has collected on the mattings and carpets an inch deep. Walking is attended with much difficulty, and the undertakers and attendants, with arms bared, slide about the slippery surface at a tremendous rate. The chancel is filled with coffins, strips of muslin, boards and all undertaking accessories. Lying across the top of the pews are a dozen pine boxes each containing a victim of the flood. Printed cards are tacked to each. Upon them the sex and full description of the enclosed body is written with the name of the known."

[21] The living set up tents, often near to the places their former homes had been located and began what must have been perceived of as the impossible task of cleaning up and starting life again.

[22] Clara Barton and her Washington, D.C. contingent of the Red Cross built hotels for the people to live in and warehouses to store the many supplies the community received. By July 1, stores opened on the Main Street for business. The Cambria Iron Company reopened on June 6. Five years later, an observer would have been hard pressed to imagine the destruction in the valley on May 31, 1889.

[23] Yet, no city, county, or state legislation was enacted to protect people from similar disasters in the future. Suits were filed against the members of the South Fork Fishing and Hunting Club, but in keeping with the times, the courts viewed the dam break as an act of God, and no legal compensation was made to the survivors.

[24] The city would continue to suffer nuisance floods, with water in the streets and in people's basements especially in the spring. It would be another 47 years, and not until more property was destroyed and more lives lost, until some constructive efforts were made to control the waters that flowed through Johnstown.

Thinking and Responding to the Reading

1. What were the causes of the Johnstown Flood?
2. Describe what happened once the flood began.
3. Gertrude Quinn Slattery described how she was saved. She tells us that Maxwell McAchren was a hero. Do you agree? Explain.
4. Why did it take so many years before "constructive efforts were made to control the waters that flowed through Johnstown"?
5. Hutcheson uses many descriptive sentences so the reader can see in his/her mind's eye what the disaster was like. Pick three descriptions that allowed you to be there in your mind's eye.

Springboard for Composing

What are the benefits and risks of building homes and businesses on land where natural disasters occur? Consider, for example, those who have homes by the ocean, a lake or a river.

THE HUMAN MECHANISM IN RELATION TO HEALTH

Dr. Jean Broadhurst

Vocabulary Words

grist to the mill (par. 5)   putrefying (par. 8)   constitutions (par. 12)   caisson disease (par. 15)
submerged (par. 6)   vibrations (par. 10)   decompose (par. 13)   pellagra (par. 15)
corpuscles (par. 7)   predispose (par. 11)   convalescent (par. 14)   implication (par. 19)

1   For years the human body has been likened to an engine, a watch, or some similar mechanism. And old as the comparison is, it is difficult to find a better one. While this likeness fails if carried too far, there are many striking points of similarity, the most striking of which are listed below.

2   **Both Engine and Body are Complex Structures.**—Both the engine and the body are complicated structures composed of many different specialized parts—some of them highly specialized, such as the human eye and the carburetor in a motor car.

3   **Automatic Control.**—Some of the parts are so constructed as to make possible a remarkable degree of automatic control; this is well illustrated by the heat regulatory power of the skin and the thermostat device used in heating systems.

4   **Foundation Substances.**—There is a suggested similarity in the fact that in each there is a foundation substance modified to form various parts differing not only in use but in appearance, elasticity, hardness, etc. In the engine this foundation substance, iron, appears in such different forms as cast iron, wrought iron, and such an alloy as the carbonized iron called steel. In the body the foundation substance called protoplasm is modified into many different types of tissue; these are well illustrated by such familiar tissues as the skin, the muscle fibres composing lean meat, the glandular tissue making the bulk of liver and "sweetbreads," and bone, in which the lime deposits wholly change the appearance and elasticity of the protoplasmic foundation substance.

5   **Fuel Necessary.**—The likeness most often emphasized is with regard to fuel. Fuel is needed by the body and by the engine; and both must have suitable kinds of fuel and enough of it. This oldest and most familiar parallel is, strange to say, the one least often carried to its proper conclusion. No one would think of not choosing carefully the type of fuel to be supplied to an engine; this engine needs coal, that one uses oil, and another must have natural gas, or perhaps, gasoline. But with our own bodies we carelessly assume that "all is grist that comes to our mill." If there is any selection, it is too often based on cost or taste rather than fuel value; "anything to fill them up" is a vulgar expression of this same attitude. An engineer selects his fuel with care, refusing to buy coal he has found to yield large amounts of such waste residue as "slag" or clinkers; but we calmly go on supplying our more sensitive human mechanisms with unsuitable materials, as if mere bulk were the chief or sole consideration

6   In the body we often fail to relate properly the amount of fuel to the amount of work to be done. Those who care for furnaces or stoves constantly use such expressions as

"need but a low fire," "keep piling on coal," and "running the furnace for all it is worth, if it takes a ton a day." But we are just beginning to consciously adapt the amount and kind of body fuel to the body needs. We may unconsciously eat less in warm weather, but it is quite unusual to find people reducing the amount on a day when the physical demands are going to be less—for example, on stay-at-home holidays and Sundays. The sense of over-fullness after the Sunday dinner is too common a sensation to make further illustration necessary. The impossibility of doing full work on half fuel is apparent to anyone. We never attempt it with engines, but human beings try it all too often. A clearer recognition of the impossibility of continuing to yield any required output on insufficient food is necessary before we can get community support for satisfactory feeding of the submerged part of our population, where lack of fuel is evidenced by the large number of undersized, anemic or low-vitality individuals.

7   **The Need of Oxygen.**—The human body is like an engine in that plenty of oxygen must be provided to secure complete and economic utilization of the fuel. Motor car engines have a device for the proper admixture of air and fuel; in furnaces the air spaces between the coal are constantly filled with fresh air sucked in by the draft; or larger amounts of fresh air may be secured by forcing or pumping air with its necessary element, oxygen, through the burning bed of coal. In the human body this necessary oxygen is absorbed in the lungs and supplied to all parts of the body by the circulating blood. A lack in red corpuscles, the store houses of oxygen, decreases the amount that can be absorbed and carried, and therefore the amount distributed to the cells. In disease (e.g., pneumonia) the lung area available for absorption is decreased. Providing the proper amounts of oxygen may, therefore, be more of a problem than for engines.

8   **Disposal of Wastes.**—A sixth likeness is the necessity for prompt disposal of waste substances. The ashes must be removed, or they choke off the draft and clog the fire. In the human body it is just as essential that wastes should be eliminated (though the reasons are not exactly the same). Delayed intestinal elimination is harmful, because the blood in that region has increased opportunity to absorb certain poisonous wastes normally formed in the intestine; these poisons irritate and poison the cells to which they are carried, causing the headache, etc., characteristic of constipation. In constipation there is another danger that should be recognized. Bacteria in such held-back putrefying masses of food material may more easily invade the intestinal wall, causing serious diseases, e.g., appendicitis.

9   **Variations and Limits in Activity.**—A seventh likeness lies in the fact that it is possible to speed up the activities of the body and the engine. As stated before, increased output demands increased fuel, increased oxygen, and increased elimination of waste. Too much may be demanded in both cases. In machines we have more definite indications when the limit is reached; there is a positive limit to the number of revolutions a wheel can make, the piston rod breaks, etc. In the body we do not have the same marked evidences as warnings: bones do not crack as piston rods do; nerve stimuli may carry one far past the danger line of physiological breakdown without sounding a warning; a lack in the food supply can be made up temporarily at the expense of body substance, etc. Though delayed in evidence in the body, the cumulative results are the same in both cases; physiological speed-limit regulations, too, should be observed strictly under penalty of the law.

[10]   **Rest Necessary.**—The need of rest furnishes an eighth parallel. There is an ingenious machine for testing the strength of metals. Strips of the metals to be tested are put into this apparatus and made to vibrate rapidly—thousands of times per minute; the number of vibrations occurring before the strips break indicates the relative strength of the metals. The number of vibrations a strip can stand is directly related to the rate of vibration; for the rate affects the degree of recovery possible between vibrations. A single long rest period is also an aid, enabling a strip to stand a higher total of vibrations than it can without such a rest period. Strips breaking after vibration, hammering, etc., show very different broken surfaces from those shown by strips broken without such treatment. This is taken to indicate that a decided rearrangement of molecules takes place during action, and that normal arrangements are reassumed during periods of rest. Engineers and motor drivers realize the value of such rest periods for machines in avoiding hot boxes; that such rest periods actually prolong the life of essential parts of the car, engine, etc., is not so generally realized. The value of rest periods for the human machine cannot be questioned. We have always recognized the value of long unbroken rest periods (sleep at night), but investigations have also proven beyond a doubt the value of frequent short rests in delaying or preventing over-fatigue. The method one naturally pursues when he can control his own time is now scientifically supported and recommended for commercial and industrial life.

[11]   **Other Likenesses.**—There are many other minor likenesses. Accidents cut short the life of but a small percentage of both engines and human beings—less than 5 percent, probably. Too much inactivity or rest is not good for either, for both rust out. The engine does this literally, but the body suffers the same impairment through the accumulation of fat, the loss of elasticity and adaptability in muscles, heart and other blood vessels. Then, too, engines, like people, always have a weakest spot. There never was a second "one-hoss shay," and the people who likewise wear out all at once, and die of "old age," are almost as rare. Environmental influences are important for both human beings and machines. Excessive dampness and irritating gases may predispose to respiratory diseases and tuberculosis; these same agents may cause rust and corrosion in important parts of an engine.

[12]   The body-engine parallel is imperfect in two important respects: (1) The engine cannot repair itself. Its fuel is fuel only, and cannot serve as material for growth and repair. While the human body uses foods mainly for energy or power, certain of our foods also supply the essentials for growth and repair. (2) The second important difference is with regard to bacterial diseases. Poor construction, poor materials in machines may be likened to weak constitutions, low vitality, etc., in human beings, but there is not a complete parallel for disease, for the machine is not subject to bacterial invasion as human beings are.

[13]   **Bacterial Action.**—Bacteria may invade and weaken any organ of the body; less often they distribute themselves quite generally throughout the body. By their action they interfere greatly with health. They sometimes secrete poisons or toxins which irritate or injure the body; they may decompose our normal foods into irritating or non-nutritious substances; and they may actually disintegrate or destroy tissue, as in ulcers.

[14]   The results of such bacterial action are more serious than we realize. We "get well," but that does not tell the whole tale. Occasionally one seems better after an illness than before, due probably to the long rest, better food, or improved care taken during and

even after the convalescent period. Quite often, serious effects are more evident and persistent. One's chances for a long and vigorous life are lessened by every illness; for the few who seem uninjured (and we can never predict what their possibilities might have been without the illness) there are thousands who must "walk softly all their days."

[15] **Keeping Well.**—Keeping well, however, includes more than avoiding infection by bacteria. Such diseases as nervous affections, eye weakness, caisson disease, and pellagra may interfere just as completely with one's happiness and life work as diseases caused only by bacteria. Such diseases and decided predisposition to many other diseases often come from ignoring the laws that apply to man and machines both. Yet, it is not an uncommon thing to find an individual giving more real consideration and more time to the well-being of a motor cycle or a motor car than to his own health or to the health of members of his own family.

[16] This is not intentional, of course. It is because a poorly cared for machine stops running. It won't work. But the body machine braced up by stimulants, helped by high nervous tension, works on until we forget that there is "a limit to what flesh and blood can stand."

[17] The body must be fed, exercised, rested, and cared for to avoid any predisposition to disease. Its environment must be made safe and healthful. The environment includes the next-door neighbor who has smallpox; water from the watershed polluted by the typhoid carrier on a Pullman train; milk from a farm four states away where septic sore throat prevails; the smoky pall in the air which delays the germicidal action of the sun 90 millions of miles away; in fact, as Sedgwick once defined it, "Our environment is that part of the universe that lies outside ourselves." To control wholly such an environment is a mighty task.

[18] **Personal and Community Hygiene.**—The relation between the individual and the environmental factors that may affect his health is very close and also very far reaching. It is often difficult to say where personal hygiene ends and public health begins. What is a matter of personal hygiene to you individually may become an important phase of sanitation when you are responsible for the health and food of a family or a group of school children. You, from habit, never drink from a public drinking cup; but the removal of public drinking cups from the school attended by your children is a matter of public health or sanitation.

[19] To live up to the implication of the slogan, "Woman's place is in the home," would take her out of it. She is responsible for safeguarding in every way the well-being of the members of that home. She becomes thereby interested in pure water, safe milk, warm lunches for school children, health examinations for the waiters who serve the older boys' downtown luncheon, the enforcement of quarantine for the lawless cases of measles next door, the flies in the meat market and the piles of refuse at its back door, the tubercular clerk in the laundry who folds articles ready for deliver, the broken sewer pipe on the hillside within fly-distance of the house, the proposed local enactment requiring health examination for domestic helpers, and the election of the mayoralty candidate who favors school nurses and free school clinics. The hygienic interests of the individual, the home and the community are essentially one and the same.

Thinking and Responding to the Reading

1.   This article describes the human body by extended analogy, yet Broadhurst mentions two differences between humans and machines. Explain the differences she describes.
2.   Based on the descriptions of hygiene and the role of women, when do you think this article was written?
3.   Are there any parts of the analogy that you think don't hold true? Which one(s)? Why?   Are there any parts of the analogy that helped you to understand better how your body works? Which one(s)? Why?
4.   What are some ways that you can draw an analogy from two unrelated objects that are considered part of technology, for example, the mind and computer chips?

Springboard for Composing

Think of an area where we have a new understanding of the human body and how to care for it that is not described in this article. How has this new understanding been important in how you care for your body? Explain.

THE BAMBOO GROVE BY THE TANSHUI RIVER IN TAIPEI

Hai Tao Tang

Vocabulary Words

bamboo (par. 1)	manifest (par. 3)	vicariously (par. 5)	introspection (par. 6)
Taipei (par. 1)	boring (par. 3)	pensive (par. 6)	continuous (par. 7)
serenity (par. 1)	vitality (par. 4)	perseverance (par. 6)	solitude (par. 7)
cicadas (par. 2)	diligence (par. 4)		

1   I like bamboo. For three and a half years, I took a walk in the bamboo grove by the Tanshui River in Taipei at dusk, almost every day, except when the weather was terribly bad, or when I had an important engagement such as tutoring a high school student or attending an important party. An hour-long walk in the grove provided me with great serenity and a time to reflect on myself and the things that happened during the day.

2   I like nature better than human society. Though at times I went there with a friend, most of the time I went there alone. While walking, I was in no mood for talking. I enjoyed listening to the soothing sounds of the bamboo leaves rustling in the wind, the chirping sounds of the returning birds, the shrilling sounds of mating cicadas and the rippling sounds of the river water.

3   At those times, I felt peace and harmony inside. At dusk, the color of the sky changed rapidly; the slanting sun's golden gleam would shine upon the river and make the water glitter, but soon the clouds near the sun would turn to orange, rose, and then gradually fade into purplish grey. In the meantime, these colorful clouds would manifest themselves in all kinds of strange shapes, allowing me to fantasize with imagination. In springtime, when the frozen earth began to thaw, grass started boring through the hard ground, and the bamboos became greener and more moist. After a heavy rainfall, the bamboo shoots would mushroom right in front of my eyes. What a sight! And the smell of life they gave forth was pleasant and refreshing, beyond any verbal description. I like bamboo.

4   I first noticed this place in the spring of my freshman year in college. Since then it soon became the favorite place for me to linger about. That spring my health improved quickly after a long illness, for which I had been discharged from military service the previous year. It was the vitality of nature that helped me to regain my health and my self-confidence. I could spend half an hour watching old men on boats fishing, marveling at the remarkable skill of these fishermen in catching fish and the strong will of the fish struggling to break away from the fishing line. When I walked on the path in the bamboo grove, I took great care not to step on earth worms, ants or other tiny insects. I admired them for their diligence and pitied them for their hardships in life. We were all a part of the great nature, after all.

5   Summer time brought many children out to swim in the river, and I enjoyed with them vicariously. The "gu-gu" sounds of frogs were also amusing. Obviously these poor musicians did not care whether their music was pleasing to human ears; they just enjoyed

themselves. A man in his late thirties or early forties also came to the grove every day, and we nodded to each other whenever we met on our ways. He always carried a bamboo flute and occasionally played with it; the sound of it was somewhat saddening. He often chanted poems to himself, but in most cases he was just repeating the same poem, composed by Wang Han, a poet in the eighth century:

> Vintage wine in a jade cup, glittering at night
> I want to keep drinking, but the guitars on the horse back were calling the fight.
> Don't laugh at me should I lie drunken on the battle ground,
> Since antiquity, how many actually returned from war-bound?

He must have been a soldier away from home. I felt sad but didn't have the heart to ask because I was one, too.

6   In the fall my mood was generally more pensive. The grass turned yellowish and dry. The bamboos would shed some of their shells, and these shells would tumble in the wind, like wanderers with nowhere to go. Autumn was the time for reservation and perseverance. A brisk walk would energize my body and clear my mind. The poem-chanting, lonely man stopped coming while I kept my daily routine, as if visiting an ailing old friend. Observing from a distance the bustling vehicles and people going one way or the other on the Ying Bridge, which was built to cross the Tanshui River, was a sobering thing: human lives did not differ from those of the busy ants and bees, after all. I would then heave a sigh. I was one of them too; I needed some time for introspection.

7   Winter time in Taipei is characterized by days of continuous rain. I went to the grove only when the weather allowed me, usually twice or three times a week. There was no one else roaming. In solitude, I felt I was ever stronger standing in the cold wind. Only the bamboos remained there solemnly; they were my true friends. I like bamboo.

8   This was over forty years ago, and I was then in my early twenties. Things have changed drastically since that time. When I revisited the site in the summer of 1983, I could not find a single bamboo there. All the bamboos had been cut down, and the entire place had been turned into a training ground of a driving school. I regretted very much the change that had taken place. But who knows? I might be wrong. Maybe youngsters nowadays do not need a quiet place to walk around and do some soul-searching. They may prefer driving around in a fancy car instead.

Thinking and Responding to the Reading

1.   Why does the author like to walk in the bamboo grove? He gives several reasons throughout the essay. Be sure to mention all of them.

2.   The author uses many of the five senses to give the reader a picture of his experiences. What are some of these? Do you find them effective?

3.   In paragraph 5, the author refers to the old man singing the 8th century poem by Wang Han. Explain the meaning of the poem line by line. Explain how the poem relates to the men's lives.

4.   In paragraph 7, the author says that the bamboos "were my true friends." What evidence does Tang give to support this statement.

5.   In the last paragraph, the author discusses the change to the bamboo grove. What are his two reactions? Which one do you think he believes more? Why?

6.   Are the bamboo trees a metaphor of his life? Explain.

Springboard for Composing

List some of the benefits the author derived from walking in the bamboo grove. Would you consider some of these to be biological needs? What do you think the effect upon him was when he found a parking lot in the grove's place forty years later? Think about a place in nature you like to use as a retreat, explaining what you do and the benefits you derive.

MARIJUANA: WEIGHING THE EVIDENCE

Carl Wellman

Vocabulary Words

reliable (par. 2)	illusion (par. 4)	congenial (par. 7)
discount (par. 2)	profound (par. 4)	endure (par. 8)
neurosis (par. 2)	justification (par. 5)	inhibit (par. 9
psychosis (par. 2)	skepticism (par. 5)	ample (par. 9)
partisans (par. 3)	intrinsically (par. 6)	infer (par. 10)
claims (par. 3)	hedonism (par. 6)	crucial (par. 11)

1   My own belief is that, everything considered, marijuana as used in our country under present conditions is bad.   Although I have come to this conclusion after considerable investigation and careful reasoning, I am far from claiming to be certain of the truth of my negative evaluation.

2   One of the major difficulties in reaching any reliable evaluation of marijuana is that one must discount the many exaggerated assertions made about it. Those who wish to discourage the use of marijuana too often paint it in the darkest possible colors. They assert that it is addictive just as heroin is, that it frequently causes violent antisocial acts, and that it is a direct cause of mental illness. It seems to me that these claims are simply not supported by the evidence. It is misleading to classify marijuana with narcotics like opium or heroin, because its continued use produces neither tolerance nor physical dependence. There is no convincing sociological or psychological evidence that smoking marijuana arouses violent emotions and often leads to acts like assault, murder or rape. Nor is there any real reason to believe that the use of marijuana can transform a normal person into someone in a state of neurosis or psychosis.

3   On the other hand, the alleged virtues of marijuana seem greatly exaggerated, too. Partisans of pot often assert that it vastly increases the communication between human beings, that it gives knowledge of the meaning of reality and the nature of oneself, and that it heightens creativity. I am suspicious of these assertions for three reasons. First, such strong claims should be accepted only if they are backed up with strong evidence, but this is seldom even attempted. The usual strategy is to say that anyone who has smoked pot knows them to be true by firsthand experience and that the person who does not use marijuana simply lacks the experience to make any rational judgment on the matter.   But the reliability of an experience is not, I believe, to be determined by the experience itself; the experience of seeing a mirage in the desert appears thoroughly real when judged entirely on its own terms.

4   Second, certain characteristics of the experience produced by marijuana could easily explain the illusion of communication, knowledge and creativity. The experience is strikingly different from ordinary experience; sensations and emotions are much more intense, and fantasy increases markedly. Because the impact of the experience is great

and because judgment is impaired by intoxication, the user of marijuana imagines that the experience is particularly profound and reliable.

5   Third, there is a limited amount of evidence against these assertions. Observations of pot parties suggest that individuals are absorbed in their own experiences and not sharing their thoughts, feelings, or activities on anything but the most superficial level. Alleged truths discovered with the aid of marijuana often conflict with our specific knowledge, and we have no rational justification for rejecting the reliability of science. Objective critical evaluations of literary and artistic works produced under the influence of marijuana indicate that these works are of lower, not higher, quality than those produced by the same people at times when they did not use drugs. Although none of these three reasons is decisive, together they seem to justify skepticism with regard to these claims on behalf of marijuana.

6   After exaggerated assertions have been discounted, the serious business of responsible evaluation remains. What are we to say of the experience of smoking marijuana? After a little practice, most people find this experience very pleasant. The Le Dain Commission concluded that a major factor in the contemporary marijuana explosion in the adult population as well as among young people is the simple pleasure of the experience. For example, a teacher and mother of four testified, "When I smoke grass I do it in the same social way that I take a glass of wine at dinner or have a drink at a party. I do not feel that it is one of the great and beautiful experiences of my life; I simply feel that it is pleasant." Marijuana typically produces an experience free from anxiety, unusual in interesting ways, including intense sensations and emotions, and stimulating to the imagination. For these reasons it is no exaggeration to say that the experience is *very* pleasant. Since I believe that pleasure is intrinsically good, I conclude that the experience is good for its own sake. I do not conclude, however, that it is very good for its own sake. Why not? It seems to me that traditional hedonism has misinterpreted the nature of valued experience because it has emphasized the role of feeling and ignored the element of significance in such experiences. If an experience feels good it is good (judged in itself and apart from its consequences), but the intensity of the feeling is no reliable measure of the degree of value. Most of the value or disvalue of our experiences comes from their significance or meaning. The experience of receiving an A on an exam feels good, but most of its value comes from the awareness that this grade is the product of past effort and one step toward passing the course, earning a degree, and pursing a vocation. Only as one is aware of the place an experience has in the larger context of one's own life and the lives of others does the experience have any great value or disvalue. Because the experiences of smoking marijuana tend to be isolated from the mainstream of the user's life and to contribute very little to achieving personal goals or to advancing the welfare of others, these experiences, although very pleasant, are relatively meaningless. In my judgment, the experience of using marijuana usually has a genuine but very limited value.

7   For some young people, however, the experience of smoking marijuana is far from trivial. The use of marijuana represents a rejection of the competitive work ethic of their parents and the adoption of a very different ideal of life in which work should be intrinsically rewarding and not a mere means to material success. For them the good life consists more in shared enjoyments than in wealth and status gained at the expense of their competitors. Thus for many members of the drug subculture in our country, the use

of marijuana offers far more than immediate and trivial pleasure; it provides a highly meaningful pleasure because it signifies both protest against an alien way of life and participation in a more congenial and more morally acceptable community. Nevertheless, since most of those who use marijuana do not belong to this drug subculture, it remains true that for most people the experience of smoking marijuana lacks this degree of intrinsic value.

8   What of the consequences of using marijuana? These vary considerably from case to case, but after predictions of the direst consequences and promises of easy salvation are discounted, two considerations remain before us. First, the use of marijuana releases one from the pressures of society and the anxieties deep within oneself. This immediate result is genuinely good, but it must be considered in the light of further consequences. Sometimes the use of marijuana will enable a person to live through a period of crisis or to endure a harsh environment without breaking down emotionally. It can sometimes supply a temporary relief from tensions that prepares the individual to return to reality and to cope with it. So far, so good. In other cases persons who turn to marijuana become psychologically dependent upon the drug. They may retreat into their dream world and become unable to face up to the problems they must solve if they are to live a fully satisfactory life. Although these bad consequences probably occur in a relatively small minority of users, they are serious enough to constitute a real and considerable danger. It seems to me that the release afforded by the use of marijuana is sometimes beneficial and sometimes harmful; that the benefits are probably more common than the harms; but that the harm, when it does occur, is so great that it outweighs the benefits. On balance, I think it better to find less dangerous means to escape, or change, the harsh realities of our lives.

9   Second, marijuana is said to be a steppingstone to highly undesirable drugs like heroin or LSD. There is nothing necessary or inevitable in this progression. The person who uses marijuana is not psychologically compelled to go on to use heroin or LSD, and in fact the majority of those who smoke pot never even try these more dangerous drugs. Nevertheless, a significant minority does progress from marijuana to heroin or LSD, and I believe that their use of marijuana is one factor that predisposes them to use these other drugs. This seems to be so for several reasons. Most people in our society have been educated—or brainwashed—so that they are strongly inhibited about the use of drugs. When a person breaks through these inhibitions sufficiently to use marijuana, his inhibitions against the use of other drugs are also weakened. In addition, those who use drugs often form groups, even subcultures, within our society. Thus a person who begins to use marijuana may become associated with other drug users, some of whom use the much stronger drugs. This community of drug users provides ample opportunity and some social pressure at least to try other drugs.

10   Finally, because the sale and possession of marijuana are illegal, those who use marijuana must obtain their supply through the black market. In times when anti-marijuana laws are strongly enforced and supply is consequently diminished, there is evidence to suggest that users may turn to other available drugs—often more potent and harmful ones. The same persons who peddle marijuana often push heroin and LSD also. Moreover, it is to their personal advantage to encourage their customers to progress to the stronger drugs. The heroin addict is a sure customer, and the user of more potent drugs can sometimes be charged very high prices. Since I believe that the use of marijuana

leads, in a significant minority of cases, to the use of heroin or LSD, and since I believe that these drugs are far worse than marijuana, I infer that the use of marijuana is, in this respect, undesirable.

[11]   Although the experience of using marijuana seems to have some positive value in itself, the use of marijuana seems to have more bad consequences than good ones. Everything considered, it seems to me that the use of marijuana under present conditions in our country is bad. The qualification "under present conditions" may well be crucial. That marijuana is sometimes a steppingstone to the use of more dangerous drugs seems to be due to the fact that users tend to form semi-isolated groups and that it can be obtained only on the black market. Both of these facts about our society probably stem in large measure from the fact that the use of marijuana is forbidden by law.

[12]   It is also possible that social conditions lie behind the frequency with which users of marijuana become psychologically dependent upon it. The fact that its use is socially condemned and practiced in groups of people who are often rather alienated from our society may be an important factor in turning users away from reality and making it hard for them to return to the normal pattern of life in our society. The analogy with alcohol, so often used in discussing drugs, may be enlightening here. Quite possibly the use of alcohol, whatever one may say of it today, was less good or more bad during Prohibition. The quality of booze was inferior, sometimes dangerously so, because much was made at home by those with limited knowledge and the rest was manufactured by people out for a quick profit. Again, those who drank during Prohibition tended to be the least law-abiding citizens, and buying liquor contributed to the financial resources of criminal organizations whose other activities were clearly harmful to society. Just as the repeal of Prohibition eliminated these socially conditioned disvalues of alcohol, so reforming the drug laws might significantly alter the harmful consequences of using marijuana. The lesson to be learned, however, is not that marijuana is good. The most that can properly be inferred is that marijuana as used under present conditions in our country really is bad, and that some of its badness is conditioned by social factors. Until these factors change, I will continue to believe, somewhat tentatively, that the use of marijuana is undesirable.

Thinking and Responding to the Reading

1.   What is Wellman's argument, his overall thesis?

2.   List the evidence Wellman gives to support his argument. List the claims that Wellman discounts. Do you find his reasons for discounting them sound?

3.   Paraphrase the meaning of the lines found in paragraph 6: "Marijuana typically produces an experience free from anxiety…I do not conclude, however, that it is very good for its own sake."

4.   Explain whether Wellman uses inductive or deductive reasoning. Use the definition of induction and deduction to explain your answers.

5.   Make a side-by-side list of the positive and negative effects of marijuana according to this article. On which side of this argument do you stand? Can you add additional points to it? Make another list using some other drug.

Springboard for Composing

Explain what Wellman means when he writes regarding marijuana, "Most of the value or disvalue of our experiences comes from their significance or meaning." Decide if you agree with Wellman. Use a personal value you hold to support your answer.

A FABLE FOR TOMORROW

Rachel Carson

Vocabulary Words

harmony (par. 1)	stricken (par. 3)	counterparts (par. 9)
blight (par. 3)	moribund (par. 4)	specter (par. 9)
maladies (par. 3)	withered (par. 6)	stark (par. 9)

1 There was once a town in the heart of America where all life seemed to live in harmony with its surrounds. The town lay in the midst of a checkerboard of prosperous farms, with fields of rain and hillsides of orchards where, in spring, white clouds of bloom drifted above the green fields. In autumn, oak and maple and birch set up a blaze of color that flamed and flickered across a backdrop of pines. Then foxes barked in the hills and deer silently crossed the fields, half hidden in the mists of the fall mornings.

2 Along the roads, laurel, viburnum and alder, great ferns and wildflowers delighted the traveler's eye through much of the year. Even in winter the roadsides were places of beauty, where countless birds came to feed on the berries and on the seed heads of the dried weeds rising above the snow. The countryside was, in fact, famous for the abundance and variety of its bird life, and when the flood of migrants was pouring through in spring and fall people traveled from great distances to observe them. Others came to fish the streams, which flowed clear and cold out of the hills and contained shady pools where trout lay. So it had been from the days many years ago when the first settlers raised their houses, sank their wells, and built their barns.

3 Then a strange blight crept over the area and everything began to change. Some evil spell had settled on the community: mysterious maladies swept the flock of chickens; the cattle and the sheep sickened and died. Everywhere was a shadow of death. The farmers spoke of much illness among their families. In the town the doctors had become more and more puzzled by new kinds of sickness appearing among their patients. There had been several sudden and unexplained deaths not only among adults but even among children, who would be stricken suddenly while at play and die within a few hours.

4 There was a strange stillness. The birds, for example—where had they gone? Many people spoke of them, puzzled and disturbed. The feeding stations in the backyards were deserted. The few birds seen anywhere were moribund; they trembled violently and could not fly. It was a spring without voices. On the mornings that had once throbbed with the dawn chorus of robins, catbirds, doves, jays, wrens, and scores of other bird voices there was now no sound; only silence lay over the fields and woods and marsh.

5 On the farms the hens brooded, but no chicks hatched. The farmers complained that they were unable to raise any pigs—the litters were small and the young survived only a few days. The apple trees were coming into bloom but no bees droned among the blossoms, so there was no pollination and there would be no fruit.

6 The roadsides, once so attractive, were now lined with browned and withered vegetation as though swept by fire. These, too, were silent, deserted by all living things.

200

Even the streams were now lifeless. Anglers no longer visited them, for all the fish had died.

7   In the gutters under the eaves and between the shingles of the roofs, a white granular powder still showed a few patches; some weeks before it had fallen like snow upon the roofs and the lawns, the fields and the streams.

8   No witchcraft, no enemy action had silenced the rebirth of new life in this stricken world. The people had done it themselves.

9   This town does not actually exist, but it might easily have a thousand counterparts in America or elsewhere in the world. I know of no community that has experienced all the misfortunes I describe. Yet every one of these disasters has actually happened somewhere, and many real communities have already suffered a substantial number of them. A grim specter has crept upon us almost unnoticed, and this imagined tragedy may easily become a stark reality we all shall know.

Thinking and Responding to the Reading

1.   What is a fable? Why does Carson title the essay "A Fable for Tomorrow"?
2.   What is the impression you get after reading the first two paragraphs?
3.   Carson uses contrasts throughout the essay. What are some of these contrasts? Why does she use them?
4.   Although Carson doesn't tell the readers what "strange blight crept over the area," she implies it. What do you think caused the change? What evidence makes you think this?
5.   This essay is full of description. Pick out three descriptive passages that you think are particularly effective. Paraphrase each.
6.   Compare Rachel Carson's prediction of the "imagined tragedy" to Chief Seattle's characterization of the white man's disregard for the earth and its creatures. (Seattle states, "Every part of this earth is sacred to my people.")

Springboard for Composing

Compose a list of the effects of the "evil spell [that] had settled on the community." Do we now have "safe" chemicals to be used on the likes of crops and lawns, or even ponds and lakes? Are alternate methods being sought or practiced? Tell about a time when you used chemicals to try to influence nature.

RUBE GOLDBERG

Patent Fan

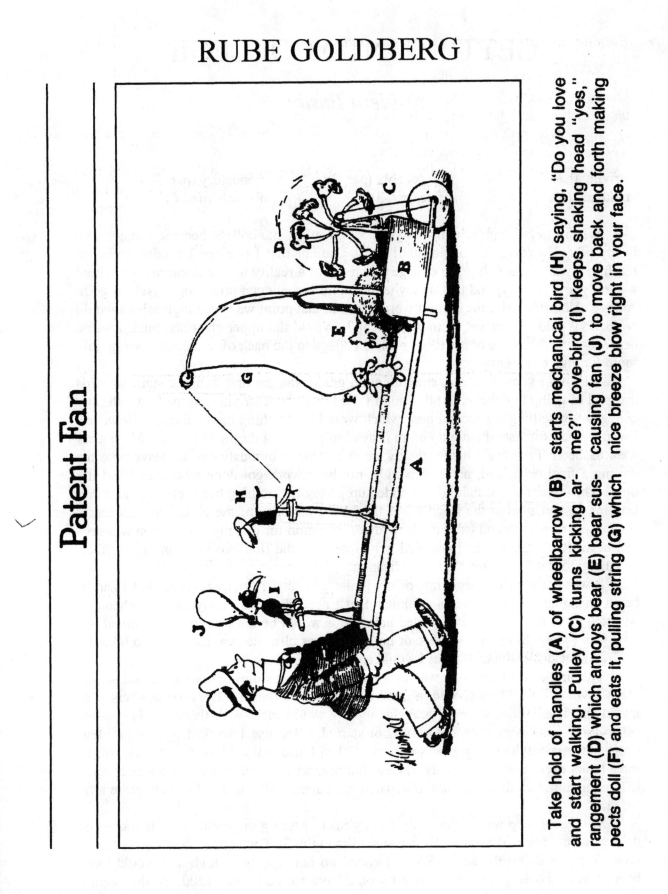

Take hold of handles (A) of wheelbarrow (B) and start walking. Pulley (C) turns kicking arrangement (D) which annoys bear (E) bear suspects doll (F) and eats it, pulling string (G) which starts mechanical bird (H) saying, "Do you love me?" Love-bird (I) keeps shaking head "yes," causing fan (J) to move back and forth making nice breeze blow right in your face.

GETTING INTO COLLEGE

Student Essay

Vocabulary Words

striving (par. 2)	regrettably (par. 2)	mandatory (par. 5)
indulged (par. 2)	fate (par. 3)	obstacle (par. 6)

1   When I began high school four years ago, getting into college became a major goal in my life. However, it was not until I was a junior that I realized I needed a plan to reach my goal. In eighth grade college was more of a reality for me because high school was only a year away, and this was when I should have begun preparing myself to go to college. Unfortunately, the biggest worry I had at that point was what high school would be like. Would the classes be more difficult? Would the upper classmen think I was a nerd? During this stage of my life, I pushed college to the back of my mind, leaving only room for high school matters.

2   Whether I knew it or not, entering ninth grade was the first stepping stone towards my goal of going to college. At this point I did think about striving for the best—the Ivy colleges—or settling for second best, which would be anything below them. However, I would study for tests the night before instead of preparing during the week. My papers were dashed off the night before they were due, which obviously did not leave time for writing a final draft, and, not surprisingly, my homework got done whenever I had the time. This system I had indulged in ended up giving me nothing but average grades and learning less than what the teacher had taught the majority of the class. My academic standing during ninth and tenth grade made the decision for me; my only option was second best. Regrettably, I had not tried my hardest for the first two years in high school, and my grades reflected my lack of dedication.

3   It was not until the beginning of my junior year that I finally realized that I had to begin changing my study habits. I knew that I needed to start studying in a scheduled way and go to my teachers if I needed help. This would be the year that determined my fate: was I going to get into college or not? This was also the year that I had to take the SAT and decide to which colleges I would apply.

4   The first step of my plan was to improve my grades during my junior and senior years—which I did. I succeeded in this by going to receive help from the teachers who taught the classes that were difficult for me. I would meet with them regularly after school and sometimes even before school started. Because I worked on my problem spots and repaired them, my grades improved. But I also learned how to set aside two to three hours every evening to study, review and prepare my homework. I no longer studied the night before for a test, and I prepared my papers with plenty of time to write a final draft.

5   My second step was to get ready for my SAT. During my junior year, it was mandatory that my class take the PSAT, a test similar to the SAT which would allow us to see how we might do on the actual SAT. I ended up not scoring as high as I would have liked. I earned only 1015 points when I should have scored at least 1200. At this point I

became very nervous about whether I would get into college at all owing to my poor performance, so I decided to enroll in the Princeton Review, a course designed to allow college-entry level students to improve upon their PSAT. The course did help me to improve my PSAT scores and prepared me for the actual SAT. When I finally took it, I scored 1210 points. As a result, I was accepted at eight of the ten schools that I wished to attend.

6   Now that I am finally in college and have reached the goal I set for myself in eighth grade, I feel as though I can conquer just about any obstacle that gets in my way; however, without a plan, I would not have gotten as far as I have. Because I followed up on the system that I set up for myself, I have found the courage to pursue my goals. Nothing will stop me from achieving what I set out to accomplish. In fact, I can take my planning experience with me through college and apply it towards my far more difficult study needs!

Thinking and Responding to the Reading

1.   What lesson does this student learn about striving to achieve a goal in life?
2.   What are some of the setbacks that this student encounters along the way and how does he/she remedy them?
3.   Why does this student think that preparing for the SAT is useful? Is his/her prediction correct?
4.   What obstacles do you face while studying and managing your time while in college? What plans do you have for overcoming them?

Springboard for Composing

In paragraph 4, the student writes about how he/she consciously implemented a plan to enter college. What tool, system or program do you think you will use to achieve your academic goals? First, sketch the general points (your general plan), and then add the details.

DRILL PRESS CLAMPING TIP

from *Woodsmith*

Vocabulary Words

C-clamp (par. 1)   ribs (par. 1)   punch (par. 2)

1   Whenever I want to clamp a work-piece to my drill press with C-clamps, the ribs that are cast into the underside of the table are always in the way. The ribs are spaced so they're always right where I want the clamp to be. And they're so narrow that if I try to clamp to the edge of one, the clamp slips off as it's tightened. To solve this problem, I cut and glued some scrap blocks to fit between the ribs.

2   Because I occasionally use the slots in the table, I didn't want to permanently fix the blocks to the table. So I just put a few drops of glue from a hot glue gun on each scrap. Then I stuck the blocks between the ribs. (You could also use double-sided carpet tape to mount the blocks.) When I want to remove the blocks, I insert a small punch through the slot and tap them out, or pry them off with a screwdriver.

Thinking and Responding to the Reading

1.   State the main idea of the passage
2.   Paraphrase the author's method of solving his problem.

Springboard for Composing

The drill press clamping tip provides a simple yet very effective way of solving a problem. Think of a time when you had to figure out a "quick-fix" way of solving a problem. Explore beyond traditional machinery with its accompaning tools and consider a program or system that you took your time to customize in order to accomplish your goal.

Drill Press Clamping

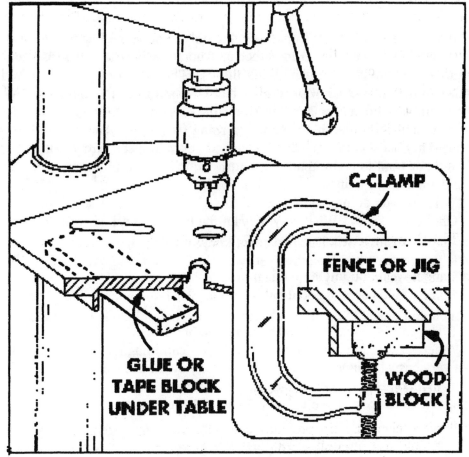

CHAIN SAWS AND CHIGGER BITES

Marie Cobb

Vocabulary Words

crosscut (par. 1)   respectable (par. 13)   thoroughly (par. 23)
apprehensive (par. 11)   acquisition (par. 20)   brainwashed (par. 23)
relative (par. 12)   chigger (par. 21)

1   As I was growing up in Tennessee, the only experience I had with tools was on my grandparents' farm with my grandfather and uncles who thought girls—and especially blind girls—had no business using such things. The most I ever was allowed to do was pull one end of a crosscut saw or screw a black walnut in a vice to hold it while I cracked it with a hammer. Power tools of any kind were certainly off limits.

2   Bright and early one hot summer morning five or six years ago the telephone rang and I heard my dad ask in a voice that sounded very chipper, "Are you alive?"

3   I did not want to admit that I was sitting in my bed drinking my first cup of tea and reading a good book. I answered, "Certainly."

4   "What are you doing today?" he asked.

5   "Oh, I don't know. What do you want me to do?" I asked with no idea of what the answer might be since with Dad one never knew.

6   "If you haven't had breakfast yet, why don't you come over, and we'll have a bite and talk about what you might do this morning."

7   I said I would come in about half an hour after I had taken a shower and dressed.

8   "You don't need to do all that. Just put on some old clothes and come on now. I'm hungry. The gate is open." And he hung up the phone.

9   While we were having fruit and cereal, you can imagine my delight when he asked me in a very casual manner if I had ever learned how to use a chain saw. Of course I had to admit that somehow I never had but that I would like to since I shared his love of gadgets. "Well as soon as we're finished here I'll teach you. A girl ought to know how to use a chain saw," he said.

10   When we went out to the wood garage, he got out a contraption that looked like a vice on legs and took a tree branch about four feet long and about the size of my forearm and secured it with the clamps. He showed me the controls and how to place the blade exactly on the spot I wanted to cut before pushing the power switch. Then, he told me to put my hands on top of his while he made the first cut.

11   As those of you who are familiar with my father know he was blind from birth, but what you may not know is so was I. Therefore, I was just a wee bit apprehensive since chain saws are so noisy and neither of us could see what we were doing, although I knew he wouldn't have been showing me how to do something that wasn't safe, and besides I didn't want him to think I was a coward.

12   After he had done a couple of pieces it was my turn, and I discovered that it was great fun to zip through pieces of wood with such relative ease. When he was sure I

could handle the saw competently he said, "Now over here I have a big stack of these limbs you can cut up for me to burn in my fireplace."

13 In a couple of hours I had what I thought was a very respectable pile of wood, of which I was quite proud.

14 Getting the wood cut up was a good and productive thing to do, but the most important thing that happened that day was that I gained a little more confidence in my ability to use power tools.

15 On the following Saturday I happened to mention to Dad that I knew where there was a lot more wood about the size of the limbs we had cut earlier in the week. He wanted to know where they were, and I told him in the woods a block or so from his house.

16 "Show me," he said, and off we went.

17 By the middle of the afternoon when I was tired and bathed in perspiration I wasn't so sure it had been such a good idea to tell him about the dead branches in the woods.

18 I had dragged many long pieces of wood back to his driveway, and some of them were too long and heavy for me to handle by myself. Of course Dad had a solution for that problem.

19 "Take this little hand saw over and cut the long ones into more manageable pieces," he said. I said somewhat sheepishly that I had never been able to use one of those successfully. "Nonsense. I know exactly what you are doing wrong," he said. Of course he really did. I had always put too much pressure on the saw instead of letting the blade just ride along the top of the wood until it caught on its own.

20 After several more trips to the woods I finished cutting the wood. Later that night I discovered that I had made another acquisition that day besides learning to use a saw.

21 I woke up itching in several places, and realized from past experiences that I was covered with chigger bites. It was definitely time to get out the nail polish to seal off the little holes they had made in my skin for breathing purposes.

22 Using a hand saw proved to be much harder work than using an electric chain saw, but I was glad to have the knowledge and to have learned a new skill. Sometimes it is necessary to remind myself that blindness is not the reason why I can't or don't do certain things. It is simply that I haven't tried yet, and there is the big difference.

23 We are all so thoroughly brainwashed concerning the so-called limitations of blindness that we have to guard against not allowing ourselves the freedom to accept all the exciting challenges the world has to offer.

Thinking and Responding to the Reading

1. Define perception.
2. Early in the narrative, Marie Cobb is asked by her father to learn how to use a chain saw. Do you find this unusual given that she is both a female and blind? If so, which do you think is more unusual—being female or being blind? Explain why.
3. Summarize how one can learn a new task without vision.
4. Is this story written inductively or deductively? Explain your reasoning.

5. In paragraph 22, Cobb writes: "Sometimes it is necessary to remind myself that blindness is not the reason why I can't or don't do certain things. It is simply that I haven't tried yet, and there is the big difference." Do you have a limitation that has prevented you from trying new things? If so, what is it and what is it that you have shied away from attempting?

Springboard for Composing

Think of a time when you had to use a tool, system or program for the first time. What were you attempting to achieve? Discuss how you went about it. Did you encounter problems? How did you resolve them?

from *ANATOMY OF A MURDER*

Robert Traver

Vocabulary Words

irked (par. 4)   catharsis (par. 8)   rhetoric (par. 9)   abstractions (par. 9)
blithely (par. 4)   anarchy (par. 8)   buttress (par. 9)   liberty (par. 9)
layman (par. 4)   Magna Carta (par. 9)   lofty (par. 9)   justice (par. 9)
bristling (par. 7)   archaic (par. 9)

1   "It's a pretty unscientific thing," my man the Lieutenant said thoughtfully. "This insanity business is pretty damned unscientific."

2   "Why do you say that?"

3   "Well, we can't prove insanity without a medical expert, you tell me. Yet you and I have already decided I was insane, we know that we're going to plead insanity—you tell me it's the only legal defense I've got. And even I can see that now. In other words you a mere lawyer and I a dumb soldier have between us decided that I was medically and legally insane. Having decided that, we must now go out and shop around for a medical expert to confirm our settled conclusion. Yet you tell me an ordinary medical doctor won't do." The Lieutenant shook his head. "It all sounds damned unscientific to me."

4   It irked me unaccountably to hear this Mister Cool so blithely undertake to criticize my profession. It was all right if a member of the family did, but for a perfect stranger... "Lieutenant," I said, "the easiest thing in the world is for a layman to poke fun at the law. Lawyers and the law are sitting ducks for ridicule and always have been. The average layman may in all his lifetime collide with but one small branch of the law, which he understands but imperfectly. He usually knows whether he won or lost. He may also remember that Dickens, grumbling through Mr. Bumble, once called the law an ass. So for him all the law is henceforth an ass, and, overnight, he becomes its severest critic."

5   "But I still don't get it," the Lieutenant said. "On this score at least, the law looks like a prime ass."

6   "Granted," I said. "But the point I wish to make is that from this people may not safely proceed to damn all law. You of all men should be grateful that the massive structure known as the law really exists. It so happens that it represents your only hope."

7   "How do you mean?" the Lieutenant said, bristling.

8   "I'll try to tell you," I said. "Mr. Bumble was only partly right. He was only part right because, for all its lurching and shambling imbecilities, the law—and only the law—is what keeps our society from bursting apart at the seams, from becoming a snarling jungle. While the law is not perfect, God knows, no other system has yet been found for governing men except violence. The law is society's safety valve, its most painless way to achieve social catharsis; any other way lies anarchy. More precisely, Lieutenant, in your case the law is all that stops Barney Quill's relatives from charging in here and seeking out and shooting up every Manion on sight. It is also what would keep the heavily mortgaged Manions of Dubuque from in turn coming a-gunning for the Quills, in

210

other words what keeps the fix you're now in from fanning out into a sort of Upper Peninsula version of Hatfield-McCoy."

⁹   I paused, warming to my unfamiliar role as a defender of law. The law is the busy fireman that puts out society's brush fires; that gives people a *nonphysical* method to discharge hostile feelings and settle violent differences; that substitutes orderly ritual for the rule of tooth and claw. The very slowness of the law, its massive impersonality, its insistence upon proceeding according to settled and ancient rules—all this tends to cool and bank the fires of passion and violence and replace them with order and reason. That is a tremendous accomplishment in itself, however a particular case may turn out. As someone has well said, "The difference between an alley-fight and a debate is law." I paused. "What's more, all our fine Magna Cartas and constitutions and bills of rights and all the rest would be nothing but a lot of archaic and high-flown rhetoric if we could not and did not at all times have the *law* to buttress them, to interpret them, to breathe meaning and force and life into them. Lofty abstractions about individual liberty and justice do not enforce themselves. These things must be reforged in men's hearts every day. And they are reforged by the law, for every jury trial in the land is a small daily miracle of democracy in action."

Thinking and Responding to the Reading

1.   In paragraph three, the Lieutenant states his plea. What is it? How does he feel about it?
2.   What is the lawyer's explanation of this?
3.   In paragraph six, the lawyer says, "It so happens that it represents your only hope." Is he referring to the law or the plea of insanity? Explain your answer.
4.   The law is presumed to provide its society with reasoned, logical arguments, not only to provide answers that are true. How does the author explain this?
5.   Explain the last four lines of paragraph 9. Do you agree with these statements? Explain why or why not.

Springboard for Composing

The narrator in this excerpt, a lawyer, says, "While the law is not perfect, God knows, no other system has been found for governing men except violence." Do you agree? Why or why not? Now choose a law that you have some familiarity with and explain not only its content and meaning but also what this law accomplishes. What would happen if it did not exist? Have you ever had an encounter with the law, perhaps as a defendant, juror or plaintiff? What happened? Do you think the law worked effectively?

GRAMMAR, PUNCTUATION, AND OTHER CONVENTIONS OF WRITING

THE NINE PARTS OF SPEECH

I. **Noun**: a word that names a *person, place, thing, idea* or *condition*

Ruth jogs past the *White House*, watching the *tourists* with their *cameras* and the *protesters* marching for *peace* and *democracy*.

Practice 1: Underline all the nouns in each of the following sentences.

1. Jeff and Maryanne went to the Nickelback concert last Saturday night with their friends Sam and Josh from Miami, Florida.

2. "The milk will spoil if you leave it out on the counter," said the mother to her child.

3. A dark sky, rumbling thunder and high winds are common signs of a storm approaching.

4. Skateboarding and rollerblading are two sports that require a great deal of balance and coordination.

5. I had never heard of quasars and black holes before I read about them in last month's *Discovery* magazine.

Practice 2: Underline all the nouns in each of the following sentences.

1. Joan is a hypochondriac because she imagines she has all kinds of ailments, such as arthritis, asthma and cancer.
    [handwritten: Proper noun, Pronoun]

2. "You'll never understand love if you insist on setting all these rules for our marriage," huffed the frustrated bride-to-be.

3. When you cannot make up your mind, try talking to someone about your choices.
    [handwritten: Pronoun]

4. At the SGA meeting this afternoon, several items were discussed: where to hold the fundraiser, whether to charge admission, and who would supply the food.

5. An old woman with a cane hobbled through Sunset Park just as the snow began to fall in heavy flakes.

6. The judge told the lawyer to quiet his client.

7. The president of the college attended the fundraiser at the Scythe Convention Center.

8. The maintenance workers rolled the airplane into the hangar for repairs.

9. The movie premiere was held at the Palace Theater in Trenton, New Jersey

10. The cat cried at the back door to be let in for dinner.

Collective Nouns

A collective noun is a noun that names a collection by a singular form, for example, *assembly*, *band*, *jury*, and *majority*. When the group is thought of as one unit (for example, *The committee is meeting today*), use a singular verb. When the individual members of the group are acting separately (for example, *The committee are unable to agree on a plan of action.*), use a plural verb.

You as the writer must decide how you intend the collective noun to be understood, and then you must be consistent in how you use that noun.

Certain collective nouns—for example, *athletics*, *contents*, *politics*—appear to be plural because they end in s. However, they are treated as singulars (for example, *Statistics is not my best subject.*). The writer is discussing a single course called statistics so the verb must be singular. These words are treated as plurals when they are thought of as plurals (for example, *Statistics are said to mislead the unwary.*). The writer is thinking of the individual statistics separately, which are plural.

With a collective noun as an antecedent, use a singular pronoun if you are considering the group as a unit (The *militia* increased *its* watchfulness.). A plural pronoun is used if the individual members of the group are thought of as separate (The *band* raised *their* instruments at the conductor's signal.).

Practice: In the following sentences underline the collective nouns and indicate whether they are singular or plural.

1. In many schools, athletics is funded from football receipts.

2. The geology class is glad that trip to Florida was funded by the SGA.

3. He asked the group to take its time in reading a decision.

4. The opposition is meeting quietly to organize their forces.

5. Politics are not for the faint of heart.

II. <u>Pronoun</u>: a word that stands in for a noun

There are many different types of pronouns. Some are as follows:

<u>Subjective</u>—indicates that the pronoun is acting as the subject of the sentence

	Singular	**Plural**
1st **person**	I	we
2nd **person**	you	you
3rd **person**	he, she, it	they

<u>Objective</u>—indicates that the pronoun is acting as the object of the sentence

	Singular	**Plural**
1st **person**	me	us
2nd **person**	you	you
3rd **person**	him, her, it	them

Possessive—indicates that the pronoun is acting as a marker of possession and defines who owns a particular object or person

	Singular	**Plural**
1st person	my, mine	our, ours
2nd person	your, yours	your, yours
3rd person	his, her, its	their, theirs

Indefinite Pronoun: does not specify the person or thing to which it refers. Here is a list of some indefinite pronouns:

all	both	everything	nobody	several
another	each	few	none	some
any	each one	many	no one	somebody
anybody	either	most	nothing	someone
anyone	everybody	much	one	something
anything	everyone	neither	other	such

Practice 1: Circle each pronoun in the sentences below and then list which type of pronoun it is.

1. Fran and I have never been good friends because she and I have different ideas about most things.
2. "You have read more books than I have," said Janice to her classmate.
3. Our team voted him and his buddy as captain and co-captain.
4. If anyone wants to succeed in life, he or she has to have a plan.
5. Kareem and Shanda often jog in their favorite park.
6. Somebody left her handbag on the bench in the railway station.
7. My dog barks during thunderstorms.
8. She and I share the same taste in music.
9. The police officer gave her and me a ticket for loitering.
10. "Please pass the report," my boss said to me.

Practice 2: Circle all the pronouns and then list what type each one is.

1. They saw themselves reflected in the large windowpane of our store.
2. Neither would own up to having broken her dollhouse.
3. The football team won its first game.
4. "Why don't we ship it to them by UPS?" suggested Marlon.

216

5. His cat arched its back at the sight of us in our costumes.

6. With you, him and me on this team, we are sure to win.

7. Whether it is yours or mine is for her to decide.

8. This time, sit across from him and me instead of them.

Pronoun Agreement, Reference and Point of View

Pronoun Agreement: Pronouns must agree in number and gender with their nouns.

Joe takes long walks when he needs to think about a problem. ("He," the pronoun, agrees with "Joe," the subject.)

Indefinite pronouns sometimes confuse students because they are not sure if they are singular or plural. Here is a chart to which you can refer if you are unsure whether the pronoun is singular or plural:

Singular

another	each	neither	one
any	each one	nobody	other
anybody	either	none	somebody
anyone	everybody	no one	someone
anything	everyone	nothing	something

Plural

all	few	none	several
anybody	many	no one	some
both	most	other	such

You should write, "<u>Each</u> of the boys <u>is</u> eligible for a scholarship" because <u>each</u> is the subject and it is singular. For this sentence, "<u>All</u> of the boys <u>are</u> eligible for scholarships." <u>All</u> is the subject and it is plural so the verb <u>are</u>, which is also plural, is correct.

Sometimes writers get confused about which pronoun to use: subject or object. An easy way to remember is that subjective pronouns act as the subject of the sentence (usually in the front) and objective pronouns are the direct or indirect object of the verb or the object of the preposition (usually in the back). Look at this example:

Alexandra and I are driving across the country this summer.

"Alexandra and I" is the subject of the sentence. In speech you might say (incorrectly), "Alexandra and me are driving across the country this summer." A way to test the correctness of your pronoun use is to separate the subjects: Alexandra is driving…Me is driving…No!

Pronoun Reference: The pronoun must refer to only one word in the sentence. Readers can be confused if a pronoun appears to refer to more than one word or not to any specific word at all. Look at these sentences and see if you can spot the errors:

At the shops downtown, *they* are all ready for the July 4th celebration.
Samuel told William that *his* hair was turning gray.

In the first sentence, "they" doesn't refer to anyone. Rewrite the sentence to make the "they" clear:

At the shops downtown, the owners are all ready for the July 4th celebration.

In the second sentence, we don't know whose hair is turning gray. Is it Samuel's or William's? This sentence also needs revision:

Samuel told William, "My hair is turning gray" or Samuel told William that William's hair was turning gray.

Pronoun Point of View: When you write your essay, you need to keep the point of view, or person, consistent. If you start to write in the first person, then you must continue to do so. Look at the inconsistencies in the following sentence:

Whenever *I* travel to another country, *I* like to talk to the natives because *you* can learn so much.

The sentence should be consistent and remain in the first person:

Whenever *I* travel to another country, *I* like to talk to the natives because *I* can learn so much.

Whether you write in the first, second, or third person, you must stay in that person.

Pronoun Agreement
Practice 1: Correct all the mistakes in agreement and reference in the following sentences.

1. One can view many educational TV programs today, but you often have to have special channels to do so.

2. Very surprised, Ted exclaimed, "Somebody wrote their notes in my notebook!"

3. Each of the contestants are to wear a nametag.

4. Another of the personnel files were missing from the cabinet in the office.

5. Neither of the boys were listening to the long speech.

6. Each student must see their counselor before the end of the semester.

7. If every student writes the required 6,000 words for the research essay, they will keep poor Prof. O'Brien busy grading papers until the end of the semester.

8. Many people choose someone to marry even though they are not from the same culture.

9. Luis bought two records by Natalie Cole and lent it to me.

10. During early rehearsals, an actor may forget their lines.

Pronoun Reference
Practice 2: Correct all the mistakes in agreement and reference in the following sentences.

1. We seldom visit that museum because they have such boring exhibits.

2. Craig squeezed a plastic sheet over the thin book cover and tore it.

3. Sean told David that he was going to be the captain of the team.

4. The students shoved the books off the boxes and sat on them.

5. The angry customer said that they had sent her the wrong part.

6. Danna told Marne that it was her turn to go grocery shopping.

7. Fred told Tony that polka-dotted underwear was showing through the ripped seat of his dress pants.

8. Mrs. Schiff told her neighbor Marge that she was going to set all of Windsor aglow with the thousands of holiday lights in her yard.

Pronoun Point of View
Practice 3: Correct the mistakes in point of view in the following sentences.

1. I just love the spring. You can finally go for a walk without wearing a heavy coat.

2. A teenager who is looking for her first job knows you'll find help at the guidance counselor's office.

3. When people watch silly or violent programs, they often try to imitate the actors and usually end up making a fool of yourself.

4. In learning, you must be able to slow down and consider what one has been experiencing.

5. People are crazy to think one can become a radiologist without studying many hours because he or she just cannot learn it all by cramming at the last minute.

6. As a species, humankind has always responded well when our survival has been challenged, and they will do so again now.

7. Every father deserves a day off; they need their time to rest too.

8. I dislike my job; you are overworked and underpaid.

9. When one travels to exotic lands, you should always take along mundane supplies such as Band-Aids, aspirin, and Kaopectate.

III. <u>Verb</u>: generally carries the essential **meaning** of what we write. Verbs tell what the subject *does*, *is* or *receives*. A complete thought can't be accomplished without a verb. One of the most important things a verb conveys is a **sense of the time** of an action. *Tense means time.*

This tense expresses	this meaning.	It's formed by	and called.
PRESENT			
The bird flies past my window.	an actual fact at the moment	verb or verb+s	present
I walk to school every-day	the action happens regularly	verb or verb+s	present
Birds fly south in winter	historically true or continues to be true now action	verb or verb+s	present
I am walking to the classroom	the action is going on right now	present of "to be" + (verb+ing)	present continuous
The bird has hunted for food.	the action has been completed before the present	present of "to have" + (verb+ed or d)	present perfect
PAST			
I walked to the class-room yesterday	the action happened before now	regular: verb+ed or d	past
The bird was hopping on the ground when it saw a worm.	the action was going on before the present	past tense of "to be" + (verb+ing)	past progressive or continuous
I had walked to the classroom before I realized I'd forgotten my textbook.	the action is completed before some other action in the past	past of "to have" + (verb + ed or d)	past perfect
FUTURE			
I will walk to school to-day	the action has not yet happened	will + verb	future
The bird will be flying back to its nest.	the action will be happening some time after the present	will + be+ (verb +ing)	future progressive
I will have walked twenty minutes before I arrive at the school	the action will have been completed before another one in the past	will + have + (verb + ed or d)	future perfect

REGULAR VERBS

PRESENT TENSE

	Singular	Plural
1st person	I talk	We talk
2nd person	You talk	You talk
3rd person	He, she, it talks	They talk

PAST TENSE

	Singular	Plural
1st person	I talked	We talked
2nd person	You talked	You talked
3rd person	He, she, it talked	They talked

FUTURE TENSE

	Singular	Plural
1st person	I will talk	We will talk
2nd person	You will talk	You will talk
3rd person	He, she, it will talk	They will talk

AUXILIARY VERBS (Helping verbs)

TO BE

PRESENT TENSE

	Singular	Plural
1st person	I am	We are
2nd person	You are	You are
3rd person	He, she, it is	They are

PAST TENSE

	Singular	Plural
1st person	I was	We were
2nd person	You were	You were
3rd person	He, she, it were	They were

FUTURE TENSE

	Singular	Plural
1st person	I will be	We will be
2nd person	You will be	You will be
3rd person	He, she, it will be	They will be

TO HAVE

PRESENT TENSE

	Singular	**Plural**
1st person	I have	We have
2nd person	You have	You have
3rd person	He, she, it has	They have

PAST TENSE

	Singular	**Plural**
1st person	I had	We had
2nd person	You had	You had
3rd person	He, she, it had	They had

FUTURE TENSE

	Singular	**Plural**
1st person	I will have	We will have
2nd person	You will have	You will have
3rd person	He, she, it will have	They will have

TO DO

PRESENT TENSE

	Singular	**Plural**
1st person	I do	We do
2nd person	You do	You do
3rd person	He, she, it does	They do

PAST TENSE

	Singular	**Plural**
1st person	I did	We did
2nd person	You did	You did
3rd person	He, she, it did	They did

FUTURE TENSE

	Singular	**Plural**
1st person	I will do	We will do
2nd person	You will do	You will do
3rd person	He, she, it will do	They will do

Some other auxiliary verbs are **may**, **can**, **must**, and **should**.

Irregular Verbs
Some verbs are irregular, meaning they don't conjugate as neatly as regular verbs. Here is a list of some irregular verbs in the present, past and past participle:

Infinitive	**Present**	**Past**	**Past Participle** (use with has, have or had)
to be	am	was	been
to bear	bear	bore	born, borne
to begin	begin	began	begun
to choose	choose	chose	chosen
to dive	dive	dived, dove	dived
to drink	drink	drank	drunk
to eat	eat	ate	eaten
to fall	fall	fell	fallen
to fly	fly	flew	flown
to forget	forget	forgot	forgotten
to forgive	forgive	forgave	forgiven
to freeze	freeze	froze	frozen
to fry	fry	fried	fried
to get	get	got	got, gotten
to go	go	went	gone
to grow	grow	grew	grown
to have	has, have	had	had
to hide	hide	hid	hidden
to know	know	knew	known
to lay	lay	laid	laid
to lie (recline)	lie	lay	lain
to ride	ride	rode	ridden
to ring	ring	rang	rung
to rise	rise	rose	risen
to see	see	saw	seen
to shake	shake	shook	shaken
to shine (polish)	shine	shined	shined
to shine (light)	shine	shone	shone
to shrink	shrink	shrank	shrunk
to sing	sing	sang	sung
to speak	speak	spoke	spoken
to spring	spring	sprang	sprung
to steal	steal	stole	stolen
to swear	swear	swore	sworn
to swim	swim	swam	swum
to tear	tear	tore	torn
to throw	throw	threw	thrown
to wake	wake	woke, waked	woken, waked
to write	write	wrote	written

Practice 1: Underline each verb in the following sentences and indicate in which tense it is written.

1. The bicyclists were riding downhill during the race when they hit black ice.
   Past progressive · *Past*

2. This whole-wheat pasta is perfectly cooked and nutritious.
   present perfect

3. When the performance started, the dancers moved to center stage in a circle.
   Past

4. Power bars and other nutritional bars each contain 4 grams of protein.
   present

5. Most investors will not be buying stock right now.
   Future progressive

6. The swimmers took their marks on the starting blocks and waited for the start gun before diving into the pool.
   Past

Practice 2: Underline each verb in the following sentences and indicate in which tense it is written.

1. The yellow roses have bloomed profusely every summer for five years.
   Past perfect

2. After the movies, Joey and Sasha went out to Friendly's for ice cream.

3. The computers were shut down all day after the power failure on campus.

4. Charles left the office and boarded a bus downtown for the African Art Exhibit.

5. Gandhi ate a diet of fruits during some of his spiritual quests which further led to his periods of fasting.
   Past

6. Meteorologists are predicting heavy snow and sleet for the month of February.
   present

Practice 3: Use the correct form of the verb in each of the following sentences.

1. Last night the moon (to shine) _shown_ very brightly.

2. I have been (to choose) _chosen_ for the lead in the play.

3. For the last two years, Mildred has (to swim) _swum_ for five miles each day.

4. Joey (to lay) _laid_ the carpet in the family room.

5. The lock for the window has (to spring) _sprung_ again.

6. I finally (to write) _wrote_ my essay last night.

Practice 4: Use the correct form of the verb in each of the following sentences.

1. We (to fly) _flew_ to Venice, Italy for our honeymoon.

2. Stella has (to grow) _grown_ vegetables in her garden for years.

224

3.   The cotton shirt (to shrink) _Shrank_ in the dryer.

4.   The witness in a trial (to swear) to tell the truth to the court. _Swore_

5.   The child (to tear) _tore_ his shirt while climbing the tree.

6.   The tired father has (to lie) _laid_ down to rest.

Consistent Verb Tense

You must keep your verb tense consistent when you are writing your essays. If you start to write your essay in the present tense, you must keep it in the present tense and not suddenly and without reason shift to the past tense. The same is true about the past tense. If you start in the past tense, then you must remain in the past tense unless there is a good reason to switch to another tense. Look at the underlined verbs in the following sentences:

> When Deborah sits to write in her journal, she turns off the television or radio, and she unplugs the telephone. She likes to work uninterrupted.

Did you realize that all the verbs are in the present tense?

Look at these sentences:

> When Deborah sat to write in her journal, she turned off the television and radio and she unplugged the telephone. She likes to work uninterrupted.

The first sentence is written consistently in the past tense. The verb "likes" changes to the present tense because it is something Deborah does all the time. This is correct. To avoid confusing your readers, be sure to write your verbs in the correct tense.

Practice 1: Correct the verbs so that the tenses are consistent.

1.   I am eager to go to see *Bye-bye Tomorrow* because I loved the lead actor.

2.   The council believes it belongs to the best political party and had elected the correct candidate.

3.   The president of SAX Warehouses says he had done the right thing.

4.   I wanted to go home because I will miss my dog.

5.   Karin knew she had made the right decision when she will break up with Joe.

Practice 2: Correct the verbs so that the tenses are consistent. One sentence is correct.

1.   The medieval people believed that the earth is flat.

2.   ~~"I will be so sad if they are not fixing my car yesterday," said Marina.~~

3.   The note on the blackboard read: "You will pass the quiz if you are studying for it."

4. She mops her kitchen every morning; she likes her floor to be clean.

5. The job market looks bleak right now, so it has been better to go to college.

IV. **Adjective**: describes or tells more about a noun, usually telling what kind or how many

    The *happy* beagle ran through the *six red* rosebushes.

Practice 1: Circle all the adjectives in the following sentences.

1. All the new guides in the national park tried hard to please their many customers.

2. She was disappointed with the poor service at the small bus terminal.

3. Red, white and blue vinyl ribbons decorated all the children's bikes.

4. "Is the tuna salad better than the chicken salad?" the customer asked the waiter.

5. Mr. Arvin has a quick mind, an eagle eye and a sharp tongue.

Practice 2: Circle all the adjectives in the following sentences.

1. I liked the original movie, but the sequel was incredibly boring and too long.

2. Time travel is a difficult concept to grasp fully.

3. Six-foot Sven was the fastest and tallest skater on the hockey team.

4. "Which looks better on me: the plain, white cotton shirt or the flowered polyester one?" the young man asked the sales associate.

5. The boys' mud-spattered uniforms lay on the locker room floor.

V. **Adverb**: describes or tells more about a verb, adjective or adverb

    Michelle plays the piano *well*.
    Shanista is an *extremely* sophisticated chess player.
    Lauren has *very* long black hair.

Practice 1: Circle all the adverbs in the following sentences.

1. Marilee spoke softly to the lost child who was crying loudly on a street corner.

2. My ninety-year-old grandfather can't hear very well.

226

3.	After polishing the glass box, the magician (carefully) stored it away in his cabinet.

4.	Surprisingly, the students wrote their essays (quickly) and (well.)

5.	Because Myrtle whines (aggravatingly) every time she has to do the dishes, her sister prefers to do them herself.

Practice 2: Circle all the adverbs in the following sentences.

1.	(Oddly,) today's temperature rose (considerably) from yesterday's record low.

2.	I always wanted to learn how to ski (gracefully.)

3.	Ann's friends (constantly) call her after midnight, which (rightfully) annoys her parents.

4.	"This is an (incredibly) tasty hamburger!" the guest compliments his host.

5.	Felipe plays soccer very (aggressively,) which (always) annoys some of his teammates.
	modifier

Practice 3: In the paragraph below, adjectives and adverbs are left out of the twenty-five blank spaces. Choose words you think fit best.

The colors and sounds of early spring are fresh and bright. (1) _____ the sky lightened to (2) _____ blue. An (3) _____ (4) _____ cloud (5) _____ drifted by, its underside (6) _____ from the rising sun. (7) _____ birds made (8) _____ sounds in the (9) branches of the trees (10) _____ against the eastern sky. The (11) _____ chorus of the "peepers" in the (12) _____ meadows dwindled to a (13) _____ soloist. As the sun rose, the sky grew (14) _____ and the clouds lost their (15) _____ bottoms. The tree branches changed from (16) _____ gray and brown to a (17) _____ green. The birds, (18) _____ now, chirped and trilled and sang. Trees in (19) _____ greens formed a (20)

_____ background for an oak tree whose (21) _____

leaves were (22) _____ balls of (23) _____. Above the chorus

of singing birds, a cardinal made his (24) _____ comment, "bir die, bir die, bir die."

The colors and sounds of spring bring in the new season, driving out (25)

_____ winter.

VI. **Preposition**: It usually refers to a position in time or space.

There are over 100 prepositions. Here is a list of some common ones:

aboard	about	above	across	after
against	ahead of	along	alongside	among
apart from	around	as	at	away from
of	before	behind	below	beneath
beside	besides	between	beyond	by
down	during	for	from	in
in between	inside	into	near	of
on	onto	on top of	outside	over
through	throughout	to	toward	towards
under	underneath	up	upon	up to
with	within	without		

Practice: Circle each preposition in the following sentences.

1. The Outward Bound Program consists of intensive hiking, rafting and mountaineering for those wanting to have an incredible experience with nature.

2. Video games are for anyone who likes to spend free time facing a screen.

3. In July, for the second time, we decided to take a cross-country trip to California.

4. Looking up from the check in her hand, Tasha said to her fiancé, "Between us we have enough money to buy that beautiful house with the white picket fence!"

5. Whenever Carlo visits us, he knows he is among friends.

VII. **Article**: "determiners" that come before a noun or adjective. There are three: *a, an, the*. "A" and "an" are indefinite, meaning they are used when there is a general category that is singular—a cat (meaning any cat). "The" is definite, meaning it refers to a specific one, singular or plural—the cat (meaning a specific cat) or "the" cats (specific cats). *The* teenager decided to

228

take *a* trip. In this example, a specific teenager (*the* teenager) decided to take an unspecified trip (*a* trip).

Practice 1: Circle the articles in each sentence.

1. The textbook for the geology course is unique, colorful, and expensive.

2. Sally made an appointment with her guidance counselor for Tuesday.

3. The *New York Times* does a fair job covering events in the Middle East.

4. When I go to the movies, I pick an action film because I'm a martial arts buff.

5. The washer and dryer cost $500 at Sears' end-of-the-year sale.

Practice 2: Circle the articles in each sentence.

1. We broke up because he became an annoyance to me.

2. A programming position that Jack had yearned for was just about to be given to him by the head of the department when the CEO cancelled it.

3. As the saying goes, "An apple a day keeps the doctor away."

4. The bicycle trip begins in the Bronx and ends in the north of California, a course of 3,000 miles.

5. The dogs in the shelter wagged their tails in hopes of finding an owner.

VIII. <u>Conjunction</u>: words that act as connectors between words, phrases, or sentences.

There are several different types of conjunctions:

<u>Coordinating</u>: join items of equal value—*for, and, nor, but, or, yet, so.*

An easy way to remember these seven conjunctions is to think of the acronym FANBOYS. Each of the letters in this somewhat unlikely word is the first letter of one of the coordinating conjunctions. Remember, when using a conjunction to join two sentences (independent clauses), use a comma before the conjunction; otherwise, don't use a comma. (For additional information and examples of independent clauses, see the sections on "Clauses" and "The Four Sentence Types.")

We walked five miles to get to the store, <u>but</u> we forgot our money. (The coordinating conjunction "but" is joining two sentences.)

Janice <u>and</u> Rae will share the lead female role in the play. (The coordinating conjunction "and" is joining two words.)

Practice: Circle all the coordinating conjunctions below; change or add any punctuation as needed.

1.   That purple suit and bright green tie is a disastrous combination.

2.   Nobody wants to work today for it's too hot today.

3.   "It's pouring right now," Rick said trying to sound enthusiastic "but the sun will come out later."

4.   The police investigated the crime for three months yet they found no tangible evidence to convict the suspect and his apparent accomplice.

5.   I did all the typing so you will have to do all the proofreading.

Subordinating: join clauses of unequal value. These adverbs act like conjunctions at the front of a subordinate (dependent) clause and show *cause and effect*, or *time*, or *opposition*, or *condition*. If the subordinating clause starts the sentence, use a comma after the clause. (For additional information and examples of dependent clauses, see the sections on "Clauses" and "The Four Sentence Types.")

Cause and effect: because, since, now that, as, in order that
Because we missed the bus, we will have to wait ten minutes for the next one.

Condition: if, unless, only if, whether or not, even if
If Sharon goes to Long Beach Island, I will ask her for a ride.

Opposition: although, though, even though, whereas, while
The sun is shining now *although* the sky was cloudy this morning.

Time: after, before, when, while, since, until
We will ride the roller coaster *after* Steve finishes his hot dog.

Practice: Circle all the subordinating conjunctions below and change any punctuation as needed.

1.   Because the cabbie got him to the station in record time, Jay gave him a five-dollar tip.

2.   "Nothing will happen until you add the oxygen to the mixture," said the science teacher.

3.   Alexandra excels at every sport since she is a natural athlete.

4.   When the clock struck the hour it filled the house with a melody.

5.   Whereas I like to be prepared for all eventualities you enjoy being surprised.

__Correlatives__ are always used in pairs. They join similar elements. When joining singular and plural subjects, the subject closest to the verb determines whether the verb is singular or plural.

both…and   not only…but also

either…or   neither…nor

Both my brother *and* my sister play the saxophone in a local band.
Not only did Ron go to state finals *but also* his brother Bob.

__Practice__: Circle all the correlatives below and change or add any punctuation as needed.

1.   Both the cocker spaniel and the calico cat were prizewinners.

2.   Either they or we must deliver the papers, but someone has to do it.

3.   Not only Sam but also his friend Chen was selected as winners in the art contest.

4.   Neither this door nor that one will lead to the back yard of this complicated house.

5.   In the morning, with both the fan and the air conditioner left on over night, the building remained cool.

IX. __Interjection__: familiar words that show strong feelings

Oh!   Gosh!   Wow!   No!   Hey!

__Practice 1__: In the sentences below, insert exclamation marks in the appropriate places.

1.   "Wow I can't believe he asked me to marry him " Suzie exclaimed excitedly.

2.   Hooray for us

3.   Oh no I lost my job and my car keys on the same day.

4.   Hey there, watch where you're going

5.   Oh, my mother can be so frustrating at times

6.   Ouch That hurts

7.   Hey Where are you going?

8.   Darn Our team only lost by two points

9.   Ah, now I understand

10.   Dear me That's a surprise

Subjects

The subject of a sentence tells *who* or *what* the sentence is about.

Maria enjoys dancing salsa. (Who enjoys dancing? Maria.)

The acid spilled in the laboratory caused a delay in the investigation. (What caused a delay in the investigation? The acid spilled in the laboratory.)

Computer and management skills are in demand in today's workforce. (What are in demand in today's workforce? Both computer and management skills.)

An easy way to identify the subject in a sentence is to ask *who?* or *what?* right before the verb. Remember that a subject can be a person or a thing and doesn't have to be only one. There can be multiple subjects in a sentence.

Practice 1: Underline the subject(s) in each of the following sentences.

1.   Exams, quizzes and tests can be stressful.

2.   The nurse administered the right dose of penicillin to the patient.

3.   The conference members studied the literacy rate of the nation.

4.   The Johanssons added a double garage to their house.

5.   Have you and your brother eaten breakfast yet?

Practice 2: Underline the subject(s) in each of the following sentences.

1.   In a sentence, every verb needs a subject.

2.   One of my contacts lenses fell on the floor.

3.   The tall grass needs to be mowed, and the hedges need to be trimmed.

4.   Did you study for the vocabulary test with Susanne?

5.   Once again, Francine burned the toast.

Subject-Verb Agreement

The verb in a sentence must agree with its subject in number. A singular subject takes a singular verb and a plural subject takes a plural verb. A quick way to remember is that, as a general rule, there is one "s" per subject-verb unit.

The <u>kitten cries</u> when its mother won't feed it anymore. (The "s" at the end of "cries" does not make it plural.)

All the <u>kittens cry</u> when their mother won't feed them anymore.

Be careful not to confuse a descriptive phrase between the subject and the verb as the subject.

Renee, unlike other four-year-old girls, shuns dresses and other frilly attire.

Notice that the subject is "Renee," a singular noun, and the verb "shuns" matches the subject by also being singular. "Girls" is not the subject; therefore, the verb is not plural.

Watch out for collective nouns that look plural but act singular; they take a singular verb. Here is a list of some of the more common collective nouns:

administration	committee	fleet
audience	crowd	government
band	faculty	public
class	family	team

Practice 1: Rewrite the following sentences by changing each italicized subject to its plural form and then making all other necessary changes.

1.   The *school* needs more support. _____

_____

2.   The *house* was sold at auction. _____

_____

3.   Does the *shoe* fit? _____

_____

4.   The *pigeon* picks up crumbs of bread. _____

_____

5.   The *car* has increased speed. _____

_____

6.   The recent *rain* is a relief to farmers. _____

_____

7.   The *top* of the *tree* catches the sun's rays. _____

_____

8. The *pupil* relies upon the teacher's guidance. _____

9. No *newspaper* has been delivered this morning. _____

10. The *robin* pecks at the ground searching for worms. _____

Practice 2: Underline the subject and then circle the correct verb to match the subject in number.

1. The crowd around the bulletin board (is/are) always large.

2. On the stove (was/were) a teakettle and two saucepans.

3. A basket of oranges (stands/stand) on the table.

4. A card or slip of paper (is/are) posted over the name.

5. The coffeepot and the ceramic creamer (was/were) broken when the cat jumped onto the table.

6. A man with a live goose and a young girl hugging a toy elephant (was/were) standing on the train platform.

7. Neither the carpenter nor the plumber (has/have) done any work on the house since Monday.

8. Everything in the houses (was/were) clean and neat.

9. Why (doesn't/don't) someone tell her not to talk so much?

10. Every one of the soldiers (was/were) expecting a package from home.

Practice 3: Underline the subject first and then fill in the present tense form of the verb to agree with the subject in number.

1. This old skeleton key _____ the front door (to fit).

2. The brown recluse spider _____ caught the fly in its web (to have).

3. The children in the play _____ nervous (to be).

4. The black billowing smoke from the chimney _____ over the neighboring valley (to sweep).

234

5.   Absolutely no food or beverage _____ allowed in the computer lab (to be).

6.   The buildings behind my house _____ in disrepair (to be).

7.   The bank committee _____ more members (to need).

8.   The child, anxious for the candy, _____ for the jar full of colorful mints (to reach).

9.   Patches of snow _____ in the woods (to linger).

10.   The horse and her two colts _____ across the field (to run).

Practice 4: Circle the mistake in verb use and then write the correct form of the verb on the line.

1.   There was no corrections on my paper. _____

2.   A scratch or even a paper cut can sometimes causes a serious infection. _____

3.   Either of these pages fit the envelope. _____

4.   Every one of these sunflowers need water. _____

5.   Here is the names of all the participants in the *Dare to Be* show. _____

6.   Because we arrived late, there wasn't any sandwiches left for us. _____

7.   The results of the blood drive was much better than expected. _____

8.   July or August are the best time to take a vacation. _____

9.   Ms. Robin's choice of clothes show her artistic side. _____

10.   Snow and sleet damages highways. _____

Active and Passive Voice

Active Voice
When the subject of a sentence is the <u>doer</u> of the action, the active voice is used.

Rachel <u>dropped</u> the cake. (<u>Rachel</u>, the subject, did the action, which is <u>dropped</u> the cake.)

Beau <u>is hitting</u> Miguel. (<u>Beau</u>, the subject, is doing the action, which <u>is hitting</u> Miguel.)

Sentences written in the active voice let the reader see what is happening in the sentence more clearly since the subject is doing the action. You should try to write your sentences in the active voice unless the object (the receiver of the action) is important.

Passive Voice

When the subject of the sentence is receiving the action, the sentence is written in the passive voice.

The cake <u>was dropped</u> by Rachel. The cake, the receiver of the action, is in the subject position. Rachel, the doer of the action, is in the object position.

Miguel <u>is being hit</u> by Beau. Miguel, the receiver of the action, is in the subject position, and Beau, the doer of the action, is in the object position.

You can see that the passive voice is wordier than the active voice and seeing the action is more difficult.

Practice: Change the following passive-voice sentences into active-voice sentences.

1.	The beds were made by Dylan. _____

_____

2.	The car was drive by Erin. _____

_____

3.	The robber was given the money by the clerk. _____

_____

4.	The camp was run by the Krotowski family. _____

_____

5.	The essays were graded by the professor. _____

_____

Phrases and Clauses

Phrase: a group of words that *does not* contain a subject-verb unit; it functions as a single part of speech. The most common phrase is a prepositional phrase. It usually begins with a preposition and ends with a noun or pronoun. It answers the question by whom? by what? with what? into what? or it shows location, exclusion, ownership or identification or time.

In the morning…   With telephone in her hand…

By willpower…   Under the desk…

Practice: Underline each preposition and then place brackets around each prepositional phrase for each sentence below.

1.   Studying for that final exam put me over the top, but I did well anyway.

2.   At the Happy Beginnings Day School, the teacher told the four-year-olds to stay within the boundary of the playground.

3.   "The cats keep running under the thorn bushes, and I can't catch them," shouted Linda to her mother standing by the kitchen door.

4.   In the story, "Around the Block," the author recounts how he learned to find his way back home.

5.   Throughout the night, the baby birds kept me awake with their persistent chirps.

Clause: a group of words that *does* contain a subject-verb unit. There are two types of clauses: dependent and independent.

An **Independent Clause** also has a subject-verb unit and it <u>can</u> stand alone as a sentence. Notice how each independent clause below makes sense by itself.

> Kelly exercises.
> Samuel is an avid reader.
> I love ice cream.

A **Dependent Clause**, since it is a clause, contains a subject-verb unit but <u>cannot</u> stand alone as a sentence. See coordinating conjunctions for more information. Here are some of the words that start dependent clauses:

after	even	so long as	whenever
although	if	that	which
as	in order that	though	whichever
because	since	until	while
before	so that	when	who

Notice that the dependent clauses give information, but they do not make sense by themselves.

> Because she races motorcycles.
> Whenever he skateboard.
> If I miss the bus.

A **Noun Clause** is a dependent clause used as a subject or object of a sentence often introduced by *when, what, that, whatever, whenever* or *how*

Example: <u>Whoever wrote this essay</u> deserves an "A." (subject)

Notice that when the clause functions as a subject, there is no comma between the subject and its verb.

Marianne never forgot <u>what she learned in her algebra class</u>. (object)

Practice: Identify the noun clauses in each sentence below as either subject or object clauses.

1. We hope that you develop your ideas very carefully.

2. When he will show up is as much a mystery to you as it is to me.

3. What the professor attempted to do was explain the uses of a comma in one class session.

4. People once thought that the sun revolved around the earth.

5. Penny's teacher frowned whenever she struck the wrong note on the piano keyboard.

An **Adjective Clause** is a dependent clause that modifies (tells more about or describes) a noun or a pronoun often introduced by *who, whom, which,* or *that* (sometimes referred to as relative pronouns)

Examples: Janice needs a tutor <u>who will explain compound sentences to her</u>. (describes the tutor)

This car <u>that once ran so well</u> now barely creeps along at 15 mph. (describes the car)

Practice: **Identify all the adjective clauses below.**

1. Here is the poem that Sivan wrote.

2. People who smile often find life easier to handle.

3. Green, which is known as a soothing color, is often used on peace posters.

4. The child, to whom the lecture was addressed, continued playing

5. Jill, whom they had counted on the least to help mail the flyers, turned out to be their best assistant.

An **Adverb Clause** is a dependent clause that modifies (tells more about or describes) a verb, an adjective or another adverb. It can often be moved around in a sentence; is introduced by a subordinator (since, when, until, after, because and so on); and explains *when? where? why? under what conditions?* or *to what degree did something occur?*

Examples: <u>When</u> you run out of ideas, let me know. (When? When you run out of ideas)

This would be an excellent essay <u>if</u> it weren't for the spelling errors. (Under what conditions? If it weren't for the spelling errors.)

Practice: Identify all the adverb clauses below:

1. Although Ari and Ethan have not surfed in years, they are going to surf this evening.

2. Alvin should to take cooking lessons before he gets married, for his girlfriend is a confirmed gourmet.

3. Because Mary Jo likes exercising, she bicycles whenever she can.

4. Next semester, since I will be taking only two classes, I will be able to work again.

5. Many people book cruises to the Bahamas during the winter months because it is sunny and warm there.

Four Sentence Types

To be a sentence, a group of words *must* contain 1) a subject, 2) a verb and 3) a complete thought. There are four types of sentences: simple, compound, complex, and compound-complex. By learning them and using them, you can work toward sentence variety in your essays.

I. <u>Simple</u>: contains one independent clause

> Shannon passed all her courses last semester.
> Come here.
> We need volunteers.

II. <u>Compound</u>: Made up of two simple sentences (independent clauses) connected by a coordinating conjunction or a semi-colon (;). There are seven coordinating conjunctions: *for, and, nor, but, or, yet, so*. An easy way to remember this is to think of the acronym FANBOYS:

1. <u>for</u> – an explanation of the first clause
2. <u>and</u> – an additional fact of equal importance
3. <u>nor</u> – carries over the negative idea from first clause
4. <u>but</u> – an exception, qualification or reversal
5. <u>or</u> – an alternative to the first clause
6. <u>yet</u> – an exception, qualification or change
7. <u>so</u> – a result of the statement made in the first clause

> We ran for the bus<u>, but</u> we missed it.
> Billy called me yesterday<u>, so</u> I called him today.
> You can go to the movies<u>, or</u> you can go to the party.

Look at the following sentence:

Lenny earns only fifty dollars last week**, yet** he charged two hundred on his VISA card.

This sentence contains two simple sentences: "Lenny earns fifty dollars last week" and "he charged two hundred on his VISA card." The word "yet" with a comma joins the two thoughts and shows their connection to one another.

The **semi-colon (;)** also connects independent clauses when the independent clauses are closely related and approximately the same length. (For more information on uses of the semi-colon, see the section on punctuation.)

The rain clouds rolled in from the **south; the** sky darkened as if it were midnight.

This sentence also contains two simple sentences: "The rain clouds rolled in from the south" and "The sky darkened as if it were midnight." They are joined by the semi-colon (;) to show they are closely connected in meaning.

Practice 1: Finish the following sentences to create your own compound sentences by adding meaning to replace the…. Remember to put in the correct punctuation.

1.   The winning soccer team….. but…..

_____

_____

2.   The burned dinner…. so….

_____

_____

3.   My younger sister Karen didn't …. nor….

_____

_____

4.   The writing student…. for….

_____

_____

5.   Either…. or….

_____

_____

6.   The plump kitten.... and ....

_____

_____

7.   The muscular bus driver.... yet....

_____

_____

8.   Benjamin rode the bus.... ; he ....

_____

_____

Practice 2: Write a compound sentence for each one of the coordinating conjunctions, and use a semi-colon. Be sure that you join two complete thoughts.

(and) 1.   _____

       _____

(but) 2.   _____

       _____

(for) 3.   _____

       _____

(so)   4.   _____

       _____

(or)   5.   _____

       _____

(nor) 6.   _____

       _____

(yet) 7.   _____

       _____

(;)   8.   _____

       _____

Practice 3: Place a comma before the coordinating conjunction in the following sentences only if it is needed. Be sure that you join two complete thoughts.

1.   We need plenty of food for the hikers will be hungry.

2.   A sudden gust caught the sail and a wave rolled over the leeward side of the boat.

3.   Nobody saw us but Kathy.

4.   Keep the machine covered with oilcloth or dust will get into the bearings.

5.   The girls caught the fish and I cooked it.

6.   Grace invited all the girls but Jaclyn to the party.

7.   Nobody saw us but Henry heard us talking.

8.   I tried all the tricks I knew for getting the heavy truck out of the soft sand.

9.   Christina missed her workout class so she jogged five miles instead..

10.   The play was a success to everyone but Huasong who directed it.

Practice 4: Place a comma before the coordinating conjunction in the following sentences only if it is needed. Be sure that you join two complete thoughts.

1.   The rain ceased and the sun came out.

2.   The sauce must be stirred or it will stick.

3.   At the party, the manners were not polished nor was the language eloquent.

4.   The Wilsons must have driven for they arrived in 15 minutes.

5.   Gianna studied regularly all semester so she passed her finals with ease.

242

III. Complex: contains one independent and at least one dependent clause

Remember that the dependent clause starts with a subordinator:

after	even	so long as	whenever
although	if	that	which
as	in order that	though	whichever
because	since	until	while
before	so that	when	who

If David misses the bus, we will have to pick him up.

Caitlin wore a new outfit **since** she was the guest of honor.

Practice: Underline the dependent clause with one line and the independent clause with two lines. Add a comma after the dependent clause if it comes first.

For example: Whenever Mr. Weinberg taps his pencil, we know we are going to get a lecture.

1.   While we were eating paper hats were distributed to the guests.

2.   The fire was still burning when I ran out.

3.   Before the day was over the students began to circulate rumors.

4.   Just as he began to read the paper was blown out of his hand by a gust of wind.

5.   The magician entertained the guests after they finished their dessert.

6.   As we moved along the shore became hardly visible through the dense fog.

7.   My grandfather told me that when he was a boy about twelve people in this town owned automobiles.

8.   If we like to do a thing usually we do it well.

9.   Mr. Sanchez called to his dog Sparky to follow him so that could return home.

10.   As the hiker continued the path became steeper and more dangerous.

IV. Compound-Complex: contains two or more independent clauses and one or more dependent clauses

If Jen's car breaks down again, we'll have to walk; my car is in the repair shop.

("If Jenna's car breaks down again" is a dependent clause; "we'll have to walk" is an independent clause; "my car is in the repair shop" is an independent clause.)

Practice 1: Each of the sentences below is either simple, compound, complex or compound-complex. First, indicate what type of sentence it is in the blank provided. Then, insert any needed punctuation in the appropriate place. Some sentences should have commas added; some should have semi-colons added; and some should have nothing added.

1. _____ The bike trail ran next to the lazy, winding river.

2. _____ I can't hurry because I'm out of breath.

3. _____ As soon as the picnic party spotted the snake by the bushes they decided to move to the open field.

4. _____ Sports drinks work great just before and during a run but they don't supply enough calories and carbohydrates if they are all you consume after a run.

5. _____ The developers planted many flowering pear trees but they all died because of the severe draught that summer.

6. _____ We need to buy all our texts before we go to class.

7. _____ The office supply company donated the following articles: pens, paper, and computers.

8. _____ When Marty received his first paycheck from ABC Hardware he decided to frame it.

9. _____ This yogurt tastes funny it might be over the expiration date.

10. _____ Laura found a ten-dollar bill in the tin box that lay beneath the pile of old magazines.

Practice 2: Complete each **COMPOUND** sentence. Be sure each clause can stand on its own.

1. The soccer team…, or….

_____

_____

2. She didn't…, nor….

_____

_____

3. Elsie studied the menu; Ralph…

_____

_____

244

4. ...., so they left without them.

_____

_____

Practice 3: Complete each **COMPLEX** sentence. Be sure one clause can stand on its own and one clause is dependent.

1. Whenever ..., the dog swam out to retrieve it.

_____

_____

2. Monika likes.... even though....

_____

_____

3. Since ..., I will have to ....

_____

_____

4. After the electrician installed the wiring, he...

_____

_____

Practice 4: Complete each **COMPOUND-COMPLEX sentence**. Be sure two clauses can stand on their own and one clause is dependent.

1. We have no ..., but we do have .... because....

_____

_____

2. Before he went out, Robert checked ..., and then ....

_____

_____

Fragments, Run-ons, and Comma Splices

Another advantage to learning the sentence types is that you will not write sentence fragments, run-ons, or comma splices.

Fragment: a word group that lacks a subject or verb or complete thought. There is a sense of incompleteness when it is read, much as you experienced when identifying phrases and dependent clauses.

> After I stopped drinking coffee.
> During the night.

Notice that the first example is a dependent clause and the second example is a phrase. Neither contains at least one independent clause (a subject-verb unit and a complete thought).

Practice 1: Correct the fragment (unfinished thought) by completing it as a sentence. Remember to use proper punctuation.

1. in China, just before the last trade agreement

   _____

   _____

2. will be running as fast as I can

   _____

   _____

3. some of the students reading in Professor Rumson's class

   _____

   _____

4. which was hard

   _____

   _____

5. although it has been exceptional

   _____

   _____

6. walking out of the room

   _____

   _____

7. those who were in the conference room

   _____

   _____

246

8.   a winner in New Jersey

_____

_____

9.   have dashed off my paper

_____

_____

10.   helped by her

_____

_____

Practice 2: Connect the fragment to an adjoining related sentence. Add words as necessary.

1.   I tried to help him, ~~Although~~ *but* he didn't ask me to.

2.   Since yesterday morning, ~~The~~ the accountant had been trying to call his client with the good news.

3.   Hang gliding is an exciting sport, ~~E~~*e*specially when one has an ideal location.

4.   Spinning around makes me sick, ~~Dizzy, mostly.~~ *and mostly dizzy*

5.   To call the prize awarding company immediately, ~~That~~ *that* was the urgent message left on Louise's answering machine.

6.   We all went to the mall, ~~Since~~ *because since* there was nothing else to do on that Friday evening.

7.   Because the carpenter needed to finish the cabinets by four o'clock, ~~He~~ *he* hurried too much and hit his thumb very badly with his hammer.

8.   Marvin didn't know what to do, ~~U~~*u*ntil told.

9.   The cashier's job was boring, ~~But~~ *but* necessary to pay her bills.

10.   Whenever the cook felt happy, ~~That~~ *that*'s when he would turn on some soft music.

<u>Run-on</u>: two complete thoughts that are run together but not properly connected:

    Deanna decided to stop smoking cigarettes became too expensive.

    The baseball game was postponed the rain soaked the field.

These sentences are incorrect because the two independent clauses run together.

Here they are corrected:

> Deanna decided to stop **smoking; cigarettes** became too expensive. (The semi-colon connects the two complete thoughts.)

> The baseball game was postponed **because** the rain soaked the field. (The second independent clause was changed to a dependent clause with the word "because.")

There are four main ways to correct a run-on sentence:

1. Break the independent clauses into two separate sentences.
The baseball game was postponed. The rain soaked the field.

2. Separate the independent clauses with a semi-colon.
Deanna decided to stop smoking; cigarettes became too expensive.

3. Connect the independent clauses with a coordinating conjunction (FANBOYS) and a comma.
The baseball game was postponed, for the rain soaked the field.

4. Make one of the independent clauses a dependent clause.
Since cigarettes became too expensive, Deanna decided to stop smoking.

Practice 1: Correct the following run-ons. Be sure to use each method at least once.

1. The sun is dangerous you should wear sunscreen.

2. The next chapter requires careful reading you should start doing it now.

3. Mr. Robbins has sent his children to camp however he has to work day and night to afford it.

4. This cell phone does not work for me it came without instructions.

5. Most of the tape recorders in the library are unused this proves my belief that they are outdated.

Practice 2: Correct the following run-ons. Be sure to use each method at least once.

1. Cathy has the perfect life she never seems to have any problems.

2. Amtrak has new super-fast trains there is no better time to take a train trip than now.

3. The movie starts in twenty minutes meet me in the lobby.

4. Marcus always knows how to drive in Manhattan obviously, it is a skill not everyone possesses.

5.   Rajesh prepared for the accounting exam and burdened every friend to help quiz him it was the hardest test of his career.

Practice 3: Correct the following run-ons. Be sure to use each method at least once.

1.   The cat jumped from step to step it gracefully landed with each jump.

2.   Anthony did not agree with the method he was taught he found other means to solve the problem.

3.   Vicky sculpted the statue she also painted the picture.

4.   The Civil War was a triumph it was also a struggle.

5.   This next chapter has a lot of difficult information in it you should start studying right away.

Comma splice: two complete thoughts separated by a comma instead of a semi-colon, comma and FANBOY word, or a period.

> The examination was difficult, Emily was worried. (The comma splice occurs between "difficult" and "Emily.")

> We hung up the painting, the room looked better immediately. (The comma splice occurs between "painting" and "the.")

In both examples the comma should be replace with either a semi-colon; a comma and the appropriate FANBOY (for, and, nor, but, or, yet, so) word, or by breaking the independent clauses into two separate sentences.

Like the run-on sentence, here are four main ways to correct a comma splice:

1. Break the independent clauses into two separate sentences.
The examination was difficult. Emily was worried.

2. Separate the independent clauses with a semi-colon.
We hung up the painting; the room looked better immediately.

3. Connect the independent clauses with a coordinating conjunction (FANBOYS) and a comma.
The examination was difficult, so Emily was worried.

4.   Make one of the independent clauses a dependent clause.
As soon as we hung up the painting, the room looked better.

Practice 1: Correct following comma splices. Be sure to use each method at least once.

1.   It was a frustrating experience, the seams were crooked and the armholes too small.

2.   Finally, the day arrived, it was opening day, and I was ready.

3.   Our car had slid off the road into the ditch, we didn't know what to do.

4.   I can clearly remember, he first came to visit in 1991.

5.   Leah has worked ten years for the state, not once has she taken a sick day.

Practice 2: Correct following comma splices. Be sure to use each method at least once.

1.   Sometimes Charles would listen, occasionally, he would give advice.

2.   The officer called him a scofflaw, he did not understand what she meant.

3.   The old man loved mystery novels, he read at least one a week.

4.   A surfboard floated on the waves, no one knew where it had come from.

5.   Lisa was tall and blond, Michael was short and red-haired.

Practice 3: Correct the following comma splices. Be sure to use each method at least once.

1.   He enjoys hiking, he often goes backpacking on his vacations.

2.   He watched TV even when there were only reruns, she preferred to read instead.

3.   I didn't know which job I wanted, I was too confused to decide.

4.   Michaela loves to draw comics, she is a talented artist.

5.   The night was cold we forgot to bring our coats.

HOW TO PUNCTUATE

Russell Baker

When you write, you make a sound in the reader's head. It can be a dull mumble—that's why so much government prose makes you sleepy—or it can be a joyful noise, a sly whisper, a throb of passion.

Listen to a voice trembling in a haunted room:

"And the silken, sad, uncertain rustling of each purple curtain thrilled me—filled me with fantastic terrors never felt before…".

That's Edgar Allan Poe, a master. Few of us can make paper speak as vividly as Poe could, but even beginners will write better once they start listening to the sound their writing makes.

One of the most important tools for making paper speak in your own voice is punctuation.

When speaking aloud, you punctuate constantly—with body language. Your listener hears commas, dashes, question marks, exclamation points, quotation marks as you shout, whisper, pause, wave your arms, roll your eyes, wrinkle your brow.

In writing, punctuation plays the role of body language. It helps readers hear you the way you want to be heard.

"Gee Dad, have I got to learn all them rules?"

Don't let the rules scare you. For they aren't hard and fast. Think of them as guidelines.

Am I saying, "Go ahead and punctuate as you please"? Absolutely not. Use your own common sense, remembering that you can't expect readers to work to decipher what you're trying to say.

There are two basic systems of punctuation:

1. The loose or open system, which tries to capture the way body language talks
2. The tight, closed structural system, which hews closely to the sentence's grammatical structure

Most writers use a little of both. In any case, we use much less punctuation than they used 200 or even 50 years ago. (Glance into Edward Gibbon's "Decline and Fall of the Roman Empire," first published in 1776, for an example of the tight structural system at its most elegant.)

No matter which system you prefer, be warned: punctuation marks cannot save a sentence that is badly put together. If you have to struggle over commas, semicolons and dashes, you've probably built a sentence that's never going to fly, no matter how you tinker with it. Throw it away and build a new one to a simpler design. The better your sentence, the easier it is to punctuate.

Choosing the right tool

There are 30 main punctuation marks, but you'll need fewer than a dozen for most writing.

I can't show you in this small space how they all work, so I'll stick to the ten most important—and even then I can only hit highlights. For more details, check you dictionary or a good grammar book.

Generally speaking use a comma where you'd pause briefly in speech. For a long pause or completion of thought, use a period.

If you confuse the comma with the period, you'll get a run-on sentence: *The Bank of England is located in London, I rushed right over to rob it.*

Semicolon [;]

A more sophisticated mark than the comma, the semicolon separates two main clauses, but it keeps those two thoughts more tightly linked than a period can: I steal crown jewels; she steals hearts.

Dash [-] and Parentheses [( )]

Warning: Use sparingly. The dash SHOUTS. Parentheses whisper. Shout too often, people stop listening: whisper too much, people become suspicious of you. The dash creates a dramatic pause to prepare for an expression needing strong emphasis: I'll marry you—if you'll rob Topkapi with me.

Parentheses help you pause quietly to drop in some chatty information not vital to your story: (*Despite Betty's daring spirit "I love robbing your piggy bank," she often said*), she was a terrible dancer.

Quotation Marks [" "]

These tell the reader you're reciting the exact words someone said or wrote: *Betty said, "I can't tango,"* or: *"I can't tango," Betty said.*

Notice the comma comes before the quotation marks in the first example, but comes inside them in the second. Not logical? Never mind. Do it that way anyhow.

Colon [:]

A colon is a tip-off to get ready for what's next: a list, a long quotation or an explanation. This article is riddled with colons. Too many, maybe, but the message is: "Stay on your toes; it's coming at you."

Apostrophe [']

The big headache is with possessive nouns. If the noun is singular, add 's: I hated Betty's tango.

If the noun is plural, simply add an apostrophe after the s: Those are the girls' coats.

The same applies for singular nouns ending in s, like Dickens: This is Dickens' best book.

And in plural: This is the Dickenses' cottage.

The possessive pronouns *hers* and *its* have no apostrophe.

If you write it's, you are saying it is.

Keep Cool

You know about ending a sentence with a period [.] or a question mark [?]. Do it. Sure, you can also end with an exclamation point [!], but must you? Usually it just makes you sound breathless and silly. Make your writing generate its own excitement. Filling the paper with !!!! won't make up for what your writing has failed to do.

Too many exclamation points make me think the writer is talking about the panic in his own head.

Don't sound panicky. End with a period. I am serious. A period. Understand?

Well...sometimes a question mark is okay.

Punctuation

Like mathematical symbols, punctuation marks guide the reader through your sentences. Each piece of punctuation is a code for the reader, so each must be used correctly or you will confuse your reader.

End Punctuation

Each sentence gets one end punctuation mark. There are three end punctuation marks:

- **Period (.)** ends a statement: George took the bus.
- **Exclamation point (!)** shows strong feelings: Gwen swam 500 meters!
- **Question mark (?)** ends a question: Where is your next class?

Practice: Add the appropriate end punctuation to each sentence.

1. Are you getting a degree and then transferring ?

2. Frank woke up early to take the train .

3. "Wait I'm coming too," said Berry.

4. I already took test two, Did you ?

5. He asked me what my name was .

6. The owner wanted to know if we could pay for the boat in cash .

7. "Will you marry me ? asked Stephen.

8. How many pages did you read last night ?

9. Wow, I can't believe she ate twenty brownies !

10. My sister asked, "Can you drive me to the mall ?"

Internal Punctuation

Unlike end punctuation, internal punctuation can occur many times in a sentence. Learning how each piece of punctuation works, will make you a more careful, focused writer.

Comma (,) has eight main uses:

1. Between three or more items in a series:

   - Please give a copy of the minutes of the meeting to the president, vice-president, and treasurer. (The comma before the "and" is optional unless without it the sentence would be confusing.)

With a coordinating conjunction (FANBOYS) to separate independent clauses:

- Ian won a scholarship for his track and field abilities, **so** he won't have to work during the school year.

2. To separate the speaker from his/her quotation:

- "Let's hike the Blue Ridge Mountains**," said Morgan**.

3. To set off parenthetical elements. (By "parenthetical element," we mean a part of a sentence that can be removed without changing the essential meaning of that sentence.):

- The Trenton-Makes Bridge**, which spans the Delaware River,** is a favorite among the locals.

4. To separate a phrase or clause that is introductory:

- **Because you covered my shift for me last Tuesday,** I will cover for you tomorrow.

5. With other conventions of writing—direct address, addresses, letter salutations and closings, and dates:

- Carol**,** please come here.
- 1200 Old Trenton Road**,** Trenton, NJ
- Dear Mom**,**
- Sincerely**,** Hannah Deckler
- Friday**,** May 19, 2004

6. To set off phrases that express contrast:

- It was her money**, not her charm or personality,** which first attracted him.

7. To separate coordinate adjectives. If you can put *and* or *but* between the adjectives, a comma will probably belong there:

- He is a tall**,** distinguished man.

Practice: Insert commas where needed.

1. "You never know when you might need a dictionary thesaurus and encyclopedia" the librarian said as she pointed them out to Aaron.

2. Success is usually a matter of course of preparation and attitude.

3. Keith's basketball coach who is also a math teacher is always checking on his grades.

4. "Until you straighten up your room," her mother said to Tracy, "you can't go over to Janice's house."

5. "Well, well, well," joked the clown, as he pulled coins, stamps and buttons from the little girl's ears. "What have we here?""

6. The hikers enthusiastically walked ten miles on the first day, but the next day, they decided to go home, because it was raining.

7. After her dental session, Sheila rewarded herself with an ice cream cone.

8. The plumber could not locate the leak, nor could he suggest what to do about it.

9. As the bear family moved slowly along through the trees, the forest rangers watched them through their binoculars.

10. The children knew that squirming, whining, and throwing popcorn at each other was not allowed during the long car ride to visit their grandmother.

11. Tyco, a Newark New Jersey-based company, is moving to another state.

Semicolon (;) has two uses:

1. To separate independent clauses:

- My history professor requires perfect attendance; my painting professor allows us three absences.

2. To separate items in a series that already have commas separating the items:

- The three officers of the club are Esther, the president; Louis, the vice-president; Diane, the treasurer; and Annie, the recording secretary.

Practice: Insert semicolons where necessary.

1. I do not like reality shows; however I do enjoy adventure movies.

2. Mr. Bates was the sales associate; Mrs. Bates was the accountant.

3. The power plant malfunctioned on a hot summer's day; residents were without air conditioning for most of the afternoon and evening.

4. Marvin bought his girlfriend a bouquet of roses for her birthday; moreover he tucked a diamond necklace into one of the petals.

5. Last spring the elderly couple cashed in their life savings then they retired to a little community in Arizona.

6. "I have a meeting on Monday, April 12 from 9:00 to 10:00 a report due the next day April 13 and a follow-up meeting on Thursday, April 15," Pat sighed resignedly.

7. The marathon started with twenty runners only five made it to the finish line.

8. The doctor advised Bernie, his cousin, Elaine, his sister and Harold, his brother to eat healthful meals if they wanted to feel better.

9. Eugene is studying political science at Rutgers University this year and he plans to attend Berkley University for law next year.

10. As program director, she had several responsibilities: planning, budgeting, contracting, and hiring staff for the summer projects managing the projects and supervising the staff and at the end of the summer, closing the offices, distributing remaining funds to agency departments, and writing final reports.

Apostrophe (') has two uses:

1. To show contraction: don't, wouldn't, hasn't

2. To show possession: the dog's collar, the general's wrath

   The general rule for adding apostrophes is if the word is singular add an **'s—book's** cover or **Charles's** car.

   If the word is plural and ends in "s," add just an apostrophe— **books'** covers. The exception is for plural words that do not end in "s." In these cases, treat them as if they were singular and add **'s--children's**, **men's**, **women's**.

Practice: Insert apostrophes where necessary.

1. Its the best game Ive ever played.

2. Theyre going to the ballgame at Tylers Park today.

3. Youre my best friend and well be together for the rest of our lives!

4. Janes class is in the south wing of the math building. Ours is in the north.

5. Dont worry about dinner. Ill warm up the left over meatloaf.

6. Marta wouldve gone if she couldve.

7. Rachel got four Bs for the last term of classes.

8. Sunshine is a child of the 60's.

9. Theirs is the best entry of all the posters submitted.

10. His heavy texts filled the shelves of his bedrooms sagging bookshelf.

<u>Quotation Mark (" ")</u> has three uses:

1. To set off the *exact* words of the speaker:
    - "To be or not to be," says Hamlet in Shakespeare's play by the same name.

2. Around the title of a *short* work, such as a poem, short story, or essay, but not your own work.
    - Here is a list of types of common works considered "short":

Poem	"Sonnet 130"
Short story	"The Story of an Hour"
Essay	"A Modest Proposal"
Song	"My Own Prison"
Article	"Titanic Sinks!"
TV episode	"Kissing Up"
Scene	"Act 1, Scene 3"

3. Use quotation marks to indicate words used ironically, with reservations, or in some unusual way:
    - History is stained with blood spilled in the name of "civilization." (Note that the period is inside the closing quotation mark.)

Practice: Add quotation marks where needed. Some sentences do not need any change.

1. My favorite poem is The Road Not Taken by Robert Frost.

2. My mother still says, Look both ways before crossing the street.

3. Come here, said the angry father, before I count to three.

4. Last night I was reading a short story called The Mist.

5. When Jessica felt she needed a good laugh, she would watch *The Holy Grail*, a Monty Python movie.

6. In Da Club is my favorite song on 50 Cent's CD *Get Rich or Die Tryin*.

7. Rae thought a long time before she entitled her essay Winning the Word Battle.

8. Mr. and Mrs. Weiss, owners of a family farm, said, We refuse to use that pesticide because it might pollute the nearby wells.

9. The audience was shocked when two actors fell off the stage in the first act of *Cats*.

10. In many ways progress has left millions unemployed, poor and hungry.

Italics or __underlining__ is used for the titles of longer works. If you are writing on a computer, use italics. If you are writing by hand, use underlining.

- Here is a list of types of works considered long:

Long poems	*Iliad, Paradise Lost*
Books	*The Open Mind, Sula*
Plays	*A Midsummer's Night's Dream*
Journals/Magazines	*Nursing, U.S. News and World Report*
Newspapers	*Los Angeles Times, The Trentonian*
CDs or records	*Sheryl Crow Live, Mr. Smith*
Television shows	*CSI: New York, Friends*
Works of art	*Guernica, The Artist's Mother*
Long Musical Pieces	*Madame Butterfly, Nutcracker Suite*
Famous speeches	Lincoln's *Gettysburg Address*
Pamphlets	*New Developments in AIDS Research*

Practice: Add italics (by underlining) where needed in the following sentences.

1. The New York Times is the best newspaper in the U.S.

2. Will Smith's film Men in Black is very funny and well acted.

3. Walt Whitman's poem Leaves of Grass runs over forty pages.

4. We saw the Venus de Milo when we went to Rome last year.

5. Seinfield is off the air as a regular TV show now.

6. The very funny play The Producers is still playing on Broadway.

7. All students should read James Baldwin's novel Go Tell It on the Mountain.

8. In U.S. History class we studied Washington's Second Inaugural Address

9. I love Dr. Seuss's Horton Hatches An Egg.

10. The Drama Club is putting on Fiddler on the Roof this year.

Hyphen (-) has two uses: Divide a word at the end of a line of writing or typing, and attaching compound adjectives (three-year-old boy)

Practice 1: Insert hyphens where needed in the following sentences.

1. Only twenty-three raffle tickets remained to be sold.

2. A white-haired lady slowly picked her way across the ice-covered sidewalk.

3. Sea-green-emeralds and wine colored-rubies lay shining on the jeweler's workbench.

4. The dark-as-night paint makes the house look eerie.

5. For desert, Ivan served chocolate-covered-strawberries.

Practice 2: Insert hyphens where necessary in the exercises below.

1. "Hand me another of those four-by-four beams," Mike called out.

2. Our new wall-to-wall carpeting has brightened our office considerably.

3. Mr. Jamison recommended a first-rate-hotel to the visiting couple.

4. Low-level-ambition had plagued him all his life.

5. "Live-rent-free" proclaimed the too good to be true ad.

Dash (--) signals a degree of pause longer than a comma but not as complete as a period. Use it to set off words for dramatic effect.

Practice: Insert dashes where needed in the exercises below.

1. A beautiful wife, a comfortable home and a well-paying job that is what Francisco wanted out of life.

2. "Yes but then maybe not," said Jamie hesitantly as she tried to decide whether to break her diet.

3. I love no I absolutely adore Lady Godiva chocolates.

4. Never had the biologists seen such a sight penguins stretched across the ice as far as the eye could see.

5. After decorating the hall for the prom for six hours straight, the five girls wanted to do only one thing go home and go to sleep.

Parentheses ( ) has three uses: It signals additional information that is not essential to understanding the sentence; it encloses numbers or letters indicating the items of a list; and it encloses dates.

- All the teachers I have ever had in elementary school (except Mrs. Snyder) were old and fat.

- I decided to study at the University because (**a**) I wanted to improve my chances at finding a good job and (**b**) I thought it would be fun.

- John F. Kennedy (1961-1963) was the youngest man elected President

Practice: Insert parentheses where necessary.

1. You will need the following items for the test (1) a calculator (2) scrap paper, and (3) two pencils.

2. *The Joy of Cooking* (a famous culinary art book) is popular among newlyweds.

3. The singles dance (ages twenty-five to thirty-five) was a huge success as a fundraiser for the fire department.

4. Mrs. Beaver the (main character in the play) was played by Juliette Simms.

5. Only a small number of those who signed up for the contest (10 percent) had all the required criteria for qualification.

<u>Colon</u> (:) has three main uses: After an independent clause which announces a list, explanation, or illustration; between the hour and minutes in designating time; at the end of a sentence introducing a long quotation; between the verse and line in biblical references.

- Li's mother was busy all <u>**week: she**</u> cooked, cleaned, did laundry, and played with Li.

- "The test will begin at **8:15** a.m.," said the professor to the students.

- Victor Hugo **said:** "The invention of the printing-press is the greatest event in history. It was the mother of revolutions. It was the total renewal of man's mode of expression, the human mind sloughing off one form to put on another, a complete and definitive change of skin by that symbolic serpent which, ever since Adam, has represented the intelligence."

Practice: Insert colons where necessary.
1. Dear Mr. Harvey,

2. The kitchen table groaned under the weight of the guests' contributions, salads, main dishes, rolls, desserts, drinks, paper products and a huge basket of fresh fruit.

3. Greg looked over the old computer books before he threw them out Using Netscape 3, How Computers Work, Using the Internet, and Windows 3.1.

4. Last Sunday, Rev. Joshua Smith quoted from Genesis 1 5. This Sunday he spoke about Luke 2 10.

5. In Winston Churchill's defining speech of WWII, he said "We shall go on to the end, we shall fight in France, we shall fight on the seas and oceans, we shall fight with growing confidence and growing strength in the air, we shall defend our Island, whatever the cost may be, we shall fight on the beaches, we shall fight on the landing grounds, we shall fight in the fields and in the streets, we shall fight in the hills; we shall never surrender…."

6. All semester long, my English class ended promptly at 3 10 which gave me plenty of time to get to my job at the Lobster Shack by 4 30

Capitalization

Capital letters are used to call attention to words used in special ways. The following list tells when to capitalize:

- The first word of every sentence:

  Mike Myers's television career started in 1988, when he joined *Saturday Night Live*.

- Proper names including persons; places; days and months; countries, peoples and tribes; buildings and monuments; organizations and clubs; businesses and services; titles; and specific course names:

  Dr. David Rexrode
  San Francisco, California
  Monday, October 30
  Brazil, Europeans, Blackfoot Indians
  Liberal Arts Building, Washington Monument
  Student Government Association
  ABC Plumbing Company, Forest Service
  Psychology of Children II

- All words in a title except prepositions and articles that don't start the title:

  "Angels on a Pin"
  For Whom the Bell Tolls
  "How I Learned to Read and Write"

Practice: Insert capitalization where necessary.

1.   dr. shah is the president of the mercer county pediatric association.

2.   to get to pennsylvania take the new jersey turnpike south.

3.   many students take biology 101 in their freshman year.

4.   the secretary of state is responsible to the president and citizens.

5.   the fourth of july is the celebration of united states independence from great britain.

Sentence Variety/Unnecessary Repetition

Sentence variety is important in your writing because it keeps your writing from being monotonous and boring, and it helps to alleviate unnecessary repetition. Below are some methods to add variation to your sentences.

I.   **Sentence Beginnings:**

- adverb: *Unfortunately,* he came too late to take the quiz.
  Never is he on time.

- preposition   (for, with, at, on, etc.): *With* great style, the pitcher delivered a curve.

- ing modifier: *Diving* into the ocean, she touched the sandy bottom.

- ed modifier: *Frustrated* by the assignment, he went to work with a tutor.

Practice 1: Rewrite each sentence so it begins with an adverb.

1.   The falcon passed silently over the meadow.

Quietly, the

2.   The head of the forensics occasionally visits the lab.

Weekly,

262

3. Carry these phone numbers with you always.

   Carefully, _____

   _____

4. Fred and Denise sometimes spend the summer in San Juan.

   Occassionly, _____

   _____

5. Dawn foolishly forgot where she had left the package.

   _____

   _____

Practice 2: Begin each of these sentences with an appropriate adverb. Punctuate correctly.

1. _Quietly,_ _____ the hunter approached the angry wolf.

2. _____ Edith attended every play rehearsal.

3. ~~The estatic~~ _Quickly,_ she cashed her one-million-dollar check from The State Lottery Commission.

4. _Ignorant_ _____ Joe admitted his mistake.

5. _Slowly,_ _____ the child slept, curled up on a blanket with his teddy bear.

Practice 3: Combine each pair of sentences so the initial word begins with "ing."

1. _Camping_
   We ~~camped~~ in the Pinelands,
   We learned a lot about self-reliance.

   _____

   _____

2. _Squaking_
   The rooster ~~squawk~~ed loudly,
   The rooster fluttered out of our path.

   _____

   _____

3. The design consultant checked our blueprints. *thinking*
    He discovered a flaw in the design.

    _____

    _____

4. Freud analyzed his own dreams. *analyzing*
    He developed a theory of dream interpretation.

    _____

    _____

Practice 4: Combine each pair of sentences so that the initial word starts with "ed."

1. The soccer game will take place on Friday evening.
    It was rained out twice.

    _____

    _____

2. The essay is very easy to read.
    It is typed on the computer.

    _____

    _____

3. Dr. Berman will address the architecture students.
    He has been recognized for his unique yet functional buildings.

    _____

    _____

4. The azalea bush is withered and yellow.
    It needs a thorough watering.

    _____

    _____

264

Practice 5: Rewrite each sentence by shifting a prepositional phrase to the beginning. Punctuate correctly.

1.   The band members arrived at seven o'clock sharp.

    _____

    _____

1.   A thick-clouded sky obscured the buildings across the bay.

    _____

    _____

3.   We must develop a thesis from these facts.

    _____

    _____

4.   The children played with the electric train for hours.

    _____

    _____

5.   A group of men talked about the state of the country inside the coffee shop.

    _____

    _____

II.   **Sentence Combining**

Short sentences that are closely related can be combined to make a longer more coherent sentence. Here are some ways to combine your sentences:

- Join sentences with a compound <u>predicate</u> (verb). The audience *hissed* and *booed* at the singer's performance.

- Use an <u>appositive</u>: Beer, *the cause of much rowdiness*, should not be sold at games.

- Use a <u>relative clause</u>: Jack, *who is an outstanding swimmer*, practices everyday.

- Use <u>parallel structure</u>: The children *sang*, *danced*, and *recited* poetry.

Practice 1: Rewrite each group of sentences using one of the above methods.

1.   Don made baked fish with coconut for the party.
     He is a fine cook.

     _____

     _____

2.   Eric bikes ten miles a day to stay in shape.
     He also swims 100 laps.

     _____

     _____

3.   The Cromwell Hotel was built in 1806.
     It is an elegant example of Mexican architecture.

     _____

     _____

Practice 2:   Rewrite each group of sentences using one of the above methods.

1.   Her car is a bit too flashy for me.
     It is a yellow 1939 Buick.

     _____

     _____

2.   The children ran from case to case in the museum.
     They were happy and excited.

     _____

     _____

3.   The elevator shudders violently and begins to rise.
     It is an ancient box of wood and gears.

     _____

     _____

266

4.	Zoë hummed while working on her painting.

	Zoë tapped her foot while working on her painting.

	_____

	_____

Practice 3: Combine the following sentences into one complex or compound sentence. Use all of the components. Omit nothing important. Add sparingly. Be sure your punctuation is correct.

1.	Dorothy Parker was a writer who lived in New York.
	Dorothy Parker wrote reviews, poems, short stories, plays and screenplays.
	In 1937, Dorothy Parker won an Academy Award.

	_____

	_____

	_____

2.	Alice Walker is an African-American writer.
	She wrote *The Color Purple*.
	The Color Purple was made into a movie.
	It was a successful movie.

	_____

	_____

	_____

3.	Gary Soto is a poet.
	He is Mexican American.
	His poems have appeared in many literary magazines.

	_____

	_____

	_____

4.	Smallpox is a serious disease.
	Smallpox is a contagious disease.
	The only prevention is vaccination.

	_____

	_____

	_____

5.   LL Cool J writes hip-hop.

He performs hip-hop.
He has ten albums.
He is a veteran in the music business.

_____

_____

_____

6.   Bill H. Gates is chairman of Microsoft Corporation.
Bill H. Gates is chief software architect of Microsoft Corporation.
Microsoft Corporation is a worldwide leader in computer technology.
Microsoft Corporation employs more than 55,000 people in 85 countries.

_____

_____

_____

Practice 4: Combine these short sentences into three or four rather long sentences.

1.   A football stadium before the game begins

    a.   Before the game begins, a football stadium teems with excitement.
    b.   Fans pour into the stands.
    c.   They carry woolen blankets.
    d.   They carry mugs of steaming coffee.
    e.   They carry bright red cans of Coca-Cola.
    f.   They wave to friends.
    g.   They chatter brightly.
    h.   They cheerfully settle themselves.
    i.   There is a bustle of last-minute activity.
    j.   Some people hustle to their seats carrying popcorn.
    k.   They also carry hot dogs.

_____

_____

_____

_____

_____

2.   A concert on the beach

    a.   The beach is empty.
    b.   The crowds have gone.
    c.   The litter remains.
    d.   A blanket of trash covers the bleachers.
    e.   The bleachers are covered with torn candy wrappers.
    f.   They are covered with smashed Coca-Cola cans.
    g.   They are covered with crumpled napkins.

_____

_____

_____

_____

_____

3.   A car in the garage

    a.   A 1961 MGA sits on blocks in the garage.
    b.   The body was once white.
    c.   It is now chipped.
    d.   It is stained.
    e.   It is streaked with dirt.
    f.   There is a box next to the car.
    g.   It is heaped with rusty engine parts.
    h.   There is also a door handle in the box.
    i.   There are windshield wipers.
    j.   There is the rim of a wheel.
    k.   A black metal toolbox sits in the corner.
    l.   It is unopened.

_____

_____

_____

_____

_____

Practice 5: Rewrite the paragraph below, eliminating as much of the repetition as possible while keeping the original meaning. Make use of all your sentence combining strategies.

If I won a lot of money, I would spend the money on several things. The first thing I would do is that I would spend the money on traveling. I would travel all over the world. First, I would spend some of the money on buying a first-class ticket for my world trip. Then I would spend some more of the money to stay in five-star hotels. Then in the hotels I would spend money to have room service whenever I wanted. I would call room service at all hours of the day and night and be generous with my money tips. But then, I wouldn't want to spend all the money, of course, because I would like to invest some of the money in the stock market or a business so that I would have some more money to spend later on.

Practice 6: Revise the following essay so it is concise yet effective, focused, and readable.

My major area of study is biology. Biology is an open subject. It includes the study of all life forms on this planet and their interactions with non-living matter and energy. The greatest challenge that biologists face in this coming millennium is the preservation of our environment. Naturally, the environment is of great concern to biologists. Without suitable habitats for life, biologists would have nothing to study. In addition, of course, they would not be alive themselves.

The current problem with the environment is actually a conglomeration of many problems. Global warming is a problem. The overuse of non-renewable resources is a problem. Human overpopulation is a problem. The existence of Global Warming has been debated over the last few decades. The current scientific consensus is that it does exist. It cannot be blamed on a naturally occurring phenomenon. Humans are to blame for it. The new question is "How bad will it get?" not "Does it really exist?"

The over use of non-renewable resources is another pressing issue. One of these resources is oil. Oil drives our economy by driving our industries. Wars are fought to control the land where this precious commodity is found. However, according to one estimate the entire world supply of oil will run dry in the next 50-75 years. This is alarming. We are dependent on this resource.

Human overpopulation can be cited as one of the main reasons the environment is in trouble. The more we chose to live in habitats unsuitable for human life, which can only be sustained by bringing in outside resources, the more this problem will continue to grow. It is a fact that the more resources that we make available the more a population will continue to grow. Thomas Malthus wrote about this. Malthus was a political economist in nineteenth century England. The population explosion and its effects (global warming and overuse of non-renewable resources) will continue until something is done.

Some attempts at conservation have been made. However, many think that it is too little too late. Governments have imposed laws restricting pollution. Organizations have tried to educate the public about the limits of our resources. The problem is still increasing. It will take a major shift in attitude of the entire world's population, or a major catastrophe, or both before any real solutions will come about.

_____

_____

_____

_____

_____

_____

_____

_____

_____

_____

_____

Misplaced and Dangling Modifiers

Misplaced modifiers are words that, because of awkward placement, do not describe the words the writer intended them to describe. Misplaced modifiers often confuse the meaning of a sentence. To avoid them, place words as close as possible to what they describe. A modifier that opens a sentence must be followed immediately by the word it is meant to describe.

- A small book sat on the desk that Sarah had read. (Sarah had "read" the desk!?)

A **modifier dangles** when the word it modifies is not actually in the sentence.

- Having finished the homework, the television was turned on. (Who has finished the homework? Not the television!)

Practice 1: Identify the misplaced modifier and then rewrite the sentence.

1. Tony bought an old car from a crooked dealer with a faulty transmission.

   _____

   _____

2. I nearly earned a hundred dollars last week.

   _____

   _____

3. Bill yelled at the howling dog in his underwear.

   _____

   _____

4. He swatted the wasp that stung him with a newspaper.

   _____

   _____

5. I almost had a dozen job interviews after I sent out my resume.

   _____

   _____

6.   I adopted a dog from a junkyard which is very close to my heart.

_____

_____

7.   Clyde saw a three-car accident going to work.

_____

_____

Practice 2: Correct each dangling modifier by adding the missing word that is being modified.

1.   Confirming our conversation, the meeting will be on Tuesday.

_____

_____

2.   Racing through the living room, the lamp was knocked to the floor.

_____

_____

3.   Raised in Nova Scotia, it is natural to miss the smell of the sea.

_____

_____

3.   Sitting for hours in the air-conditioned office, her nose began to run.

_____

_____

4.   Our cat had kittens while on vacation.

_____

_____

Copyright Acknowledgements